How to Land Your First Paralegal Job

An Insider's Guide to the Fastest-Growing Profession of the New Millennium

How to Land Your First Paralegal Job

An Insider's Guide to the Fastest-Growing Profession of the New Millennium

Fifth Edition

Andrea Wagner

PEARSON

Prentice Hall

Upper Saddle River, New Jersey 07458

Library of Congress Cataloging-in-Publication Data

Wagner, Andrea.
   How to land your first paralegal job: an insider's guide to the fastest-growing profession
of the new millennium/Andrea Wagner.—5th ed.
      p. cm.
   Includes bibliographical references and index.
   ISBN-13: 978-0-13-206903-8 (alk. paper)
   ISBN-10: 0-13-206903-2 (alk. paper)
   1. Legal assistants—Vocational guidance—United States.   2. Job hunting—United States.
I. Title.
   KF320.L4W34 2009
   340.023'73—dc22

                                                                          2007050111

Executive Editor: Vern Anthony
Acquisitions Editor: Gary Bauer
Assistant Editor: Linda Cupp
Director of Marketing: David Gesell
Executive Marketing Manager: Leigh
   Ann Sims
Marketing Assistant: Les Roberts
Production Manager:
   Wanda Rockwell
Creative Director: Jayne Conte
Cover Design: Bruce Kenselaar
Cover Illustration/Photo:
   Getty Images

Director, Image Resource Center:
   Melinda Patelli
Manager, Rights and Permissions: Zina
   Arabia
Manager, Visual Research: Beth Brenzel
**Manager, Cover Visual Research &
   Permissions:** Karen Sanatar
Image Permission Coordinator:
   Jan Marc Quisumbing
**Full-Service Project
   Management/Composition:** Integra
Printer/Binder: R.R. Donnelley/
   Harrisonburg

Credits and acknowledgments borrowed from other sources and reproduced, with
permission, in this textbook appear on appropriate page within text.

Pearson Education LTD.
Pearson Education Australia PTY, Limited
Pearson Education Singapore, Pte. Ltd
Pearson Education North Asia Ltd

Pearson Education, Canada, Ltd
Pearson Educación de Mexico, S.A. de C.V.
Pearson Education–Japan
Pearson Education Malaysia, Pte. Ltd

10 9 8
ISBN-13: 978-0-13-206903-8
ISBN-10:   0-13-206903-2

Dedicated to my Grandchildren,

Ella and Jake Torgan,

the lights of my life,

and to my wonderful children,

son-in-law, and husband.

Brief Contents

Contents

List of Illustrations

Introduction

The purpose of this handbook is to assist new paralegals in finding satisfying and fulfilling jobs. Whether you are a paralegal student beginning your career, a recent college graduate searching for a career, or a professional changing careers, my goal is to give you that extra competitive edge to get the job you want in the paralegal market. You may use this book not only for this job search, but for all subsequent ones.

Because the paralegal profession is relatively new, there is still a wide array of entrées into the marketplace. During my 20 years as a legal assistant recruiter, placement director, human resources manager, and career counselor, I have placed and interviewed all kinds of legal professionals with all types of backgrounds. I have placed people in the largest law firms in the nation and in one-lawyer firms that had never employed a paralegal before. I know which approaches work, and which do not. I have seen the successes and the failures. Over the years I have developed a keen awareness of how successful job searches work, and what law firms and corporate employers of paralegals look for in applicants—from what kinds of resumes and cover letters work, to how to conduct yourself successfully in an interview.

This book is designed to share what I know with you. It is designed to be a practical handbook to be used again and again. In it you will find step-by-step procedures to follow when you look for a job. Included are samples of cover letters, resumes, and interview questions, as well as a suggested reading list and employment references and Internet resources.

I have also included convenient checklists for your use with each subsequent job hunt. Special Hot Tips will give you insiders' information about the marketplace. You will find these sections very helpful. Best of luck in your job hunting. You are entering the most dynamic and fastest growing profession in the nation!

1

The Paralegal Field

A Profession with Great Opportunities

If you are serious about landing a job as a legal assistant, this book is a must read for you! It is a simple, clear guidebook that will tell you what kinds of organizations have paralegal positions, the types of jobs that are available, and how you can get them. If you use this book conscientiously, you will be way ahead of your competition in pursuit of your first paralegal position.

One of the bonuses of the paralegal profession is that it is constantly evolving. Although many paralegals are doing fascinating, high-level work—on large, complex and important cases—the field still has enormous entrance flexibility. Described as a profession that will grow faster than average through 2010 by the U.S. Department of Labor–Bureau of Labor Statistics, the paralegal field is expanding so rapidly that there are, as of yet, no "etched in stone" standards for entering it. Although most paralegals have trained at one of the nation's 800 plus paralegal schools and programs, a few may enter fresh out of college with no paralegal training whatsoever; this way of getting into the field is not encouraged, as most lawyers do not have time for training beginners. Still others get their start in the profession from different fields or jump into the field from their positions inside law firms, such as legal secretaries who may want a more challenging and professional position. There is consensus that the field and role of paralegals will definitely continue to expand well into the next decade. The legal industry as a whole has become more efficient and businesslike in the last 10 years, allowing paralegals to become more important because they are extremely cost effective and their time can be charged to clients.

Moreover, the paralegal field offers the unique opportunity to do important work on absorbing matters without the commitment to years of additional education earning a law degree. Many new college graduates are becoming paralegals so they can experience a career in law before committing themselves to three or more difficult years of law school. Many other professionals—teachers for instance—are becoming paralegals because the work seems more fulfilling, with comparable or better compensation.

Whatever your present position, or your motivations for wanting to enter the profession, this book can be your ticket inside. It will not only give you practical step-by-step guidance about seeking your first job, it will tell you where the jobs are and what special requirements exist for different specialty areas. It will tell you what kinds of jobs are available for your particular qualifications, and how qualifications for entry-level positions differ from region to region within the United States.

If you are presently a paralegal student, you are learning about the tasks of your chosen profession. But knowing how to do a job and knowing how to land one are two different skills. This book will help you package yourself and your knowledge so you can land the entry-level job that will take you to the career you envision. It will provide you with invaluable information for gathering strategic facts about potential employers, how to network to get your job, and finally how to negotiate for an appropriate salary.

By the time you complete your job search, this book should be worn and dog-eared. But by that time, you also should have begun a career that can fascinate and reward you as few others can. Good hunting!

WHO ARE THESE PEOPLE? THE PARALEGAL DEFINED

Paralegals perform a wide assortment of tasks in a broad range of legal matters. Some are engaged in high-level work that was once the province of associate-level lawyers; others are doing work of less sophistication. They are all paralegals, however. There is enormous flexibility in the profession—you can start out doing rudimentary work and then quickly migrate into sophisticated, fascinating endeavors. Because of the flexibility of activity and entrance requirements, there are great opportunities available for people with a wide range of backgrounds. In short, the field is wide open; you can make of it almost what you wish.

The National Association of Legal Assistants (NALA), an umbrella organization of local paralegal associations and individual members, in recognition of the need for one clear definition adopted the paralegal/legal assistant definition of the American Bar Association that reads as follows:

> A legal assistant or paralegal is a person qualified by education, training or work experience who is employed or retained by a lawyer, law office, corporation, governmental agency or other entity who performs specifically delegated substantive legal work for which a lawyer is responsible. (Adopted by the ABA in 1997.)

The terms *paralegal* and *legal assistant* are fairly synonymous, but more and more, paralegal is being used as the term of art. I will be using these words interchangeably throughout this book, hopefully without confusion. The two terms have essentially the same meaning; they refer to people who assist attorneys with all forms of substantive legal work except those tasks that, by law, require a lawyer. This means that paralegals cannot give legal advice, represent others in court, set legal fees, sign legal documents, or establish an attorney/client privilege. Virtually all other forms of legal work are open to paralegals, and some state legislatures are currently revising statutory restrictions on the profession.

BIRTH OF A PROFESSION

Paralegals first appeared in the mid-1960s as part of President Lyndon Johnson's *War on Poverty*. Federally funded lawyers in poverty law programs used the first paralegals to reduce the cost of helping low-income clients. After that, innovative private attorneys, realizing that legal assistants could help them offer more efficient legal service at a lower cost, began hiring them. In the early 1970s, the use of paralegals spread as more conservative firms realized that they would have to use paralegals to remain competitive.

Many of the early paralegals were trained on the job by attorneys. These attorneys acted as mentors to their legal assistants, who learned only the procedures of that particular office. These newly minted paraprofessionals were taught the "hows" (legal procedures) of law but not the "whys" (substantive law). From among this early group, forward-thinking paralegal educators established the first schools to provide formal legal assistant training. The classes were designed to provide a comprehensive legal foundation and to make the students more proficient in their tasks. In-house instruction, combined with a thorough educational program, gives the best legal assistant training possible. Some schools, recognizing the value of practical experience, have instituted internship programs as well.

PARALEGAL TRAINING OPTIONS

The paralegal educational system is developing rapidly. Although some law firms hire new paralegals directly out of college and train them in-house, most legal assistants now attend paralegal programs that range in length from several months to several years. A number of colleges and universities throughout the nation have developed legal studies bachelor's as well as master's degree programs. Many institutions offer students training in legal procedures and the substantive foundation of law.

In the early 1970s, the American Bar Association (ABA) began an approval process of paralegal education programs to help standardize the training. Institutions desiring ABA approval must initiate contact and pass ABA scrutiny. The process is entirely voluntary on the part of the school. Some schools have not sought ABA approval but still offer high-quality programs. It is up to each person to decide which program is appropriate. Considerations include cost, location, length of program, and requirements for acceptance. The American Association for Paralegal Education (AAfPE), established in 1983, has developed standardized curriculum that is available to all of its member schools, whether or not they are approved by the ABA (see Chapter 3 for an in-depth discussion).

CERTIFIED VERSUS CERTIFICATED

Upon completion of a program, when a student has earned a certificate or diploma, the student is "certificated." The National Association of Legal Assistants (NALA) offers a two-day examination program through which a paralegal can become a certified legal assistant/certified paralegal (CLA/CP). This is the one of a few nationwide test that enables successful participants to describe themselves as "certified."

The National Federation of Paralegal Associations (NFPA) has also developed a nationwide test called the PACE exam (Paralegal Advanced Competency Examination). The primary difference between the two is that to take the PACE exam, a paralegal must have a four-year degree and a paralegal certificate, or an Associates Degree and six years of experience whereas for the CLA/CP exam, a person can have one of the following:

- ➤ A two-year degree in paralegal studies
- ➤ An ABA-approved paralegal certificate
- ➤ A postbaccalaureate certificate in legal assistant studies (must have a bachelor's degree to be eligible)
- ➤ A bachelor's or master's degree in paralegal studies
- ➤ A certificate from a legal assistant program that consists of a minimum of 60 semester hours
- ➤ A bachelor's degree and at least one year of paralegal experience
- ➤ A high school diploma and seven years of experience

HOT TIP

Many employers confuse certified with certificated. When you see an advertisement requiring a certified candidate, the firm usually wants someone with a paralegal certificate. Whatever the case, send your resume! The law firm may not understand the difference, enabling you to land a job.

Both tests are given frequently throughout the year and have review courses prior to the tests given by the organization or authorized by the organization. When you pass the PACE exam, you will become a registered paralegal or an RP. Passing the NALA exam you become a certified legal assistant or a CLA. You may call NFPA or NALA for further information or look on the Internet. (Web site information is provided in Appendix C.)

Other organizations offer volunteer certification for paralegals. The National Association of Legal Professionals (NALS) offers two paralegal certification programs: one for legal professionals including legal secretaries (ALS—Basic Certification for legal Professionals and the PLS—Advanced Certification for legal Professionals) and the PP or professional paralegal. In order to qualify for the PP designation, the paralegal must have at least five years of legal experience.

The American Alliance of Paralegals (AAPI) offers certification as well: American Alliance Certified Paralegal (AACP). The qualifications to take the exam are

➤ A bachelor or advanced degree in any discipline from an accredited institution; or

➤ An associate degree in paralegal studies from an ABA-approved paralegal program or a program which is avoting institutional member of the American Association for Paralegal Education; or a certificate from an ABA-approved paralegal program or a program which is a voting institutional member of the American Association for Paralegal Education.

A new concept is gaining slow acceptance across the country. Individual states are now testing experienced paralegals to allow them to become state certified. The following states have begun the process of regulating their paralegals:

➤ Delaware—Delaware Certified Paralegal is a voluntary program through the Delaware Paralegal Association

➤ California—California Advanced Specialist a voluntary program offered through CACPS which is a subsidiary of the California Alliance of Paralegal Associations

➤ Florida has a voluntary registered paralegal program through the Paralegal Association of Florida.

➤ Indiana has a voluntary registration for an Indiana Registered Paralegal designation.

➤ Kentucky is working on a voluntary state certification.

➤ Louisiana has established a voluntary Paralegal certification through the Louisiana State Paralegal Association.

➤ North Carolina has a voluntary certification program through the state bar.

HOT TIP

Check to see if your state has started the voluntary regulation process. Many states that are not included above are currently exploring the idea of regulating paralegals.

➤ Ohio has a certification program through the state bar with the OSBA (Ohio State Bar Association) Certified Paralegal designation.
➤ Texas has a voluntary board certified legal assistant certificate through the state bar.

When a paralegal has either the CLA/CP, RP, or other national paralegal credential designation and an advanced certification, an attorney will be reassured that this legal assistant is indeed qualified to do specific legal work in that state.

A WORD ABOUT SALARIES AND OTHER CONCERNS

As stated in the *Occupational Outlook Handbook, 2006–2007* edition published by the U.S. Department of Labor, salaries vary greatly depending on education, training, experience, the type and size of the employer, and the geographic location of the job. Entry-level salaries are in the range of $25,000–40,000, varying by region, some even reaching $35,000–40,000. The Northeast and Pacific Coast have the highest pay scales; the Midwest and the Southeast are at the bottom. Larger cities tend to pay more because the cost of living is higher. Experienced senior paralegals in certain specialty areas can earn upward of $85,000+. In addition to salary, many paralegals receive bonuses. Your local paralegal association will have access to local, regional, and national compensation studies that you can consult.

The issue of exempt versus nonexempt compensation policies has been a hot topic in paralegal circles. Although many firms pay their paralegals salaries that are exempt from overtime, an increasing number of firms are paying hourly/overtime rates. This method of compensation can be quite lucrative, as paralegals are often required to work overtime, especially before and during trials or at corporate and real estate closings. Some paralegals view overtime pay as a diminishment of the professional status of legal assistants. According to the latest labor laws, paralegals fall into the nonexempt or hourly category because the profession does not meet the criteria for exempt status.

This controversy is revisited each year at raise and bonus time. A few of the major firms in the country have developed a two-track system to address the arguments on both sides of the issue. In such systems, senior legal assistants are not paid overtime because they may be considered supervisors, which are exempt. However, their bonuses are significantly higher than those for employees who are paid overtime. (See Chapter 13 for salary negotiation strategies.) Generally, paralegals are recompensed for the time they work either in overtime pay, compensatory time off, or a year-end bonus.

A LITTLE ABOUT COMPUTERS

Computers are an essential part of the legal business. If you know a variety of computer applications, you will have an appreciable advantage in competing for paralegal positions because paralegals must be computer competent. A savvy legal assistant will seize the opportunity to acquire additional computer skills and become more valuable in the job market.

HOT TIP

If your paralegal school does not offer computer courses, contact your local adult high school or community college to take one. They are generally lower in cost than similar courses at colleges or private institutions.

Computer applications in each area of law are so complex that they merit an entire book. With that in mind, below is a brief overview of how computers are generally used in each area.

All areas of law are supported by programs such as MSWord or WordPerfect for drafting documents. If you are a student, you are probably already familiar with a these programs—sweating out term papers with WordPerfect or Microsoft Word on either a Macintosh or a PC. To organize and draft documents, expertise in the above programs is required for all paralegals and attorneys. Computer applications are being used for billing, accounting, and time management, calendaring, case management, and conflict checking. E-mail is now being used for court filings and for communication with clients and opposing counsel.

Database technology plays an important role in document-intensive litigation. Documents are indexed for search and retrieval on the computer. Full-text databases with scanning capabilities are also used for storing depositions and trial transcripts. The software indexes every word, enabling the legal assistant to quickly find relevant testimony.

Document assembly software is used extensively in real estate and probate law, where many standard forms are used. The legal assistant drafts documents by pulling up the master form and "marking it up" for the specific work at hand. This form then goes to the attorney, who makes the final edit.

Spreadsheet programs are used in any legal work that must compute numbers. This is particularly important in tax law, as well as in estate planning, for calculating the value of an estate, family law for tracking the assets of the husband and/or wife, and probate to follow the trail of the disposition of the assets for the deceased's estate and keeping up on estate taxes.

Finally, database systems are used to create commercial legal research banks. Lexis and Westlaw are large research databases to help the legal professional in doing simple or complicated legal research. The law firm's or corporate legal department's unique research needs rely on these major databases. Knowledge of the Internet can also assist a paralegal in doing legal research. There are many search engines that are free.

HOT TIP

If you know computers but don't know their applications in the legal profession, a single paralegal course such as "Computer Use in Litigation" can make you a valuable potential employee. With one course, you may become instantly more employable, even landing jobs over more experienced paralegals that may not have your computer knowledge. You should not stop with litigation. All specialties require competency on the computer.

SO MANY ENGAGING OPTIONS: WHAT PARALEGALS DO

There are four general specialties paralegals can train for: litigation, real estate, corporate or business law, and probate. Within these areas there are many subcategories.

One way to enter the paralegal field is by starting out as a litigation case clerk or paralegal assistant. This position is very popular with midsize and larger firms in larger cities. In general, you do not need a paralegal certificate. However, to succeed in the field, you should consider acquiring one. Your assignments will include assisting a paralegal in large-scale litigation, with such duties as organizing and indexing documents, summarizing simple depositions, and performing assignments enhancing the overall organization of the case. Many firms promote from within, and after a certain length of time, you may move from a paralegal assistant up to a paralegal.

Listed below are some of the duties an entry-level paralegal may be expected to perform:

LITIGATION PARALEGAL

➤ Assisting attorneys at trial
➤ Preparing for trial
➤ Summarizing or digesting depositions
➤ Preparing simple pleadings and discovery documents such as interrogatories
  ❑ Investigating the facts of the case
  ❑ Performing legal research to identify appropriate laws, judicial decisions, legal articles, etc.
  ❑ Organizing pretrial discovery and documents

REAL ESTATE PARALEGAL

➤ Preparing loan documents
➤ Overseeing transactions from beginning to end
➤ Drafting and reviewing leases
➤ Working closely with escrow and title companies
➤ Reviewing surveys
➤ Preparing closing binders

CORPORATE PARALEGAL

➤ Drafting minutes
➤ Forming and dissolving corporations
➤ Filing documents with the Securities and Exchange Commission
➤ Reviewing Blue Sky laws
➤ Overseeing mergers and acquisitions
➤ Assisting with leveraged buyouts

PROBATE PARALEGAL

➤ Overseeing probate proceedings from beginning to end
➤ Preparing federal tax forms
➤ Assisting at asset sales
➤ Drafting simple wills and trusts and estate plans

LEGAL SPECIALTIES AND SUBSPECIALTIES

Each major discipline of law has subspecialties. For example, you may litigate a case in the areas of bankruptcy, family law, or product liability. Listed below are some of the subspecialties for legal assistants working in each major discipline.

LITIGATION LAW
- ➤ Bankruptcy
- ➤ Environmental law
- ➤ Workers' compensation
- ➤ Personal injury
- ➤ Collections
- ➤ Commercial litigation
- ➤ Computerized litigation support
- ➤ Administrative law and Social Security
- ➤ Criminal law
- ➤ Family law
- ➤ Health care law
- ➤ Immigration and naturalization
- ➤ Insurance law
- ➤ Labor/employment law
- ➤ Medical malpractice
- ➤ Product liability
- ➤ Admiralty/maritime law
- ➤ Intellectual property
- ➤ Alternative dispute resolution

CORPORATE
- ➤ Banking
- ➤ Business and finance
- ➤ Taxation
- ➤ Copyrights
- ➤ Trademarks
- ➤ Patents
- ➤ Entertainment
- ➤ ERISA (Employee Retirement Income Security Act)
- ➤ Pension plans
- ➤ Government contracts
- ➤ International law
- ➤ Mutual funds
- ➤ Securities
- ➤ Blue Sky laws

REAL ESTATE LAW
- ➤ Eminent domain
- ➤ Environmental law
- ➤ Landlord/tenant
- ➤ Unlawful detainer
- ➤ Land use
- ➤ Development
- ➤ Condominium law

PROBATE LAW
- ➤ Estate planning
- ➤ Wills and trusts
- ➤ Probate administration

PARALEGAL JOB DESCRIPTIONS

Below is a sampling of typical duties performed by paralegals. For all of the descriptions, computer skills are essential.

Litigation Paralegal

- ➤ Processing the case and commencement of the action
- ➤ Conducting initial client interview
- ➤ Organizing client files
- ➤ Ascertaining and analyzing the facts
- ➤ Investigating
  - ❑ Interviewing witnesses
  - ❑ Conducting subsequent client interviews
  - ❑ Investigating court records, corporate records, titles and deeds, medical reports, wage analysis, loss of income, etc.
  - ❑ Visiting the scene; taking photographs and measurements, etc.
- ➤ Determining legal issues
- ➤ Formulating a plan of research
- ➤ Researching the law; briefing cases
- ➤ Drafting a memorandum of law
- ➤ Corresponding with client and opposing counsel
- ➤ Drafting complaints, answers, simple pleadings
- ➤ Preparing service of process

➤ Discovery
  ❑ Drafting requests for admissions, requests for production, and interrogatories
  ❑ Preparing for depositions
  ❑ Setting up depositions, notices, subpoenas, and the court reporter
  ❑ Preparing questions
  ❑ Taking notes on testimony
  ❑ Preparing digest of testimony
  ❑ Organizing and analyzing documents
➤ Pretrial duties
  ❑ Locating and selecting expert witnesses
  ❑ Preparing witnesses
  ❑ Drafting trial briefs
  ❑ Preparing questions for jury selection
  ❑ Preparing evidence
  ❑ Drafting pretrial motions
  ❑ Drafting opening statements
  ❑ Preparing settlements
    • Drafting releases
    • Drafting and filing motions for dismissal
  ❑ Maintaining client case dockets and tickler systems
  ❑ Preparing trial notebooks
➤ Trial
  ❑ Organizing trial exhibits and handling exhibits at trial
  ❑ Coordinating witnesses' appearances
  ❑ Coordinating and organizing trial settings
  ❑ Taking notes at trials
➤ Posttrial duties
  ❑ Summarizing trial testimony and drafting motions
  ❑ Maintaining appellate timetables
  ❑ Satisfying judgments and collection work (i.e., garnishments and levies)

Probate Administration Paralegal

➤ General administrative duties
➤ Preparing and drafting
  ❑ Composites of wills
  ❑ Petitions for probate
  ❑ Proof of subscribing witness to will

❏ Order admitting will to probate
❏ Testamentary letters
❏ Estate inventories
❏ Creditors' claims for family members
❏ Petitions and orders for family allowance consents to transfer
❏ Stock powers
❏ Affidavits of domicile
❏ Inheritance tax declarations
❏ Estate tax returns
❏ Petitions for final accountings
❏ Petitions for appointments of conservator
❏ Letters to and interviews with beneficiaries

➤ Other duties
❏ Distributing receipts
❏ Documenting sales and transferring assets
❏ Opening, maintaining, and reconciling estate checking and savings accounts
❏ Obtaining inheritance tax referee
❏ Opening safe-deposit boxes
❏ Obtaining appraisals
❏ Assisting beneficiaries in filing of life insurance claims
❏ Obtaining federal employer identification numbers for estate

➤ Estate planning
❏ Drafting wills and trusts
❏ Applying to Internal Revenue Service for taxpayer identification number for trusts
❏ Checking on asset transfers for trusts
❏ Maintaining savings account records
❏ Drafting letters to clients explaining will or trust
❏ Drafting agreements regarding ownership of property
❏ Changing beneficiary designations and titles to property
❏ Maintaining records of wills
❏ Updating will and trust form book

Corporate Paralegal

➤ Organization of a corporation
❏ Performing initial client interview
❏ Opening the client file, preparing and filing documents relative to incorporation
❏ Preparing

- Pre-incorporation subscriptions
- Reserving the corporate name
- Pre-incorporation agreements
- Articles of incorporation
❑ Drafting bylaws
❑ Drafting notices for incorporating an ongoing business
❑ Organizing meetings
➤ Routine operation of corporation
  ❑ Issuing shares
  ❑ Drafting
    - Buy/sell agreements
    - Resolutions
    - Documents required for registration of securities
    - Notices of securities exemptions
    - Subchapter S elections
    - Termination of Subchapter S elections
    - Notice of directors' meeting, waivers, minutes
    - Amendments to the bylaws
    - Amendments and restatements of articles
    - Changes in capital structure
    - Dividend resolution and declaration
➤ Basic organization changes
  ❑ Preparing and organizing
    - Mergers and acquisitions
    - Consolidations
    - Reorganizations
    - Requests for tax rulings
  ❑ Dissolution of a corporation
  ❑ Drafting dissolutions
  ❑ Preparing sales of assets
➤ General duties
  ❑ Preparing corporate tax returns
  ❑ Forming closed corporations

Real Estate Paralegal

➤ Drafting and reviewing documents relative to real estate
➤ Preparing and drafting
  ❑ Brokers and agent contracts (listing agreements)
  ❑ Options to purchase

- ❑ Sales contracts
- ❑ Exchanges
- ❑ Real property security transactions
- ❑ Deeds of trust
- ❑ Promissory notes, including installments and wraparounds
- ❑ Interim construction loans
- ❑ Restrictions on land use
- ❑ Permanent loans
- ❑ Dedication of homestead
- ❑ Real property leases
- ❑ Subdivision contracts
- ❑ Construction agreements
- ❑ Mechanics' and materialmen's liens
- ❑ Property management contracts
- ❑ Real estate syndications
- ❑ Deeds, including general warranties, special warranties, and quit claims

By now, you have gotten a feeling for the different areas of law practice and for the types of responsibilities delegated to paralegals in each area. For more information about the profession, you may want to check out the U.S. Department of Labor, Bureau Labor Statistics, at *www.bls.gov*.

The next step is to look at how legal assistants fit into law firm and corporate organizational structures, determining the likely places to find jobs and who has the hiring authority.

2

Where Do You Fit into the Organization?

Finding the Decision Makers in Law Firms and Corporations

It is crucial in seeking your first paralegal job that you determine who makes the hiring decisions in the law firm or corporation, including the accepted process of interviewing and hiring. Often, being referred to a human resources department may sound the death knell to your job aspirations. Successful applicants often find that going directly to the person making the hiring decisions is most productive.

However, the direct approach may not be appropriate in seeking a paralegal job. Law firms and corporate counsels' offices are often very formal, and this means following established procedures. Although it will ultimately be necessary to meet with the hiring authority, it may be inappropriate to try to do so at first. Initially, you should establish who is the first person in a firm or corporation you need to contact about employment. Once that contact is made, you can determine through questions the person that makes the final decision. With that knowledge, you will have a better understanding of who you are meeting and why, and you can modulate your behavior accordingly. You may, for instance, try to establish a personal rapport while interviewing with an associate who may later be your boss. With the firm's managing partner, who is the ultimate hiring authority in a number of companies, you may want to be more formal.

LAW FIRM STRUCTURES

Most large firms have a managing partner, or a management committee made up of the senior partners, who are responsible for managing the firm. The hiring authority may be any one of the following persons: partner, associate, director of administration, office manager, recruiting coordinator, paralegal manager, or paralegal and possibly human resources manager.

Usually there is an office administrator, sometimes called the director of administration or the office manager. This person is in charge of the day-to-day operations of the firm, from overseeing its financial organization to determining what kind of computer system to purchase. Sometimes this person is in charge of hiring paralegals, and you may need to meet with the administrator first. Then again, there may be a human resources department that handles this initially and then reports to the administrator.

Some firms are structured so the paralegals are managed by a paralegal supervisor (also called a legal assistant manager or coordinator). All managers are good sources of information about the firm's structure, work flow, and hiring process. Smaller firms usually have an office manager, who may be the first contact in the hiring process. Call the firm and ask the receptionist who is the appropriate person to contact about employment. Once that contact is made, you can begin gathering the additional information you need about the firm.

Many large firms (over 50 attorneys) have a formal, structured paralegal department, as mentioned before, headed by the paralegal supervisor. Supervisors have their own organization, the International Paralegal Management Association (IPMA), with chapters around the nation.

HOT TIP

For networking purposes, it might be a good idea to find out if there is a local International Paralegal Management Association (IPMA) chapter in your area. The members can be a great source of information about the opportunities available at the firm and, as most managers are former legal assistants themselves, can also be a good source for informational interviews. (See Chapter 8 for a description of the purpose of an informational interview.)

A firm's paralegal program can be seen as a career ladder you can climb as you gain experience. Several legal assistant levels may exist, all with different levels of pay, overtime and bonus schedules, and degrees of responsibility.

Some firms will also utilize case, document clerks, or paralegal assistants. Though these clerks are at the bottom of the ladder, being hired in one of these positions is an excellent way for entry-level paralegals to begin their ascent.

In an ideal world, all law firms would have a structured paralegal program, but many do not. A legal assistant with five years of experience working for such a firm may have the same rank as a new person. All legal assistants may be expected to report directly to attorneys, and there may be no structured levels. However, experienced legal assistants at such firms sometimes have found their specific niche or specialization and enjoy status, tenure, and great salaries.

> **HOT TIP**
>
> Even if you are to be interviewed by the lawyer you will be working with, it is a good idea to contact the paralegal manager both to establish rapport and to gather information about the role of paralegals in that firm.

Most small firms do not have a structured paralegal program. Legal assistants are hired to work with a particular attorney who is generally overloaded. How you get along with this person is crucial to your happiness and success on the job. Be sure to talk at length with this lawyer during the interview and after you are hired about what is expected of you.

CORPORATE LAW DEPARTMENT STRUCTURES

If you accept a position with a corporation, you will most likely be working in a legal department headed by the general counsel. You may answer directly to the general counsel, assistant general counsel, or a paralegal administrator. In some corporations, legal departments have not been established. You may be acting as the legal liaison between the corporation and a law firm hired to take care of the corporation's legal business. Ask about this structure and try to meet these people during the interviewing process. In a law firm, each partner is fairly autonomous. You may answer to partner X but have nothing to do with partner Y. In a corporate legal department, the general counsel is the boss.

Corporations can offer opportunities for career growth that are not always found in law firms. Often employees at corporations enroll in a paralegal training program—taking either a full program or just one or two courses—and then use this knowledge, coupled with their existing knowledge of the company's business, to jump into the general counsel's office. Many make this move because they believe that the work will be more rewarding.

After working as a paralegal in a general counsel's office, legal assistants may be promoted to other areas of the company where their knowledge is a specific

> **HOT TIP**
>
> There are other types of legal environments—not-for-profit, governmental offices, etc.—that have environments similar to law offices and corporations. Nonprofit organizations may be similar to the law office structure and the governmental office may have a structure similar to the corporate model.

benefit. Paralegals in corporations have aspired to administrative supervisory positions, marketing management positions, or computer information management positions (sometimes referred to as MIS, manager of information systems).

HOT TIP

If you are seeking a vertical climb up a corporate ladder through the paralegal position, be sure to find out how many vice presidents in the corporation came from the legal department. If that department has been ignored, this may not be the place for you.

WHERE CAN YOU FIND JOBS?

In Private Law Firms

Wherever there is an attorney, there will usually be a need for a paralegal. In the past, the greatest employers of paralegals have been large law firms (50 or more attorneys). Now, however, paralegals have more luck finding jobs in small law firms (2–15 attorneys) or with sole practitioners. Midsize firms (15–50) also utilize paralegals to a great extent. (See Chapter 9 for assistance in locating law firms.)

With Corporate Legal Departments

An increasing number of corporations are using paralegals, whether or not they have in-house legal departments. An in-house legal department is usually a separate department made up of attorneys and requisite staff within a company. They handle the corporation's legal work and coordinate with outside counsel—independently hired law firms that have other clients in addition to the corporation. If a corporation does not have an in-house legal department, a paralegal may be hired to act as a liaison between the corporation and outside counsel.

Virtually every industry that uses corporate counsel also employs paralegals. Among them are companies specializing in

- ➤ Health care including hospitals and health care providers such as HMOs (Health Maintenance Organizations) or PPOs (Preferred Provider Organizations)
- ➤ Oil and gas
- ➤ Entertainment
- ➤ Financial services including insurance companies, banks, and real estate companies
- ➤ Accountancy services
- ➤ Computer technology

➤ Print and electronic media
➤ Utilities
➤ Transportation
➤ Manufacturing
➤ Publishing
➤ Food production and food service
➤ Software development
➤ Construction
   ❏ Retail

. . . just to name a few.

If you want to work as a paralegal in the corporate world, it is a good idea to seek a position in an industry that interests you. This is important because the work will certainly be more fascinating to you and because this could be a stepping stone into other aspects of the business.

Nonprofit Organizations

Many state and local bar associations and nonprofit organizations use paralegals as well. They include

➤ United Way
➤ American Red Cross and other disaster relief organizations
➤ Planned Parenthood and Right to Life groups
➤ Religious organizations such as Catholic Charities, Jewish Federations, and the Anti-Defamation League
➤ American Civil Liberties Union, The Southern Poverty law Center, the Urban League, Mexican American Legal Defense Fund, and other civil rights organizations
➤ Legal Aid Groups

. . . just to name a few.

The Federal, State, and Local Government

Government agencies are the single largest employers in the United States. These entities employ paralegals in many different areas. At the state level, positions may be found with the courts, the state's attorney general's office, or within the legislature, either as a state employee or a member of a legislator's staff. Lobbying groups usually employ a significant number of legal assistants. For paralegals interested in criminal law, district attorneys' and public defenders' offices offer good chances for employment. City governmental agencies such as the city attorney's office frequently hire paralegals, especially in the housing and job discrimination divisions.

At the federal level, many agencies utilize employees with a paralegal education. Remember, not all federal jobs are located in Washington, D.C. Most federal agencies and departments have offices in major cities throughout the United States. Be sure to check the list of resource publications in Chapter 9 for additional information.

What follows is a partial list of federal agencies, departments, and commissions that employ paralegals.

- ➤ Administrative Office of the U.S. courts
- ➤ Agency for International Development
- ➤ Bureau of Land Management
- ➤ Commission on Civil Rights
- ➤ Commodity Futures Trading Commission
- ➤ Corps of Engineers
- ➤ Department of Defense
- ➤ Department of Energy
- ➤ Department of Homeland Security
- ➤ Department of the Interior
- ➤ Department of Labor
- ➤ Equal Employment Opportunity Commission
- ➤ Executive Office of the President
- ➤ Federal Aviation Administration
- ➤ Federal Communications Commission
- ➤ Federal Deposit Insurance Corporation
- ➤ Federal Emergency Management Agency
- ➤ Federal Maritime Commission
- ➤ Federal Railroad Administration
- ➤ Federal Reserve System
- ➤ Federal Retirement Thrift Investment Board
- ➤ Federal Trade Commission
- ➤ General Services Administration
- ➤ International Trade Commission
- ➤ Library of Congress
- ➤ Merit Systems Protection Board
- ➤ National Highway Traffic Safety Administration
- ➤ National Labor Relations Board
- ➤ Office of Attorney Personnel Management

➤ Office of the Solicitor General
➤ Office of Thrift Supervision
➤ Patent and Trademark Office
➤ Securities and Exchange Commission
➤ Small Business Administration
➤ U.S. Postal Service

Federal Governmental Paralegal Titles

Job titles for paralegals in government vary from one agency to another. This difference is primarily a function of the employing agency's attempt to define the purpose of the job in the title. Whatever the exact title is, all the positions listed require a legal assistant background. When scanning job listings, be on the lookout for the terms analyst and specialist. Here is a sampling of job titles:

➤ Environmental Protection Specialist
➤ Security Specialist
➤ Foreign Service Diplomatic Security Officer
➤ Foreign Law Specialist
➤ Civil Rights Analyst
➤ Employee Relations Specialist
➤ Labor Management Relations Examiner
➤ Mediator
➤ Freedom of Information Act Specialist

ORGANIZATIONAL CHARTS TELL YOU WHERE YOU FIT

Typical organizational charts of various-size law firms and legal departments of corporations are shown in Illustrations 2.1 to 2.4. As you contemplate working at a specific firm or company, try to gain an understanding of its organizational structure so that you will understand how you would fit in. In a typical small firm, for example, you may be working with an associate you like very much but have to report to an office manager who puts you off. Think twice before taking a job with that kind of structure, because you may be headed for friction that you could avoid.

ILLUSTRATION 2.1

Small Firm Organizational Chart

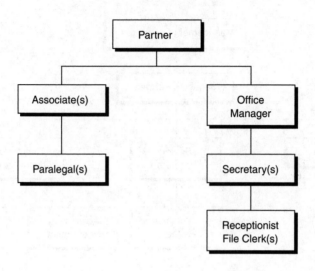

ILLUSTRATION 2.2

Midsize Law Firm Organizational Chart

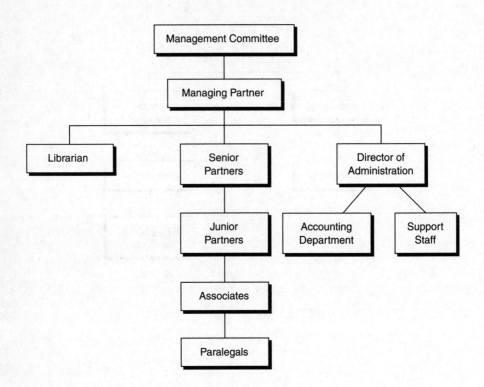

ILLUSTRATION 2.3

Large Firm Organizational Chart

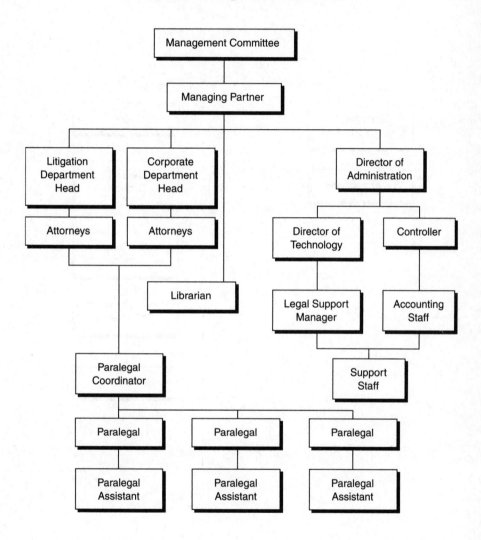

ILLUSTRATION 2.4

Corporate Legal Department Organizational Chart

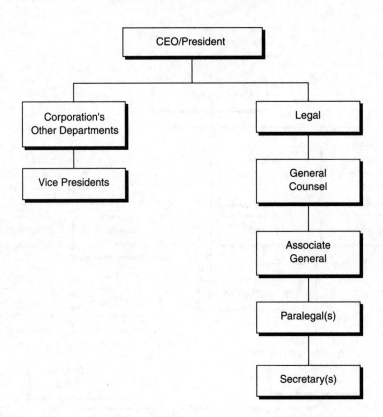

3

Straight Talk about Paralegal Schools

How to Make the Right Choice

DO YOU HAVE TO GO TO PARALEGAL SCHOOL?

You do not have to go to paralegal school to land your first paralegal job. It is a good idea; strategically, it puts you in a stronger position. But it is not absolutely necessary. That is particularly true for many law firms that hire people who are on their way to law or graduate school to work as paralegals. These firms believe that paralegals are transitional and are using the position primarily to sample the legal field as a future workplace. In other firms, paralegals are viewed more with an eye toward longevity. There it is difficult to land a paralegal job without training—difficult, but not impossible. Often, you can find both trends—transitional and career position—operating at the same firm, at the same time. But having achieved a bachelor's degree and/or a paralegal certificate will enable you to advance faster in the profession. Down the road if you decide to transition to another profession, the degree will certainly help you achieve that goal.

People from other careers—teachers, nurses, and legal secretaries, for instance—can move laterally into the paralegal field without training. The crucial determinant in such lateral moves seems to be that the candidate possess skills that ensure success as a paralegal. Teachers are skilled at digesting, organizing, and articulating vast amounts of information; nurses can be invaluable in medical malpractice litigation; legal secretaries have often learned so much about a particular legal specialty that they can make the jump to paralegal in that specialty with no trouble whatsoever.

If you have already proven yourself as a valuable employee working in a corporation, but seek more stimulating work, you may be able to transfer into the general counsel's office as a paralegal. Your knowledge of the business makes you an instantly valuable paralegal, even if you have to be trained in certain paralegal functions. I know of a woman who worked for an oil company, gathering technical information on oil well production for government-required reports. When she sought a transfer to the general counsel's office, they jumped at the opportunity because she already had great technical knowledge and had proven herself responsible in handling important, detailed information.

Still, I cannot emphasize enough the importance of paralegal training. The legal work is complex and difficult; to function properly as a paralegal you must learn a great deal about the law. While on-the-job training sounds like a fine way to learn, it can also be harrowing and, at times, debilitating. If you are the kind of person who enjoys being thrown into situations and likes to learn quickly on your own, the on-the-job training approach may be for you. On the other hand, if you are the sort who likes to feel confident about being able to perform a task before undertaking it, the basic training provided by paralegal schools can put you in a stronger position as both an applicant and an employee. However, most employers want paralegals who know legal skills that can only come through a paralegal education.

CHOOSING THE RIGHT PARALEGAL PROGRAM FOR YOU

To keep pace with the growing need for paralegals, the number of paralegal schools has been increasing, graduating paralegals by the thousands. Even though paralegal jobs are becoming more plentiful, the number of candidates vying for these positions has made entry-level competition challenging. It is important that you research several schools to make sure that you are getting the best possible education. Many schools now offer distance learning programs for those not able to attend in person. I feel it is important to actually attend class and interact with fellow students and teachers. Future jobs can be found by networking with classmates and instructors.

You will be working in a field in which your employers—lawyers—are highly educated; they want to attract employees with good academic backgrounds. Even though many paralegals are hired without a degree or paralegal certificate, or are trained in-house by attorneys, in a competitive job market, the more education you have, the easier it will be to get the higher-paying position and move up the paralegal ladder.

Types of Programs

There are many kinds of paralegal programs, which range in length from a few months to four or more years. There are degree programs within universities, as well as postgraduate courses. Other programs are associated with colleges as extension courses of study. Still others are structured more like general trade schools. Refer to Appendix B for a list of legal assistant and paralegal schools.

HOT TIP

After you have completed your paralegal certificate, it is a great idea to get a job as a paralegal and then continue your education at night to earn a bachelor's degree. The chances of your getting a better job will be greatly enhanced.

➤ Community colleges usually offer a two-year program. Some offer an associate of arts or sciences degree in paralegal studies, which incorporates a paralegal certificate. Others may offer a postbaccalaureate or postassociate certificate.

➤ Many four-year colleges and universities offer bachelor's degrees in paralegal studies; some offer master's degrees as well.

➤ Graduate and extension programs offer a shorter schedule for those who already possess bachelor's degrees. These programs can last anywhere from a few months to one year.

➤ Private (proprietary) business or trade schools also offer programs that vary in length.

All of these programs have varying admission standards. Some require only a high school diploma (or its equivalent, i.e., G.E.D.) for admission. Others have much more stringent standards, requiring a bachelor's degree with a minimum 3.0 grade point average. Some programs also require entrance examinations, covering writing and reasoning skills. These tests can be quite demanding.

Although cost is a major consideration for almost everyone, if that is your only criterion, beware! Cost is only a fraction of the total picture. Put on your detective hat and do some investigation. You should look at a number of options before selecting which school to attend. Some general questions to be asked of the school's administration when choosing the best program for you are listed below.

REPUTATION IN THE FIELD

➤ What do law firms and legal departments think of this school?

➤ Who teaches at the school?

➤ Who is on the school's advisory board?

➤ What do other educators, employers, attorneys, and paralegals think of the school?

INSTRUCTORS' QUALIFICATIONS AND BACKGROUNDS

➤ Have the instructors ever taught before and for how long?

➤ Are they working in the legal community?

➤ If they are attorneys, do they use paralegals themselves?

➤ Do the instructors generally know about paralegal job descriptions?

➤ Are the instructors teaching in their legal specialty?

ENROLLMENT REQUIREMENTS

➤ How lax or stringent are the requirements for admission?

➤ Do you need any specific educational background to be accepted?

PLACEMENT CAPABILITIES

➤ Do the law firms and legal departments that interest you accept this school's graduates?

➤ How many of the school's graduates are placed in positions?

➤ What is the average time it takes to place the school's graduates in paralegal positions?

➤ Where do the school's graduates find jobs?

➤ Does placement take a longer or shorter period of time than at comparable schools?

➤ Ask to speak to graduates directly. Get their feedback.

➤ Conduct a telephone survey of firms and corporations to determine their opinions of the school.

➤ If ABA approved, are graduate or student surveys available?

RELEVANT CURRICULUM

➤ Does the school offer a curriculum that is relevant to the paralegal practice in your region?

➤ Does the curriculum adapt to and reflect the current changes in the law?

➤ Does the school teach practical procedures as well as substantive law?

➤ Does the program have an internship or work experience as part of the curriculum?

➤ Does the school offer training in LEXIS and Westlaw?

FINANCIAL STABILITY

➤ Is the school on solid financial footing?

➤ If it is a private institution, ask for an annual report.

➤ Check with the Better Business Bureau or local chamber of commerce to find out if there have been any complaints.

➤ How long has the school existed?

STUDENT SERVICES AVAILABLE

➤ Is specialized tutoring available?

➤ What kind of financial aid is offered?

➤ Is there an active alumni association?

➤ What services do the student organizations provide?

USEFULNESS OF THE LIBRARY

➤ Is there a law library on campus?

➤ Does the school have relevant materials and books for you to use?

➤ Does it look as though the school has made an investment in proper training materials for its students?

➤ Are computers and technical assistance available for research and student use?

COST OF TUITION AND COURSE MATERIALS

➤ Find out whether scholarships or financial aid are offered.

➤ If you are choosing a private school or graduate course, shop around to find out whether the school is competitively priced.

➤ The school's tuition and fee charges should fall within 10 to 20 percent of those at comparable schools. If they are higher, try to find out why.

➤ Community colleges are usually the least expensive.

➤ Are there any hidden costs such as extra fees for books and materials, student body fees, additional training, and so on?

ACCESSIBILITY

➤ Is the school a reasonable distance from your home?

➤ Will commuting a great distance hamper you?

HOT TIP

Community colleges have the least expensive paralegal programs, and some of them are approved by the American Bar Association. It could not hurt to check with your local community college regarding program costs before you decide on which school to attend.

Importance of a Comprehensive Curriculum

Paralegal curricula vary from school to school. The American Association for Paralegal Education (AAfPE) has developed model syllabi and paralegal skills that should be mastered. Many schools are currently following the AAfPE's recommendation. (See Appendix B for schools that are AAfPE members.) The following courses should be included in order to provide you with a well-rounded legal education:

➤ *Introduction course:* provides an overview of the law and the paralegal field.

➤ *Legal research and writing course:* includes training on the use of LEXIS, Westlaw, and/or other legal research databases.

➤ *Legal ethics course:* covers the obligations owed to the client, avoiding the appearance of impropriety, and the unauthorized practice of law.

➤ *Substantive courses:* teach the "whys" of various areas of law, such as contracts, torts, and property, in which the student is required to read legal opinions and brief cases and draft documents.

➤ *Procedural courses:* teach the "how-to" of law and specific rules governing lawyers' activities.

➤ *Computer or word processing courses:* include skills specifically applicable for legal professionals such as database, spreadsheet, and word processing applications.

Course content should include the way things are done in order to enable the student to gain an understanding of areas such as the litigation process, corporate maintenance, real estate closings, and administration of probate.

The school should also offer specialty certificates and courses. The most common specialties are in litigation and corporate practices. Additional courses in other specialty areas can include

➤ Bankruptcy
➤ Family law
➤ Entertainment law
➤ Workers' compensation
➤ Wills and trusts
➤ Taxation
➤ Computerized litigation support
➤ Property law
➤ Environmental law
➤ Criminal law
➤ Intellectual property
➤ Alternative dispute resolution

Some paralegal students prefer programs offering a specialty certificate rather than a general one. For paralegals wishing to work in smaller law firms, where paralegals are usually required to know several areas of law, many schools offer a general legal program. It is certainly true that many experienced paralegals

HOT TIP

If typing and clerical courses are offered, beware! As a general rule, paralegals at a professional level are not required to perform secretarial/clerical duties unless they have the dual job title Paralegal/Secretary. If a school offers such courses, it is probably not a professionally-oriented paralegal program. Do not, however, confuse a computer training course for paralegals with secretarial training. Although both require use of a keyboard, there is a world of difference between the two! In many offices, the paralegal must do their own computer work and the secretary does purely clerical work.

find job satisfaction through specialization. On the other hand, specialty certificates are less available.

Whatever path you choose depends on your own unique wishes and desires concerning the type of firm or corporation you wish to join. I know of several legal assistants who obtained litigation specialty certificates because they thought that they would enjoy working in the litigation departments of large firms. More than a few have moved into other practice areas and to smaller firms. Investigate the legal field thoroughly before you decide.

ABA Approval

Currently, approximately 300 schools nationwide have received American Bar Association (ABA) approval, and that number is growing daily. The American Bar Association's Standing Committee on Legal Assistants originally decided to use an approval system for paralegal schools to help standardize the curriculum. The approval process is voluntary on the school's part. But many schools that have fine programs have not sought ABA approval. Check with the law firms and legal departments you may wish to work for to find out whether they require entry-level paralegals to have a certificate from an ABA-approved school.

To be approved by the ABA, paralegal schools must adhere to the following guidelines:

➤ Is part of an accredited educational institution
➤ Offers at least 60 semester or 90 quarter units (or the equivalent) of classroom work; must include general education and at least 18 semester (or 27 quarter) units of legal specialty courses
➤ Has articulation agreements with other institutions so students can continue for higher degrees

> ➤ Has qualified, experienced instructors
> ➤ Has adequate financial support from the institution in which it is situated
> ➤ Is accredited by, or eligible for accreditation by, an accrediting agency recognized by the Council on Post Secondary Accreditation
> ➤ Has adequate student services, including counseling and placement
> ➤ Has an adequate library
> ➤ Has appropriate facilities and equipment

After evaluating and investigating the legal assistant programs in your area thoroughly, choose one that meets your own personal criteria for cost, location, length, and so on, but most important, where you feel you will get the best education. If you are about to begin your paralegal training, you will want to consult the list of paralegal programs in Appendix B.

4

How to Stand Out from the Crowd

Crafting Winning Resumes, Reference Lists, and Writing Samples

A partner in a big-city law firm told me of a problem that most prospective employers face when hiring an entry-level paralegal. When he ran a help-wanted ad to fill the position, he was confronted with screening over 500 resumes. From among these, he had to select four to six candidates to interview—a few shining needles in the haystack. Although he was looking for competence in the field, he was also looking for a person with high-quality work standards, an ability to work well under pressure, and a personality that would mesh with other members of the firm.

"I realized that I was expecting a whale of a lot from a resume," the partner recalled. "I knew some of the things I was looking for would not show up except in the interview."

The purpose of every resume is to get you to the next step—the interview. It cannot win you a job, but it must win attention during the screening process. Employers typically spend 30 seconds or less reading a resume. Unless your resume gets attention, you will sit at home!

SELLING YOURSELF TO THE LEGAL INDUSTRY

Job hunting is selling yourself. Your resume is an advertisement about you. It is an example of your work product, and the prospective employer will scrutinize it carefully. Among the hundreds of paralegal resumes I have screened, I have been amazed to find many with spelling and typographical errors. One sloppy mistake can end the job hunt. Legal work is based on accuracy. You will be judged by the appearance of your resume and cover letter. Mistakes are not tolerated in the legal community! A careless mistake translates in the attorney's mind to "a person who does sloppy work."

Your resume is a brief summary of your education and professional background. Its goal is to present your qualifications to the employer in the most favorable light. As an advertisement, it should be geared toward your target market, the legal field. The resume can be further tailored for a specific area of law, job opening, or law firm. Word processing allows you to customize your resume for each application. Within one or two pages, your resume must emphasize those skills and abilities that most interest lawyers. The rest is superfluous.

There are many styles of resumes. Regardless of the format, it must be concise, accurate, and attractive. But do not get carried away with design. Try to avoid large or boldfaced headings, logos, and similar devices. Remember, the resume is going to the legal community, a very conservative and exacting audience.

UNDERSTANDING YOURSELF BEFORE SELLING YOURSELF TO OTHERS

Whatever your background, you probably possess skills transferable to the paralegal field. Carpenters have become paralegals in the field of construction litigation; persons with medical backgrounds are needed in the area of medical malpractice and personal injury; environmental experience can be applied to real estate development and environmental litigation; insurance claims handlers make great insurance defense paralegals; persons with manufacturing or engineering experience do well in product liability firms; counselors and social workers fit in family law practices; those with import and export backgrounds became international trade paralegals; entertainers and writers understand entertainment law; real estate agents have gone to work as real estate paralegals; and escrow and trust officers gravitate toward probate. I know of a firm that is enthusiastic about hiring former teachers, because the firm's management believes that teachers know how to handle difficult attorneys (sometimes viewed in the same light as difficult children)!

A self-study is helpful before you begin your resume and job search. You cannot sell anything that you know little about. Awareness of your strengths and weaknesses can help you decide on realistic and appropriate job expectations. It will also make you more aware of yourself as a product. Take time to think through the following questions and write out your answers. This process provokes thought and can be used for rehearsing interviews.

> ➤ What am I doing in my present (or past) position that brings me the most satisfaction?
>> ❑ Think about what you have done in your past jobs and write down these tasks.
>> ❑ Look at the end of Chapter 1 and see if any of these tasks or skills could be translated into similar legal skills.

➤ What do I most enjoy doing?
  ❑ There is the old saying: "Do what you love and the money will follow."
  ❑ Think about what you enjoy doing and relate that to a particular area of law, for instance: Do you like to hike? Then maybe you should set your sights on environmental law. Do you like to sail or be on a boat? Then think about maritime or admiralty law.

➤ What are my most significant accomplishments?
  ❑ We all have done something in our lives that we are proud of. Think about this and how you enjoyed the accomplishment. Mention it in your resume.
  ❑ The accomplishments could be something you've done while working, in college, or a home-based activity or volunteer work. Did you raise money for the PTA? Did you start a club at school? Did you save your company money?

➤ Would I rather work with paper or people problems?
  ❑ Answering this truthfully will tell you whether you should be a researcher or deal with clients.

➤ Do I like to give great attention to detail, or am I a "free spirit"?
  ❑ Depending on how you answer this question, your choice of law firm will be evident. Attention to detail—the best place is a corporate environment. A free spirit—maybe nonprofit should be the goal.

➤ Would I rather work 9 to 5 or make my own hours?
  ❑ If you have children or outside obligations, a 9 to 5 job would be the best for you.
  ❑ But if you want more freedom, making your own hours would best suit a freelance paralegal.

➤ What are my best and worst personal qualities?
  ❑ Being honest with yourself will help you answer interview questions.

➤ What makes me different or special from everyone else?
  ❑ Use this information in your cover letter to get the attention of the employer.

➤ Do I enjoy taking responsibility for my actions or would I rather let someone else take the risk?
  ❑ Do you want to eventually be the boss or start your own business?
  ❑ Or do you want to work for someone else and maybe move up the ladder.

➤ What are my long-term and short-term career goals?
  ❑ An important step in helping you prepare for the interview.

When you have evaluated yourself thoughtfully, you should have a good idea of the kinds of jobs where you will be most comfortable. As a result, you can create a stronger resume and have more confidence when interviewing. For more examples of self-evaluation techniques and other helpful job-hunting hints, see *What Color Is Your Parachute?* by Richard Bolles (Ten Speed Press, Berkeley, CA, updated yearly).

Only a small part of your self-evaluation will ultimately appear in your resume. More emphasis on your skills and personality will be discussed during the interview. At that time, you will be able to accent your accomplishments.

RESUME APPEARANCE COUNTS

The appearance of your resume is critical. The visual impression it makes at first glance must persuade the employer to read further. Resumes with items crossed out, or corrected with handwriting and sloppy white-out, go right into the circular file. Many resumes that I have received had informal handwritten cover letters. Some were even torn out of a spiral notebook! These make a lasting impression—the wrong kind. Always use easy-to-read 10- to 12-point font and make sure your printer cartridges are full.

Your resume should be printed on 8½-by-11-inch paper on one side only. It should be on high-quality white, off-white, or pale gray paper. Do not use any brightly colored paper such as blue, yellow, pink, or green.

Be very careful not to mar your resume with fingerprints or careless folding. Carefully fold the resume and cover letter into a Number 10 envelope. Type, never handwrite, the address. Neatness is mandatory.

If you are going to fax your resume, make sure that you have a cover letter and a professionally prepared cover sheet. It is important that you type out the information rather than handwrite it. Always include a cover letter with your resume. This means that you should be faxing a minimum of three sheets of paper. If possible, send the employer a hard copy of your resume and cover letter by regular mail. Fax copies are often of poor quality; therefore, a hard copy will look more presentable and make a better impression. You may also e-mail your

HOT TIP

Purchase a ream of high-quality paper with matching envelopes. By buying a large quantity, you can use the same paper for your cover letters, list of references, writing samples, and thank-you letters. Paper and envelopes that match look better and show the employer that you have a sense of style.

resume. If you send it as an attachment, make sure that your cover letter is also included either as an attachment or in the text of the e-mail. You could also send a copy of the e-mailed resume by regular mail, but most employers prefer only electronically generated resumes as it cuts down on the number of papers that may litter their desks. But, it is also easier for them to delete your information!

When preparing the resume, be aware of margins. Too much white space makes a resume look sparse; not enough makes it appear cramped. Employers prefer a one-page resume for entry-level paralegals. Two pages are acceptable only if you have been working as a paralegal for an extensive period of time. Never go over two pages. If you do have a second page, make sure that your name and the page number appear at the top, even if it is e-mailed. If an employer is interested in you, he/she will print out your resume, so it is very important to have your name at the top of the second page.

Law firms are very fussy about what constitutes a good-looking resume. Think in terms of the law firm: Most prefer traditional appearance and content.

Remember, the job you are seeking is detail oriented. A law firm will predict your work product by the quality of your resume. If your resume is not perfect, it reflects poorly on you, and will usually prevent your getting an interview.

RESUME DO'S AND DON'TS CHECKLIST

In a recent article in a prominent magazine, the author surveyed employers who emphasized that resumes should not be more that one page in length for staff-level employees. The most common mistakes made by novice writers are resumes that are too long; contain distortions about experience; have typographical errors, misspellings, insufficient detail, and irrelevant material; and fail to cite accomplishments.

HOT TIP

Typographical errors have a way of breeding when you are not looking. Do not assume that you will find them yourself. Ask a few objective colleagues to review your resume for typographical and grammatical errors. It should be proofread at least three or four times before the final printing or e-mailing. Do not rely solely on spell check.

DO:

➤ Place your name at the top center of the resume in bold capital letters.

➤ Make sure that your phone number is on the resume. Include two phone numbers only: home, cell phone, or work phone. Cell phones or BlackBerries are a good idea if you are thinking about working on a temporary basis. You would be available immediately for all jobs.

➤ Include your e-mail address.

➤ List your education in reverse chronological order. Include your degree or certificate and the date earned. If you lack job experience, include a list of the courses you have taken.

➤ In the work experience section, start with your most recent position and work backward through past 10 years.

➤ Illustrate your career/job accomplishments (e.g., "Reorganized company's entire filing system"). For a chronological resume, describe what you have done in a bulleted list of five items or less.

➤ Send your resume to the hiring authority.

➤ Be organized and concise.

➤ List computers skills, including software packages that you have used.

➤ List any foreign languages you speak and read fluently.

➤ Follow up by phone, letter, e-mail, or fax—you may be the only person who does.

➤ Use spell check, but also have two other people review your resume.

DON'T:

➤ Write a resume longer than two pages.

➤ Put "resume" on your resume. It is like writing "book" on a book.

➤ Use abbreviations.

➤ Include personal information such as height, weight, or age.

➤ List religious, political, or fraternal organizations. It is better to describe them as "community-based" organizations.

➤ Include salaries past, present, or desired, even if the advertisement asks you to do so. (A statement regarding salary history can be included in your cover letter; see Chapter 7.)

➤ Include your photograph.

➤ List the names of your references. References should be on a separate sheet, to be given to the employer at the time of the interview.

➤ List the names of your present or past supervisors, their addresses and phone numbers. These may be included separately on your reference sheet.

➤ Include your reasons for leaving a previous job.

➤ Use the word "I" anywhere.

➤ Send out a resume with typing, grammatical, or spelling errors.

➤ Send out a resume that is smudged or poorly reproduced and more than two pages.

➤ Include typing skills unless you really want to type, but do include computer skills.

➤ List high school activities or honors. College honors may be included if they are recent.

➤ Use brightly colored paper. It is best to use white, off-white, or light gray paper.

HOT TIP

Have a professional e-mail address. Lately I've seen some pretty unprofessional e-mail addresses on resumes I've received such as "biracialgirl," "prettyfairy," "machoman," etc. These do not leave a very good impression. Set up a separate e-mail account for your job search. Then you will be sure that you will be the consummate professional you are.

MAKING SURE THAT YOUR REFERENCES HELP YOU

It is considered unprofessional to include your references on or with your resume. "References available upon request" should be the last line of your resume. This statement is the conclusion and lets the employer know that you are aware of what is expected of you.

At some point during your job search, you may have to present your reference list. Make sure that you have a neatly typed list of at least three people but not more than five, along with their current addresses, phone numbers, and e-mail addresses, if available. Take this with you to the interview, but do not present it unless you are asked.

Your references should be people with whom you have worked or who know your work, including supervisors, colleagues, and instructors. You can also include volunteer-activity supervisors. Do not include friends, relatives, ministers, or rabbis unless you have worked for them. Employers want to know how you work, not what a great personality you have.

Ask for permission before you include a person as a reference. When asked, that person's reaction will give you some indication as to the reference you will receive. As a human resource professional, I have contacted references who did serious damage to a prospective employee. These references were given to me cheerfully by the candidate, who assumed that the reference would be positive. Ask your reference what he or she intends to say about you, or at least whether the opinion offered will be positive.

Make sure that your reference source knows you well enough to verify the information on your resume. You do not want Professor Snob to say, "Who?" To avoid this problem, send each of your references a copy of your resume. Obtaining letters of recommendation can avoid the nuisance of telephone calls for both your references and your prospective employer.

HOT TIP

Provide your references with a copy of your resume to refresh their memory regarding your dates of employment and job duties.

See Illustration 4.1 for a reference example. List references on a separate sheet of paper. It is a good idea to use the same type of paper for your references that was used for your resume. Use the same identifying information as that used on your resume: your name, address, and phone number(s). Also make sure that you list a current telephone number where your references can be reached during business hours. For each reference, include

- ➤ Full name
- ➤ Current job title
- ➤ Name of current company
- ➤ Current address
- ➤ Phone number with area code
- ➤ E-mail address, if available
- ➤ Indicate (in parentheses) how this person knows you if it is not obvious from the name of the company or the educational institution.

IMPECCABLE WRITING SAMPLES AND PORTFOLIOS CAN BE YOUR SECRET WEAPON

Writing samples are an excellent way to show your future employer the quality of your work, as well as your ability to express yourself clearly on paper. People in law firms frequently groan about the paper trail they must leave and the paperwork in which they are buried. Drafting documents, letters, and interoffice memos is an important part of virtually every paralegal job. Offering a writing sample differentiates you from other candidates and shows that you are confident about your work. Let your prospective employer know that writing samples are available by stating at the end of the resume that "References and writing samples are available upon request."

Writing samples can include writing assignments completed as a paralegal student. Documents or business letters drafted for class make good samples. Summaries of depositions, on the other hand, do not allow for much individual expression and are difficult to evaluate as an example of your writing. Articles or short papers you wrote in college may also suffice, although they may not be as relevant as an evaluation tool, especially if they are several years old.

ILLUSTRATION 4.1
Reference Example

JANE PARALEGAL
111 South Street
North Town, CA 99999
(222) 555-2222
janeparalegal@nowhere.com

REFERENCE LIST

John Doe, Esq.
Doe, Smith, & Doe
2049 Century Park East, Suite 1250
Los Angeles, CA 90067
(213) 555-1111
johndoe@doesmith.com
Supervising attorney at Do Re Me law firm

Jane Smith
Litigation Instructor
University of Paralegal Studies
12201 Washington Place
San Francisco, CA 95491
(415) 444-1111
janesmith@ups.edu
Litigation professor

Brian White
ABC Company
4534 West Fifth Street
Milwaukee, WI 48797
(505) 223-4455
brianwhite@abc.com
Current supervisor

Any original research paper is acceptable. If these items are school assignments, it is a good idea to delete any comments, including the grade. Your writing will not be graded in the real world of work! If necessary, retype your writing sample to eliminate messy white-out or to correct any errors that may have occurred in the original.

Legal memos, complaints, or other documents with points and authorities attached are good samples. However, some firms prefer to see nonlegal documents, such as detailed memos, because many legal documents (especially pleadings) contain primarily boilerplate (not original) language.

If you are going to submit a sample from work on an actual legal matter, all the confidential information must be removed. This includes all references to places and products as well as names. Failure to hold legal information confidential will immediately eliminate you as a candidate under consideration. A candidate of mine was not offered a terrific job because he forgot to redact confidential information on his writing samples. Black or white out all confidential information, then copy or retype the document to make sure that none of the covered-up writing is visible.

Your writing sample should demonstrate your grasp of the English language (sentence structure, grammar, and punctuation) as well as your ability to reason and write persuasively. Have someone proofread your sample, and then retype it if necessary. A fresh eye is more likely to see errors that you have missed. Your writing sample should not be more than two or three pages long.

Make several copies so that you can distribute the samples to your interviewers. Do not send writing samples or your list of references along with your resume and cover letter. They are reserved for interviews only.

You may also find it valuable to take a writing portfolio to your interview. This includes samples of work you have done either in school or on the job that demonstrate your knowledge of certain legal documents. You should include complaints, answers, appellate briefs, contracts, corporate minutes, and so on. Place these papers in a notebook, separated by dividers, with the name of the document on the tab. This portfolio will come in handy during the interview, demonstrating to the employer your knowledge of various written legal documents. The portfolio is for your use only; do not leave it with the employer—that is what your individual writing sample is for.

HOT TIP

On all your writing samples, make sure to include your name, address, and phone numbers. Also, copy your writing samples on the same paper as your resume and references. This will add a touch of class to your presentation.

5

Formats for Power Resumes: The Chronological Resume

This May Be the Best Style for You

There are many formats from which to choose when writing your resume. The most common in the legal community is the chronological format, which lists your educational background and work experience in reverse chronological order. This style is excellent for someone with a solid work history.

Another frequently used format is the functional style. This style is best for someone who has great skills but an insufficient employment history or is changing careers. The functional resume emphasizes abilities and experience rather than consistency or longevity in job history. Functional resumes are not as popular because they can be confusing. However, if you have been a "job hopper" or have gaps in your employment but are now ready to make a long-term commitment, the functional style presents you in the best light (see Chapter 6). Because you are starting a new career, I would recommend that you prepare one.

It is important when writing your resume to realize that the person reading it will do so in 30 seconds or less. Therefore, you want to make sure that the important information about you—your paralegal experience, education, and transferable skills—appear toward the top of the resume. The person reading the resume will generally scan across the top and then down the left-hand side of the document.

HOT TIP

Prepare several different resumes that you can use for various paralegal positions. I would suggest formulating both chronological and functional resumes to emphasize different strengths in your background.

HOW TO PREPARE A CHRONOLOGICAL RESUME

Personal Identification Data

Personal identification data are the introduction to your resume. Therefore, you
do not need to use "resume" or "curriculum vitae" as a title. This section must
include the following information, usually in the center, at the top of the page.

➤ Name (bold, in capital letters)
➤ Address [street (with no abbreviations), apartment number, city, state
   and zip code—use only five digits (the extra four digits in the nine
   digit code are not necessary); the state may be the two letters used by
   the post office (i.e., CA, NY, TX, WV, etc.)]
➤ Home telephone number, including area code

HOT TIP

When writing your phone number, you may either use parentheses
around the area code or not. It depends on your style.

➤ Optional: business or cell number, including the area code. Limit telephone numbers listed to two. If you do not have an answering machine,
   cell phone, or voice mail, now is the time to invest in one or the other.
   Busy employers become frustrated if they are unable to reach you. In
   this competitive job market, a missed call is a lost opportunity.
➤ E-mail address

HOT TIP

Make sure that your e-mail address is professional. *Hotchick@aol.com*
or *cutiepie@hotmail.com* just does not make it in the professional world.

Career Title or Objective (Optional)

Listing a career title or objective tells the employer exactly which job you are seeking. This optional part of your resume appears directly below your personal identification data. A career title such as Litigation Paralegal, Corporate Legal Assistant, or Litigation Support Specialist should be capitalized or listed in bold face type. It should be positioned two lines below the personal identification data.

A career title is an excellent way for entry-level paralegals to indicate their specialty area. However, it is limiting. If you are not sure which area you want to specialize in, omit this part. Similarly, do not use a career or professional objective that is wordier than simply a job title. A longer objective is usually filled with flowery language that does not tell the employer anything about you, such as,

> To secure a challenging position that fully incorporates my experience and provides continued growth.

I doubt you would want a position that is not challenging and provides no growth!—so leave it out.

Summary of Experience or Qualifications (Optional)

It is critical that your legal abilities are displayed at the top after your personal identification information and, if included, a job title. This can be done by developing a summary of experience or qualifications, which are a summary of your experience that includes skills you can transfer to the legal community. Only include this section if your qualifications are impressive. Remember, this section is optional.

If you have had a long or established career in another field, you should summarize your experience in words that a lawyer will understand. (See the section on professional experience in Chapter 6 for skills you have acquired that are transferable to the legal profession.) The summary should be concise and to the point, using language not repeated elsewhere. Include your strengths, skills, years of experience, and areas of expertise. Bullet the highlights for easy reading. For example,

> Six years of supervisory experience with major electronics firm specializing in the manufacturing of widgets.

Educational Background

If you have recently completed your paralegal education and have no other paralegal work experience, the educational section of your resume should be placed either just before or after the highlights of qualifications. The reason is that all your paralegal information should be placed at the top of the resume, where the reader will see it first.

HOT TIP

List institutions only from which you received a degree or certificate. By including schools attended but not completed, you open up a can of worms for employers. They will wonder why you did not complete your degree and if you are unreliable because of an inability to follow through with that degree. You do not want to have to explain all the circumstances of your dropping out. This could lead to your providing information about yourself that employers do not have the right to know, such as taking time off to have children, to care for an illness in the family, or because of your own medical history.

Another reason, albeit a superficial one, is that attorneys place great emphasis on education. Most attorneys have graduated from a four-year college and then have spent three to four years in law school. They seem to relate more easily to a paralegal that has a good educational background. That is why I encourage my paralegal students to continue their education, if they don't already posses a degree, after completing their paralegal certificates. It will not only help them gain the respect of their employers, but will aid them in getting better, higher-paying jobs in the future. An entry-level paralegal's resume with a bachelor's degree and a certificate listed first will be viewed more favorably than the very same candidate whose resume shows experience as a receptionist first, then lists the degree and certificate last.

Include only post–high school education in reverse chronological order. Do not include information about high school. Begin with your most recent degree or certificate. If you are still attending school, list that information first.

For each entry, include

➤ The name of the institution

➤ The location if it is not indicated in the school's name (for University of California at Los Angeles, you don't have to indicate that the school is located in Los Angeles, California)

➤ The date of graduation (only if less than 10 years ago), or expected graduation, in years only, not months (e.g., 1999, not May 1999)

➤ The degree or certificate awarded (no abbreviations)

➤ Your major and/or minor areas of study if relevant

➤ Your grade point average only if it is an A or a 4.0

➤ Any honors or distinctions you have received

HOT TIP

Do not list the date of graduation from college if it has been over 10 years. Even though employers are not allowed to discriminate because of age, why give them any ammunition to eliminate you even before they meet you? Once you have gotten the interview, you can prove your worth in person.

Include postgraduate and continuing education courses that reflect your preparation for the kind of work you are seeking. It will also be helpful to an employer to list paralegal classes you have completed. Include only those courses that are substantive in nature. You may list the classes in paragraph form or in columns, depending on your preference, as shown below:

PARAGRAPH FORM

Course of study included: Legal Research and Writing, Torts, Contracts, Environmental Law, Family Law, Law and Motion, Litigation

COLUMN FORM

Paralegal classes included:

Legal Research and Writing	Tort	Contracts
Environmental Law	Ethics	Family Law
Law and Motion	Property	Criminal Law

Following are two ways you can list your schooling:

➤ Name of school, degree or certificate, date of graduation (University of Paralegal, Des Moines, IA, Paralegal Certificate, 2008)

➤ Degree or certificate, date of graduation, name of school (Paralegal Certificate, 2008, University of Paralegal, Des Moines, IA)

HOT TIP

The exception to the "education first" rule applies to those career changers who are seeking a paralegal position in a specialty directly related to their work history as well as those who have just graduated and have no experience. For example, a pharmacist seeking a position as a medical malpractice paralegal, or a savings and loan director seeking a position in banking litigation, should definitely list experience first.

Whichever way you choose, remember that you want this information to influence the employer as to your qualifications and abilities. The choice must also be consistent throughout the resume, including the professional or work history.

You can divide your education into categories, such as those found in the following example:

Graduate Studies

University of Paralegal Studies, Denver, CO, ABA-approved Certificate in Litigation with Honors, 2008

Classes included: Torts, Contracts, Litigation Process, Ethics, Research and Discovery

Undergraduate Studies

University of California, Los Angeles, 2006

Bachelor of Arts in English, summa cum laude

Continuing Education

Litigation for the Practioner, Texas Bay Association, 2008

Fast Track Litigation, Practicing Law Institute, Houston, 2008

Various seminars on the litigation process, 2007 to 2008

Skills, Abilities, and Qualifications (Optional)

Describing the paralegal skills gained through your experience or schooling, together with other relevant qualifications, is a good way to catch the eye of an employer. This section should include information not found in any other place in the resume and is different from skills listed in your summary of qualifications.

If you have not attended a paralegal program, list seminars and courses you have taken that emphasize paralegal skills. For example, former real estate salespeople can list their training and licenses.

Be sure to list management, supervisory, and leadership skills as well as other personal qualities. Busy law firms look for legal assistants who can work independently, who have great attention to detail, and who can work well under pressure. If you have these qualities, you should advertise them!

Refer to your personal skills assessment for additional abilities. Be sure to include computer experience or skills. Do not mention secretarial skills such as typing, filing, faxing, photocopying, or answering phones unless you are applying for a combined secretary/paralegal position.

Computer experience is a very important asset for new legal assistants. You can highlight this asset by creating a separate section on your resume:

COMPUTER SKILLS

➤ Ability to adapt to most major software packages

➤ Familiar with Windows Vista, Excel, WordPerfect 9.0, Microsoft Word, and Lotus 123

➤ Knowledge of Macintosh, PC, and several data input systems

➤ Experienced with search and retrieval databases such as LEXIS and Westlaw

➤ Internet savvy

Also include your foreign language abilities, but only if you are fluent. If it is appropriate for your specialty, you can mention the fact that you lived in another part of the world.

EXAMPLES OF SKILLS AND ABILITIES

➤ Background skills include supervision, administration, organization; verbal and written communication; decision making and problem solving; evaluating, interviewing, analysis, and organization of data; editing and proofreading.

➤ Personal attributes include stability and assertiveness.

➤ Legal experience includes knowledge of basic legal concepts, procedures, and sources of legal research.

➤ Abilities include the analyzing and drafting of legal documents and pleadings, including complaints, answers, demurrers, motions, and legal briefs; managing files, indexing documents and records; summarizing documents and depositions; shepardizing and cite-checking cases, compiling and verifying citations; and identifying and reviewing decisions for relevance to the issue at hand.

➤ Other abilities include handling the paperwork and procedures to form and dissolve corporations: preparing minutes, drafting agreements related to incorporations, analyzing profit-and-loss statements, drafting wills and lifetime trusts, and computing federal income taxes.

You should also include skills or experience in accounting, bookkeeping, real estate, or journalism. Include any courses such as business law or another legally related matter. Mention all skills you have acquired that relate to the legal profession. Be creative, and be careful not to repeat yourself.

Legal Internship (Optional)

An internship is an excellent way to gain legal experience, especially if you have none. If you have completed or are in the process of completing an internship, it should be placed above your professional experience. Remember, all of your legal experience should be positioned as close to the top of the resume as possible. This section will be similar in appearance to your professional experience, so follow the directions below as to how to prepare your job description.

Professional Experience or Employment

Begin with your most recent job and work backward in reverse chronological order. If you have limited work experience, emphasize the skills and abilities you have gained through your education. However, you should include some work history, even if it is just a volunteer position or part-time employment while attending college. If possible, show the relevance of your previous jobs to legal work. Detail only the last four or five positions you have had in the last 10 years.

For each entry include

> ➤ Job title
> ➤ Name of employer
> ➤ Location (if it is not reflected in the name of the employer; the city and state only)
> ➤ Dates (years only) of employment
> ➤ Concise and pertinent job description

Use action verbs in the present tense for current jobs, and in the past tense for all others, when describing your experience. These verbs add dynamism to your resume. (See the end of Chapter 6 for a list of action verbs.)

Writing a Compelling Job Description

This is probably one of the most difficult sections of the resume you will have to write. The following exercise will help pinpoint the most salient facts of your past jobs.

Write each job title you have had in the last 10 years at the top of a piece of paper, using a separate piece of paper for each job. Then list everything you have ever done on that job. Include achievements as well as responsibilities. Don't worry about grammar or spelling; this is just brainstorming, refinement will come later. Include the mundane—stuffing envelopes—to the sublime—designing the set for *Phantom of the Opera*.

The next step is to cross out those things that you really do not like to do, or that will not impress an employer. It never fails that if your job description includes information about collating millions of documents and you really dislike this chore, inevitably you will be hired just because you can collate. So be aware and be wise—leave it out.

Similarly, you want to impress the person who is reading this document, the employer. Do not include information such as typing and filing, because the employer will not be impressed.

Upon completing this part of the exercise, you should be left with tasks or accomplishments that you like to do, are proud of, or will impress an employer. Choose three to five items and arrange them in order of importance, the most important things first, and the rest in descending order.

Now comes the refinement. Use bullets and action verbs to emphasize your experience. The verbs should begin each sentence. Remember to use the present tense for your current job and the past tense for all other jobs you have had. Also, use numbers wherever possible, especially if you have ever made money or saved money for your employer.

As I mentioned before, employers will be skimming the resume by reading across the top and down the left-hand side. By starting your sentences with action verbs and bullets, you will attract the reader's eye and hopefully, the employers will be so intrigued by your words, they will want to read it more slowly.

Below is a list of questions that may help you in composing your job descriptions.

➤ Have you ever been a supervisor or manager?

➤ Can you give any examples of having helped your company or firm grow?

➤ Can you give any examples of how you saved or made money for the company?

➤ Can you show that you were promoted rapidly?

➤ Did you receive any other form of recognition that would show your ability? For example, did your salary increase substantially within a year or two? Express this in percentages, if possible.

➤ What have you done that you will be doing as a paralegal? This can include writing reports, performing research, dealing directly with clients, and organizing documents. (Look in Chapter 1 for a list of paralegal duties.)

In describing former jobs, try to avoid repeating duties that you have mentioned previously. An employer is likely to favor applicants who have had some diversity of experience.

Below are two ways to list your employers that are similar to the ways to list educational background:

➤ Employer, job title, date of employment

➤ Job title, employer, date of employment

HOT TIP

A work history longer than 10 years may indicate to employers what your age is, which they have no right to know.

Again, your choice will influence the employer as to whether he or she will want to interview you. Think about what information to place first that will catch the employer's eye and be impressive.

NO LEGAL EXPERIENCE—NO PROBLEM
. . . .

If you have no legal experience, you may want to gain some by doing volunteer work. Contact the local legal aid society or other nonprofit law offices or legal corporations in your area. You will also find a list of organizations that always appreciate volunteers in "Where Can You Find Jobs?" in Chapter 2. See also Chapter 9, where a variety of resource materials are listed in the section entitled, "Where to Find the Strategic Information You Need."

If your present or past employers are not law firms and the company names are not well known, you should include a description of the size and scope of each company's business. For example,

> Retail firm with $3.8 million in annual sales
>
> Largest real estate development company in Riverside County, CA
>
> National nonprofit organization founded in 1975, based in Santa Fe, NM

OTHER ACTIVITIES AND INTERESTS
. . . .

This section should include professional legal organizations (such as your local paralegal association), volunteer activities (if not already listed), relevant hobbies, and professional licenses or credentials (such as real estate or teaching). Never include religious, fraternal, or political organizations.

Paralegal managers will sometimes look at your outside interests to see how those parallel the firm's needs or personality, particularly if your work history does not provide this match. A number of legal assistant managers have told me that these activities and outside interests can be helpful in determining whether a candidate will be a good choice for the firm. One manager liked people who had eclectic interests and showed a sense of humor in the descriptions of their outside activities. Another looked for people who demonstrated leadership abilities through organizations such as the Parent Teachers Association or scouting organizations. A third searched for paralegals with an interest in writing, especially people who have been published or have written for college journals.

Illustrations 5.1 through 5.16 show many examples of resumes.

ILLUSTRATION 5.1

Jane Doe

1234 North Maple Street
Anytown, USA 90000
Home: (213) 555-1111
Work: (213) 555-3333
jdoe@aol.com

LITIGATION PARALEGAL

Education

University of Paralegal Studies, Fremont, CA
> Paralegal Specialist Certificate, 2008, Honors graduate
> Approved by the ABA
>> Course of study: Legal Research and Writing, Contracts, Torts, Ethics, Litigation Specialization

University of California at Berkeley
> Bachelor of Arts degree in History, 2004
>> Graduated cum laude

Skills and Abilities

- Ability to analyze documents, digest depositions, draft discovery, and prepare cases for trial
- Knowledge of torts and contract law, legal research techniques, and basic civil procedure
- Fluent in French, both written and spoken
- Proficient in Word for Windows, WordPerfect 9.0, and Excel

Legal Internship

Jones, Smith, Smythe, & Smooth, Los Angeles, CA, 2008
- Digested depositions for complex litigation case
- Organized multiple documents using several software programs

Work Experience

Los Angeles Unified School District, 2004 to 2006
> Secondary School Teacher
- Arranged classroom materials
- Supervised student teachers
- Chaired English department
- Created curricula for advanced students

Professional Associations

- Los Angeles Paralegal Association
- University of Paralegal Studies Alumni Association

References and writing samples available upon request

ILLUSTRATION 5.2

Mary Paralegal

663 Hanley Avenue
Anytown, Texas 77419
(210) 222-2222
mparalegal@gmail.com

CAREER OBJECTIVE: **Litigation Paralegal**

EDUCATION

University of Paralegal Studies (ABA Approved), Los Angeles, CA
Paralegal Specialist Certificate in Litigation, 2008
Stanford University, Palo Alto, CA
Master of Arts, School of Education
University of California at Los Angeles
Bachelor of Arts,
Major–History; Minor–English and Political Science

WORK EXPERIENCE

Privilege Private School, Beverly Hills, CA, 2007 to present
Substitute Teacher
• Teach all grades and subjects
Music Center Unified Fund, Los Angeles, CA, 2005 to 2007
Manager
• Developed and implemented retail operation
• Executed data management systems for inventory control and financial statements
• Instructed volunteer sales staff in retail sales
Culver City High School, 2003 to 2005
Teacher
• Taught history, wrote curriculum, and trained student teachers
• Director of student government council
• Advisor for student councils for the state of California

VOLUNTEER/COMMUNITY SERVICE EXPERIENCE,

2003 to present
• Junior League, Finance Coordinator
• Stanford Alumni Board, Director
• Privilege Private School, Public Relations Committee

CREDENTIALS

Life Standard Secondary Teaching Credential

References available upon request

ILLUSTRATION 5.3

S. Donna Reed

465 North Avenue 51
Anytown, CA 90000
(209) 555-1234
sdreed@yahoo.com

LITIGATION PARALEGAL

ACADEMIC DEGREES AND DIPLOMAS
General Legal Assistant Certificate,
> University of Wisconsin, 2008
>> Course of study included: The litigation process, torts, contract, legal writing, and research and discovery

Master of Arts, French
> University of Michigan,
>> Department of Romance Languages

Diploma of the Cours Superieur, French
> Universite de Strasbourg, France

Bachelor of Arts, Music
> Indiana University

RELEVANT PROFESSIONAL EXPERIENCE
Summarizer Depoquick, Los Angeles, CA, 2008 to present
- Summarize depositions

Administrative Assistant/Grants Coordinator, 2008 to present
> Skid Row Development Corporation, Los Angeles, CA
- Write grants to increase funding
- Track donations to ensure correct accounting
- Manage office and staff of seven
- Administer benefits and other human resources duties

ADDITIONAL INFORMATION
- Fluent in French and German, reading knowledge of Spanish
- Versed in several major word processing and accounting programs, including:
  - WordPerfect
  - Lotus 123
  - Echo Development

REFERENCES AND WRITING SAMPLES
AVAILABLE UPON REQUEST

ILLUSTRATION 5.4

Joe Smith

1234 Main Street, No. 105
Chicago, IL 60601
(312) 555-1111
(312) 555-2222 (Cell)
jsmith@sbcglobal.net

LITIGATION PARALEGAL

EDUCATION
Roosevelt University, Extension Campus, Chicago, IL
    Attorney Assistant Training Program, 2008
Metropolitan State College of Denver
    Bachelor of Arts in Political Science

PARALEGAL INTERNSHIP
Pratt & Fall, Chicago, IL, Fall 2007
- In charge of deposition summaries and research projects
- Utilized WordPerfect 6.0

SKILLS AND ABILITIES
- Excellent communication and interpersonal skills
- Experienced in legal research
- Knowledge of Macintosh and IBM computer systems

EMPLOYMENT HISTORY
Kelly Services, Inc., Denver, CO, 2004 to 2007
TEMPORARY ASSIGNMENTS
- Sorted mail for large publishing firm
- Made and arranged copies for large document-processing company
- Prepared inventory for major department store

Jewish Community Center of Denver, 2002 to 2004
CLERK
- Supervised the Sportscenter desk
- Assisted in the physical education department

Citizens for Romer, Summer 2001
VOLUNTEER CAMPAIGN WORKER for governor of the state of Colorado
- Answered phones
- Stuffed envelopes
- Organized mailings

ILLUSTRATION 5.5

Sara Marks

2222 Market Way
Brooklyn, NY 11223
(212) 555-8634 (Home)
(212) 555-9234 (Office)
saramarks@email.com

EDUCATION
Reading College, Brooklyn NY, 2008
> Associate of Science degree, GPA 4.0
>> Paralegal Major—ABA-approved program
>> Dean's List, Vice President of the Honor Society

EMPLOYMENT HISTORY
Paralegal field work, Brooklyn, NY, 2006 to 2008
> Advisor, Small Claims Court and the Brooklyn Department of Consumer Affairs
> - Assisted claimants with small claim forms
> - Counseled individuals on consumer affairs issues

Registration and admissions clerk, Brooklyn, NY, 2004 to 2006
> Reading College
> - Registered incoming and returning students
> - In charge of organizing the filing system, creating more efficiency in the office

Cosmetologist and Barber, Brooklyn, NY, 2000 to 2004
> - Self-employed
> - Handled all phases of business, including purchasing, bookkeeping, and payroll

SPECIAL SKILLS
- WordPerfect, Microsoft Office Suite
- Excellent ability to communicate with general public

PROFESSIONAL AFFILIATIONS
Manhattan Paralegal Association

Excellent references available upon request

ILLUSTRATION 5.6

Rhonda Starr

112 Main Court
Mill Valley, CA 94440
Home (415) 555-5555
Work (415) 333-0000
rhondastarr@e-mail.com

CAREER OBJECTIVE: Entry-Level Paralegal Position

EMPLOYMENT EXPERIENCE

United States Peace Corps, Uganda, 2007 to 2008
Provincial Representative
- Managed $2000 import fund as a U.S. government subcashier, and a $4000 grant from the Peace Corps
- Mediated conflicts between volunteers and their supervisors
- Researched and analyzed prospective project sites
- Coordinated U.S. embassy staff, Ugandan government officials, and Peace Corps administrators for visits to project sites
- Arranged transportation, protocol, and adjustment of new volunteers to post

Uganda Ministry of Livestock, Fisheries, & Animal Husbandry, 2006 to 2007
Fisheries Technician/Extension Agent
- Organized logistics and protocol and helped teach a three-day seminar for 40 participants
- Conducted 60 information sessions to promote fish culture in Uganda
- Selected and trained five project fish farmers in pond construction, management, and marketing of their project

Smith College, 2005 to 2006
Archaeology Field Worker/Laboratory Assistant
- Worked in the Department of Anthropology
- Dispatcher/Secretary for the Office of Safety and Security

EDUCATION

Bachelor of Arts, Anthropology, Smith College, 2006
- Convened and presided over academic hearings with faculty and the dean of the college as head of the college's judiciary committee

COMPUTER AND LANGUAGE SKILLS

- Fluent in French
- Knowledge of IBM WordPerfect, IBM, and Macintosh Microsoft Word

ILLUSTRATION 5.7

Ronald Mans

4567 Main Avenue
Phoenix, AZ 85074
(602) 555-4444
rmans@aol.com

CAREER OBJECTIVE: NURSE PARALEGAL

EDUCATION

PHOENIX COLLEGE, Legal Assistant Certificate, 2008
> Course of study included:

Property	Criminal Law	Legal Ethics
Torts	Contracts	
Litigation	Legal Research and Writing	

UNIVERSITY OF THE STATE OF NEW YORK, Albany
> Regents External Degree in Nursing, 2003

EMPLOYMENT EXPERIENCE

REGISTERED NURSE, Phoenix, AZ, 2004 to present
> - Varied experience working for professional registries, hospitals and clinics in:
>   - medical-surgical
>   - emergency room
>   - hemodialysis
> - Able to read and interpret doctor's notes

ORDERLY AND GENERAL LABORER, Various locations
> Albany, NY, 2001 to 2003
> - Assisted with of patient care for several large hospitals in the Albany area
> - Maintained and cleaned patient rooms in a professional manner

SERGEANT, UNITED STATES NAVY, 2000 to 2001
> - Medic in combat situations in various countries

ASSOCIATIONS

> Phoenix Paralegal Association–Nurse Paralegal Division

REFERENCES AND WRITING SAMPLES
AVAILABLE UPON REQUEST

ILLUSTRATION 5.8

Andrew Dorian

2534 Bilsberg Street
Tacoma, WA 97811
(206) 555-4444 (Work)
(206) 555-3333 (Cell Phone)
Andrewd@yahoo.com

Criminal Law Paralegal

EDUCATION

Graduate Education
> Edmonds Community College, Lynnwood, WA
>> Certificate in Litigation, 2008
>> Approved by the American Bar Association
>> Course of study included: criminal law, litigation, constitutional law, torts, contracts, remedies, legal ethics, and legal research and writing

Undergraduate Education
> Southwest College, Tacoma, WA
>> Associate of Arts, Law Enforcement, 2000

EMPLOYMENT HISTORY

Seattle Unified School District, 2002 to present
> School Police Officer
> - Patrol school property and apprehend suspects
> - Investigate crimes and make recommendations for disposition of criminals and related matters involving the security of district facilities, personnel, and pupils

Edmonds Community College District, 2000 to 2001
> Campus Police Officer
> - Patrolled campus and grounds
> - Protected employees and school property
> - Composed and filed investigation reports

ADDITIONAL SKILLS

- Well-versed in criminal law
- Computer literate in MS Word and MS Office

REFERENCES Furnished upon request

ILLUSTRATION 5.9

Joe S. Smith

6789 California Street
Los Angeles, CA 90005
(323) 555-2345
jss@earthlink.net

Litigation Paralegal

Educational History

UNIVERSITY OF WEST LOS ANGELES
Paralegal Specialist Certificate in Litigation with Honors
ABA approved, 2008
Corecipient of the 2006 Leslie Ridley-Tree Scholarship

WESTLAW Training Certificate of Achievement, 2008

CALIFORNIA STATE UNIVERSITY, LOS ANGELES
Bachelor of Arts degree in Philosophy, 2004

Employment History

BEVERLY HILLS UNIFIED SCHOOL DISTRICT, 2004 to 2008
Multiple-subject elementary school teacher
- Instructed English, mathematics, language arts, and science to kindergarten through 6th grade

PATHWAYS CHILDREN'S VILLAGE, Sunnyvale, CA, 2003 to 2004
Child care worker
- Performed substitute-parental care, counseling, and behavior modification program implementation with emotionally disturbed children in a residential psychiatric treatment center

RANDOM COMPUTER CORPORATION, Palo Alto, CA, 2002 to 2003
Quality Control Supervisor
- Hired, trained, and evaluated quality assurance inspectors for printed circuit board assembly and floppy disk drive production lines

Additional Skills

- Ten years of experience with several personal computer systems
- Excellent oral and written communication skills

References furnished upon request

ILLUSTRATION 5.10

Walter C. Lee

191 65th Street
New York, NY 10010
(212) 555-8888
walterclee@verizon.net

Objective: Litigation Paralegal

Experience

USS Lewis, Long Beach, CA/Tokyo, Japan, 2006 to 2008

LEGAL OFFICER
- Conducted research on legal matters for Navy lawyers and commanding officer
- Managed the preparation of wills for entire crew
- Prepared limited powers of attorney
- Advised commanding officer on the interpretation of the Uniform Code of Military Justice, legal procedures, and the extent to which he could impose nonjudicial punishment
- Organized all administrative aspects of court martial and personnel discharges
- Coordinated depositions for trial
- Supervised and trained the ship's legal yeomen in their administrative duties
- Worked extensively with Microsoft Word and WordPerfect

ADMINISTRATIVE OFFICER
- Managed personnel assigned to administrative offices
- Tracked ship-wide personnel requirements
- Wrote all official correspondence from the Commanding Officer

Education
Dartmouth University, 2006
Bachelor of Science in Electrical Engineering

Honors
- Navy Achievement Medal, two-time recipient for outstanding professional achievement
- National Defense Medal, for Persian Gulf War service interests

Interests
Tennis, Japanese history and culture, and travel

ILLUSTRATION 5.11

Danielle Meandor

4657 Saddleback Road
Montgomery, AL 36191
(313) 444-5555 (Home)
(313) 444-6666 (Cell phone)
dmeandor@att.net

REAL ESTATE PARALEGAL

EDUCATION
Auburn University, Montgomery, AL   2008
    Legal Assistant Training Program, Litigation
Faulkner University, Montgomery, AL
    Bachelor of Arts (cum laude), Anthropology

CONTINUING EDUCATION
Society of Real Estate Appraisers   2007
    • Residential valuation
Huntington College, Huntington, AL   2006
    • Real estate appraisal, finance, law practices, and construction estimating

INTERNSHIP
Montgomery County Counsel, Real Estate Section   2007 to present
    • Assisted with research, valuation, and document organization

EMPLOYMENT EXPERIENCE
Real Estate Appraisal, Freelance Contractor   2004 to present
    • Handled research in connection with FNMA appraisals
    • Inspected property in the field and completed final reports
    • Maintained and analyzed detailed records
    • Clients included First Federal Savings Bank of Montgomery, Alabama
      Federal Savings, as well as many mortgage brokers
Montgomery County Assessor's Office   2000 to 2004
    • Appraised properties
    • Assisted taxpayers with problems and complaints
    • Kept records of government assessment data

SKILLS AND ABILITIES
    • Knowledge of WordPerfect 9.0 and MS Word for Windows
    • Drafted documents including complaints, answers, motions, and memos of
      points and authorities
    • Prepared and organized documents
    • Digested legal documents including interrogatories and depositions
    • Familiar with Lexis and Westlaw and other online research systems

ILLUSTRATION 5.12

Harriet Smith

700 Cherry Avenue, Unit 12
New York, NY 11111
(213) 445-5555
harrietsmith@tractor.com

LITIGATION PARALEGAL

EXPERIENCE

INDEPENDENT CONTRACTOR, Nassau County, NY   2006 to present
Paralegal/Secretary for various law firms
- Specialized in corporate law, city planning, probate, guardianship, and personal injury
- Organized case files
- Prepared subpoenas and proof of service
- Digested depositions

MARK DOE, ESQ., New York, NY   2004 to 2006
Legal Secretary/Receptionist in personal injury and immigration firm
- In charge of firm calendaring
- Prepared pleadings
- Performed paralegal research

SMITH, GRAVES, & DIXON, New York, NY   2000 to 2004
Legal Secretary
- Specialized in civil litigation, personal injury, workers' compensation, and family law

EDUCATION

Long Beach City College, NY   2000
    Legal Secretary Program Certificate

COMPUTER SKILLS
- Lexis, Westlaw
- WordPerfect 9.0 for Windows

ORGANIZATIONS
New York Paralegal Association
National Federation of Paralegal Associations

REFERENCES AVAILABLE UPON REQUEST

ILLUSTRATION 5.13

Jane Doe Olson

1234 Main Street, No. 5
Atlanta, GA 64810
(123) 555-0000
jdolson@me.com

LITIGATION PARALEGAL

EDUCATION
GRADUATE EDUCATION
University of Georgia, University Extension, Attorney Assistant Training Program, approved by the ABA
> Certificate in Litigation, graduated with honors, 2008

UNDERGRADUATE EDUCATION
University of Georgia
> Bachelor of Arts in Political Science, 2003

EXPERIENCE
LEGAL SECRETARY   2007 to present
Robert Baskin, A Law Corporation, Atlanta, GA
- Researched and prepared pleadings
- Administered the complete accounts receivable cycle
- Composed correspondence
- Assisted with bookkeeping for trusts
- Prepared various trust documents

EXECUTIVE SECRETARY   2002 to 2003
Dean of Administration and Finance, Harvard Medical School, Boston, MA
- Scheduled and planned meetings
- Prepared department budget and managed records
- Interfaced with various departments of the university

ADMINISTRATIVE SECRETARY   2001 to 2002
Business Services Administration, Centinela Hospital Medical Center,
San Francisco, CA
- Provided clerical support to seven quality assurance committees, the utilization review committee, and five members of the business services staff
- Managed the accounts receivable for a small subsidiary of the hospital
- Resolved patient billing problems

SKILLS AND ABILITIES
- Proficient with WordPerfect and MS Word for Windows
- Notary Public Commission

REFERENCES AND WRITING SAMPLES
AVAILABLE UPON REQUEST

ILLUSTRATION 5.14

Joan Smith

4320 Black Thorn Road
Boston, MA 01111
(615) 768-9234 (Home)
(615) 870-2384 (Cell)

OBJECTIVE: LITIGATION PARALEGAL

EDUCATION
Lester State College, Boston, MA
    Paralegal Certificate   2008
University of Massachusetts
    Bachelor of Arts degree in Radio/Television/Film   2003

SUMMARY OF QUALIFICATIONS
- Strong legal writing and research skills
- Over 5 years of experience in large corporate entities, including health care and media
- Solid technical savvy in a breadth of computer operation systems, environments, and applications
- Familiarity with medical terminology

EMPLOYMENT HISTORY
Large Health Plan, Boston, MA   2005 to present
Administration Assistant, Information Technology
- Provided comprehensive administrative support for 65 associate staff in technical services support group
- Oversaw and maintained daily calendars of management staff, including the scheduling and broadcasting of meetings and procuring resources
- Managed and maintained internal project priority lists

Administrative Clerk, Marketing Communications
- Created and verified all new projects within database system
- Assisted with reconciliation of accounts payable, including contractor and vendor invoices

Tuch and Nip, Newton, MA   2003 to 2005
Medical-Legal Transcriber
- Transcribed from dictation and edited medical-legal evaluation reports and correspondence

AFFILIATIONS AND AWARDS
- Member, Boston Paralegal Association (BPA)
- Recipient of BPA Scholarship Essay Contest Award, 2002

REFERENCES AND WRITING SAMPLES
AVAILABLE UPON REQUEST

ILLUSTRATION 5.15

Karen Anderson

476 West 36th Street, No. 23
Kansas City, MO 67608
(413) 555-3333
kanderson@aol.com

Paralegal or Paralegal Assistant

EDUCATION

Paralegal College of Missouri
    Paralegal Studies Certificate, 2008
        Course of study included:

Trials and Appeals	Law and Motion
Contracts	Tort Law and Personal Injury
Bankruptcy	Litigation Management
Commercial Law	Business Law
Legal Research	Paralegal Ethics
Criminal Law	Family Law

Universal Computing Institute
    Diploma, 2001

PROFESSIONAL EXPERIENCE

Juvenile Hall, Kansas City, MO   2004 to present
    Secretary and Personnel Office Head
    • Troubleshoot all facility work orders
    • Provide personnel services for 400 employees

Kansas City Times, Kansas City, MO   2000 to 2004
    Telemarketing, Data Entry
    • Built customer relations with excellent customer service
    • Performed data-entry activities as required

COMPUTER SKILLS

MS Word for Windows	MS Excel
Lotus 123	WordPerfect 9.0
Desktop publishing	Dbase

REFERENCES AVAILABLE UPON REQUEST

ILLUSTRATION 5.16

Thomas G. Smith

411 7th Road
Iowa City, IA 52245
(319) 388-0000
tomsmith@aol.com

EDUCATION

University of Iowa
    Paralegal Studies Program Certificate   2008
    Course of study included:
        • Survey of legal principles by case study
        • Practical experience in legal research and writing
        • Analysis and practice of litigation process from initial client interview
          to appeal

Ashbury Theological Seminary, Willmore, KY   2002
    Master of Divinity

University of Iowa   2000
    Bachelor of Arts degree in Pastoral Ministries

EMPLOYMENT

Law Offices of Gary Mark, Iowa City, IA   2007 to 2008
    Legal Assistant Intern
    • Performed case research
    • Assisted with various stages of the Litigation process

Trinity United Methodist Church, Iowa City, IA   2000 to 2007
    Ordained Minister
    • Wrote weekly sermons and monthly newsletters
    • Directed worship services
    • Supervised the financial department of the church

VOLUNTEER EXPERIENCE

    • Researched and wrote position papers for local congressman
    • Represented precinct on county political committee
    • Reported news stories for local newspaper and area publications
    • Coordinated community to host 10,000 bicyclers

REFERENCES AVAILABLE UPON REQUEST

6

Formats for Power Resumes: The Functional Resume

Show Off Your Skills

Three important reasons why you should consider the functional resume format rather than the chronological are changing careers, gaps in employment, and "job hopping." If you have unexplained discrepancies or gaps in employment, this format will not emphasize your job history. If you have changed jobs every year or so, using the functional resume will not highlight this fault. If you are changing careers, this resume will emphasize your transferable skills.

A pattern of gaps in employment and/or job hopping will land your resume in the pile of also-rans very quickly. For this reason, as a new paralegal, you should consider staying with a new job for a minimum of two years, unless you have another (and better) job offer. Firms prefer to see two to three years on a job. They do not want to invest in training someone, only to have that person leave. On the other hand, changing jobs every two to three years can indicate an enterprising person. This pattern of change is considered normal in today's paralegal job market.

TRANSFERRING YOUR SKILLS

Another reason to use this format is to emphasize your skills rather than where you have worked. Most of you will be changing careers to enter the paralegal job market. This is an excellent format for career changers. You probably have many transferable skills you would like employers to know about before the interview—and these skills will undoubtedly land you the interview. To make the employer

ILLUSTRATION 6.0

FORMER FIELD	LEGAL FIELD

FORMER FIELD

WRITING SKILLS

- Contract specialist
- Abstractor
- Micrographics services manager
- Writing, Publishing, Journalism

- Newspaper editor, Book editor, Public relations

MEDICAL SKILLS

- Hospital administration
  - ◆ Insurance companies
  - ◆ Pharmaceutical company representative
  - ◆ HMOs
- EPA specialist or Lobbyist

"GREEN" SKILLS

- Environmental consulting
- Nonprofit organizations (e.g., Greenpeace)
- Utility company employee
- Ecologist
- Environmentalist

MISCELLANEOUS SKILLS

- Pension administrators
- Project management
- Contract administration
- Problem solving
- Analysis and report generation

HUMAN RESOURCE SKILLS

- Team building

- Training new employees

INFORMATION SYSTEM SKILLS

- Database management
- System design and programming

LEGAL FIELD

- Business or contract litigation
- Summarizing documents
- Document production
- Preparation of in-house or association newsletters
- Drafting documents, proofreading
- Drafting speeches or articles for attorneys

- Medical malpractice

- Environmental law specialist

- Probate administrator
- Case management
- Negotiating and working with contracts
- Factual investigation
- Reviewing and analyzing documents, preparing follow-up reports

- Organizing trial and attorney/ paralegal teams
- Training and development

- Setting up cases on computer
- Designing support packages and computer management systems

understand what you have done in the past, your skills must be translated into "legalese." Look at the job descriptions in Chapter 1 and find those skills that can be translated from your old career into your new one. See Illustration 6.0 for some job descriptions that have been translated into the legal field.

HOW TO PREPARE A FUNCTIONAL RESUME

The personal information data, career title or professional objective, and educational background sections are the same format as the chronological style (look in the previous chapter).

Skills and Abilities

This section is the focus of your functional resume. It must outshine your insufficient legal or job history, so prepare it carefully. Condense all your experience into three to five pertinent categories that are related to the legal field. A list of possible subjects appears below. Use action verbs to describe your experience, but do not repeat yourself. Think of the law-related topics you have studied and apply them to your current skills, such as writing, supervising, or managing experience. This is also the section where your computer background should be detailed.

The format must be brief and easy to read. Each part should be no more than three to five sentences. Remember, the resume will be read in about 30 seconds or less, so you will need to highlight your accomplishments.

Determining Your Skills and Abilities: Category Paragraph Ideas

The following exercise is similar to that used in the chronological resume section when trying to describe your professional experiences in a list of five items or less. On a separate sheet of paper, one for each classification, choose three to five functional categories. Then brainstorm, thinking of everything you have ever done in your working or volunteer career in that category. Below are some questions you may ask yourself when completing this exercise:

WRITING ABILITIES
➤ What documents have you drafted or prepared?
➤ Have you written any brochures, booklets, or pamphlets?
➤ Have you corresponded with clients or customers?

SUPERVISION EXPERIENCE
➤ Have you hired or fired employees?
➤ Have you supervised or trained employees in projects?
➤ Have you taught?

MANAGEMENT EXPERIENCE
- ➤ Have you supervised a group or division of a company?
- ➤ Have you been given particular projects or suggestions upon which you have had to act?
- ➤ Have you organized or coordinated activities?
- ➤ Have you increased profits or decreased costs?

ADMINISTRATIVE SKILLS
- ➤ Have you delegated responsibilities?
- ➤ Have you had responsibility for company funds?
- ➤ Do you work with attention to detail?

ORGANIZATIONAL ABILITIES
- ➤ Have you ever established a group?
- ➤ Are you in charge of a particular division in your company?
- ➤ Have you designed or modified office systems?
- ➤ Have you arranged for a large project to be completed?
- ➤ Have you been in charge of a fund-raiser for your favorite nonprofit group?

After brainstorming, cross out the things you dislike or that will not impress an employer. Use three to five bullets in each section.

When drafting this section you should use dynamic action verbs rather than dull verbs such as work and do. Action verbs will add a sense of vitality to your resume. For example, instead of listing "research skills," write "researched and analyzed data." Remember to use the present tense for your current position and the past tense for all prior positions. At the end of this chapter you will find a list of action verbs.

The suggested functional categories listed below will add zip to your resume:

Administration	Data Organization
Analysis	Development
Banking Knowledge	Drafting
Business Management	Editing
Business Planning	Entertainment
Case Advocacy	Environmental
Client Development	Financial Management
Computer Knowledge	Government Service
Computer Skills	Human Resources
Contract Administration	Interpersonal Skills
Coordination	Investigation
Corporate Organization	Language Abilities
Data Management	Leadership

Library Skills	Public Relations
Logistics	Quality Control
Management	Real Estate
Negation	Recruiting
Oral Communication	Research
Organization	Scheduling
Planning	Strategic Planning
Problem Solving	Supervision
Program Development	Systems Development
Programming	Teaching
Project Development	Technical Skills
Project Management	Training
Proofreading	Writing

Professional Experience

The professional experience section for this style of resume should contain, in reverse chronological order, all positions you have held for the past 10 years. Include the following information:

- ➤ The name of the company
- ➤ Its location
- ➤ Your job title
- ➤ Dates of employment, using years only

Either list the job title first or the company name first, whichever you think will impress an employer. However, you must be consistent.

Below is an example of the professional experience information that should be reflected on your resume.

XYG Corporation, Philadelphia, PA, 2004 to present
   Accounting Supervisor
ABC Incorporated, Washington, D.C., 2002 to 2004
   Accounting Clerk
The Old School, Minneapolis, MN, 2001 to 2003
   English Teacher

Other Activities and Interests

The functional resume style does not differ from the chronological format in this area. See "Other Activities and Interests" in Chapter 5.

See Illustrations 6.1 to 6.6 for examples of functional resumes. Also see Illustration 6.7 for a list of action words for winning resumes.

ILLUSTRATION 6.1

Julia Somersby

4698 South Spring Street, No. 394
Boston, MA 78901
(333) 555-8888
juliasomersby@hotmail.com

LITIGATION PARALEGAL

EDUCATION

University of Boston, ABA approved
Corporate Paralegal Certificate, 2008
Tulane University, New Orleans, LA
Bachelor of Arts in English, 2003

PROFESSIONAL ACCOMPLISHMENTS

Writing
- Drafted bylaws and articles of incorporation for nonprofit corporation
- Researched and wrote honors thesis on Edgar Allen Poe's *The Raven*
- Prepared handbook for high school English department
- Created extensive lesson plans

Organizational Skills
- Founded nonprofit corporation for food distribution for the homeless
- Organized monthly distribution sites
- Administered variety of lesson plans for high school English classes

Supervision
- Recruited volunteers for homeless project
- Oversaw implementation of project from inception to realization
- Developed plan for more efficient yard supervision

Computer Skills
- Proficient with IBM PC WordPerfect for Windows, Lotus 123
- Westlaw trained

WORK EXPERIENCE

Substitute teacher with various school districts in the Boston area, 2004 to present

OTHER ACTIVITIES

Founder and president, The Homeless Project, Boston, MA, 2003 to present

REFERENCES AND WRITING SAMPLES
AVAILABLE UPON REQUEST

ILLUSTRATION 6.2

George Smartwell

PO Box 9978
Los Angeles, CA 22222
(612) 555-9922 Home
(612) 444-9999 Messages

PATENT PARALEGAL

EDUCATION

Mt. St. Mary's College, Moraga, CA, approved by the ABA
    Certificate with honors in Litigation, 2008
New York University
    Doctor of Philosophy, Experimental Atomic and Plasma Physics
Carnegie Institute of Technology
    Master of Science in Experimental High-Energy Nuclear Physics
Harvard University
    Bachelor of Science in Physics

PROFESSIONAL EXPERIENCE

Administrative
- Eighteen years experience in research and development of aerospace defense systems and associated technologies
- Project manager of large-scale defense programs
- Business development, strategic business planning, and market analysis

Publications
- Author of over 100 major reports in the areas of:
  - Military satellite systems
  - Strategic offensive and defensive missiles

Technical Knowledge
- Working knowledge of electrical and mechanical engineering
- Familiar with software development disciplines entailed in designing satellites, missiles, aircraft, and ground support systems

WORK HISTORY

Aerospace Corporation, Los Angeles, CA	2003 to 2008
Senior Systems Engineer	
Large Systems, Los Angeles, CA	2000 to 2003
Senior Scientist	
ABC Space & Technology Group, Hermosa Beach, CA	1990 to 2000
Senior Systems Manager	

REFERENCES AVAILABLE UPON REQUEST

ILLUSTRATION 6.3

Michael C. Smith

2345 Oregon Street, #A
Portland, OR 98765
(363) 282-7890
michaelcsmith@yahoo.com

EDUCATION

Paralegal Certificate, General Litigation, 2008
    University of Portland (ABA approved)
    Curriculum included:

Family Law	Paralegal Practices and Procedures
Criminal Law	Legal Research and Writing
Civil Litigation	Estates, Trusts, and Wills

Bachelor of Science Degree,
    Transportation and Distribution Management
    Golden Gate University, San Francisco, CA

EXPERIENCE

Paralegal Practice
- Drafted memos to clients
- Prepared notice of summons
- Conducted research for misdemeanor appeal cases
- Prepared points and authorities for motions
- Observed bankruptcy and family law court proceedings
- Completed necessary documents for probate
- Wrote legal memorandum

Administration and Management
- Participated in new division startup
- Dispatched and routed for the transportation of 80 to 120 special education students daily
- Supervised between 20 and 25 drivers
- Designed and implemented daily operation logs
- Liaison between drivers and school officials or parents
- Evaluated various conditions when assigning routes and equipment

EMPLOYMENT HISTORY

Susan Hildebrand, Attorney, Portland, OR Paralegal Intern	2008
Laidlaw Transit, Inc., San Francisco, CA Dispatch Manager	2002 to 2008
Hayward Unified School District Teaching Assistant	2001 to 2002
San Mateo Union High School District Office Clerk	2000 to 2001

ILLUSTRATION 6.4

Leslie Brown

12345 South Windsor Street
Green Briar, FL 33333
(432) 545-0987-Home
(432) 657-4305-Office

LITIGATION PARALEGAL

EDUCATION

Florida State College, Miami Paralegal Certificate   2008
University of Missouri, Columbia, Bachelor of Arts in Communications

PROFESSIONAL ACCOMPLISHMENTS

Writing
- Studied and drafted tax-exempt status for reincorporation of a 501c(3) nonprofit community-based organization per state and federal guidelines
- Research and wrote letters for immigration cases
- Compiled research on manufacturing processes; produced monthly operation reports for senior management

Organizational Skills
- Chaired, overhauled, and renamed annual fund-raiser, which was the most successful revenue raiser at nonprofit community-based organization
- Served on the committee of local Hunger Walk, raising over $35,000

Supervision
- Recruited and monitored volunteers for various events and projects for several community-based organizations
- Supervised and trained employees on proprietary software
- Systems coordinator for all manufacturing operations

Computer Skills
- Proficient with IBM PC, WordPerfect, and Microsoft Word for Windows

WORK EXPERIENCE

Personal Assistant and Office Manager   2003 to present
    Stone Properties, Miami, FL
East Coast Regional Sales Representative   2001 to 2003
    Ventura Industrial Products, Inc., Miami, FL
Customer Service Manager   2000 to 2001
    Strand, VCI, Miami, FL

AFFILIATIONS AND COMMISSIONS

Member of the Florida Paralegal Association
Bonded and Commissioned Notary Public for the state of Florida

REFERENCES AND WRITING SAMPLES
AVAILABLE UPON REQUEST

ILLUSTRATION 6.5

John Steward

4589 West Sixth Street, No. 2
Seattle, WA
(345) 343-4890

Objective: Real Estate Paralegal

EDUCATION

Real Estate Paralegal Certificate   2008
   Edmonds Community College, Seattle, WA, ABA approved
Bachelor of Science Degree in Business
   University of Washington

RELATED EXPERIENCE

MANAGEMENT

- Developed programs and procedures that reduced the real estate tax payment penalties by 95 percent or $25,000 per annum
- Designed and implemented an annual loan review system for evaluation loan portfolios

ADMINISTRATION

- Formulated risk management program designed to continuously monitor anticipatory potential risk areas of real estate operation
- Established new procedures for modifications on loan documents to ensure repayment, resulting in $50,000 plus in savings

SALES

- Financially analyzed and sold over 90 medium-size businesses ranging to $5,000,000
- Closed many multimillion-dollar loans in a timely manner, resulting in repeat business

EMPLOYMENT HISTORY

Coldwell-Banker, Seattle, WA   2006 to present
   Real Estate Agent
Security Pacific National Bank, Los Angeles, CA   2001 to 2006
   Assistant Vice President, Real Estate Trust Operations
Smith and Brown, Los Angeles, CA   2000 to 2001
   Real Estate Agent

PROFESSIONAL ASSOCIATIONS

Washington State Paralegal Association
California Escrow Association
National Notary Association
Professional Resource Network

ILLUSTRATION 6.6

Jane Smith

324 West Fourth Street
Milwaukee, WI 33333
(434) 434-3434
janesmith@gmail.com

LITIGATION PARALEGAL

PROFESSIONAL EXPERIENCE

Legal Procedures
- Prepared subpoenas, notice of depositions and settlement demands
- In charge of tickler and calendar system
- Composed simple contracts, declarations, and court forms
- Filed court documents and prepared instructions
- Researched state agencies' rules and procedures

Administrative Responsibilities
- Prepared office procedures manual
- Scheduled deponents and witnesses for depositions
- Designed directory systems
- Recruited clerical staff
- Calculated fee schedules

Computer Skills
- Expert in WordPerfect for Windows 9.0
- Efficient with the use of IBM PC and Macintosh
- Familiar with Lexis and Westlaw

WORK HISTORY

Day and Knight, Milwaukee, WI   2004 to present
   Legal Secretary to Litigation Department Partner
Polk, Samuels, & Daniels, Milwaukee, WI   2000 to 2004
   Legal Secretary to Litigation Partner

EDUCATION

Associate of Arts Degree, Business Administration
   Smith College, Minneapolis, MN

ILLUSTRATION 6.7

Action Words for Winning Resumes

Management
planned
revised
executed
retained
exceeded
unified
headed
operated
directed
conducted
managed
undertook
enacted
set up
governed
contracted
organized
supervised
obtained
produced
administered
coordinated
established
took charge of
controlled
implemented
maintained

Methods and Controls
installed
clarified
indexed
completed
budgeted
compiled
prepared
compared

focused
correlated
analyzed
catalogued
scheduled
increased
computed
reviewed
revised
formulated
detailed
examined
enlarged
arranged
decreased
expanded
reduced
verified
extracted
simplified
systematized
distributed
synthesized
accelerated
reorganized
restructured
redesigned
programmed

Public Relations/ Human Relations
hired
guided
harmonized
monitored
wrought
grouped
counseled
fostered

sponsored
led
delegated
advised
handled
employed
interviewed
integrated
trained
motivated
mentored
rewarded

Creativity
inspired
innovated
designed
devised
resolved
formed
excelled
effected
created
reshaped
conceived
enabled
solved
affected
converted
invented
developed
refined
founded
abstracted
transformed
performed
constructed
structured
originated

Illustration 6.7

(continued)

formulated
summarized

Advertisement/ Promotion
sparked
marketed
represented
generated
provided
influenced
recruited
secured
improved
tailored
promoted
convinced
persuaded
recommended
honored
actively engaged
was instrumental
played a key role
cultivated

Communications
moderated
facilitated
served as
edited
counseled
conveyed
presented
wrote

instructed
demonstrated
advocated
linked
straightened
presided
approved
consulted
championed
substantiated
participated in
reunited
interviewed
disseminated
exemplified
instilled

Negotiations
investigated
justified
proposed
sorted
assured
evaluated
mediated
negotiated
bargained
engineered
determined
compromised

Resourcefulness
succeeded
rectified

overcame
eliminated
achieved
doubled
digested
executed
inaugurated
initiated
awarded
won
identified
undertook
earned
fulfilled
realized
launched
trebled
halved
trimmed
pioneered
diverted
expedited
perfected
gained
attained
researched
strengthened
explored
accomplished
advanced
surpassed
supplanted
engineered
cultivated

7

Writing a Strong Cover Letter

Honest Clarity Required

A headhunter friend recently told me about a well-written resume that she had received without a cover letter. The candidate's entire experience was in the printing business. Since there was no cover letter explaining the candidate's job search goals, the headhunter simply filed the resume away because she did not know if the candidate wanted to stay in printing or make a change into law.

PURPOSE OF A COVER LETTER

Always send a cover letter with your resume, even if you are faxing or e-mailing it. The letter should focus on the position you are seeking, summarize your qualifications, and request an interview. Be sure to tell the employer that you want the job! Since the resume is the focal point of your correspondence, your cover letter should be brief. Like a resume, the cover letter should reflect your personality. This piece of paper should be engaging enough so that the reader will want to look at the resume, which, if attractive enough, will encourage the reader to call you in for an interview—the ultimate goal.

Find out the full name of the person responsible for hiring paralegals, and direct your letter to that person by name. "Dear Sir/Madam" or "To whom it may concern" never impresses anyone. Make sure that you are spelling the person's name correctly and that you have the right job title. Your resume will then be sent directly to that person's attention. If you bypass this step, your resume may take longer to reach the correct person, or it may not make it there at all.

Develop different cover letters to fit various situations. For example, if someone has referred you to the job, you are answering a want ad, or are sending out a mass mailing of resumes to firms in the Martindale–Hubbell Law Directory (see Chapter 9 for a discussion about this directory), you must address these

> **HOT TIP**
>
> Call the law firm or corporation and ask the receptionist to whom paralegal resumes should be directed. Be sure to ask for the correct spelling and job title and e-mail address. Be extremely friendly to the receptionist and all other support staff. They may become invaluable sources of information and help you get through the door!

different situations with customized cover letters. In the case of a referral, mention the name of the person who referred you in the first sentence of the cover letter. Naming a person that the employer knows and respects not only differentiates your resume from the rest of the pack, it also builds your credibility.

Use the cover letter to expand on how your background relates to the job opening. Put thought into the wording of your cover letter. The first few words are important and should attract the reader's attention. Make yourself sound interesting. Use simple, direct language and correct grammar and punctuation. Keep it short. Introduce yourself, sum up what you have to offer, emphasize your strongest qualifications, and request an interview.

Be sure not to use clichés or vulgar language. Yes, it does happen! I just received a cover letter from someone who said she was a "jack." I didn't know what she meant so I filed her resume away. The cover letter is not the time to experiment with humor. Your tone should be confident but not pushy or boastful. An honest assessment of your qualifications is enough.

If you are sending a letter in response to an ad, the language should reflect the language in that ad. Copy the phrases into the letter that reflect your abilities. The reader will be impressed that you possess the exact skills the company is seeking. If there is no ad, use some of the language found in the beginning of this book (Chapter 1) when describing your transferable experience. Try to demonstrate to the employer that you are capable of doing a great job, even though your experience in the legal field is limited.

On more than a few occasions, I have received letters that assured me that the applicant was a highly qualified paralegal because she handled her own

> **HOT TIP**
>
> Look for attorneys in Martindale–Hubbell (available at your local library or online) who are alumni of your college or the law school division of your paralegal school. In the opening sentence of you cover letter, state "As a graduate of _____ , I wanted to contact you about the possibilities of employment as a paralegal." Your resume should receive special attention.

> **HOT TIP**
>
> Many hiring authorities will judge your writing skills by your cover and
> thank-you letters. Work hard on whatever written communications
> you send out. Read them aloud to yourself and others. You need to
> sound strong and impressive; the quality of your writing provides a
> test of your abilities without your realizing it.

divorce, or he oversaw the probate of his father's estate. A colleague of mine
received a similar letter from a candidate who claimed to be qualified because he
had represented himself at his own murder trial! This experience does not necessarily present you as a qualified paralegal in the eyes of the hiring authority.

SALARY HISTORY

Often, in the classified ads, a request is made for the applicant to send in a salary
history. The employer is seeking the best candidate at the cheapest price.
To circumvent this, the following phrase can be added to the end of the first
paragraph: "I understand that you would like my salary history. I would prefer
to discuss this with you during a personal interview."

PROFESSIONAL LETTER FORMATS

The cover letter should use the same typeface as your resume, and be printed on
the same paper. Do not tape a newspaper ad to your resume as a substitute cover
letter. This is only one step up from a handwritten cover letter or attaching a
Post-It to the resume. When I receive resumes treated this way, I do not even
bother to read them.

Shown in Illustrations 7.1 to 7.10 are sample cover letters that can be used
in particular situations, like responding to a blind job advertisement. The first
sample is the basic blueprint you should use for all your letters, customized for
specific situations.

> **HOT TIP**
>
> In the first paragraph of your letter, mention the fact that you are famil-
> iar with the firm or company (if you are) and add something nice about
> it. "Your firm has a stellar reputation" or "I would enjoy working with a
> firm such as yours that has such a stellar reputation" are a few exam-
> ples. Praising the firm can only increase the credibility of your letter.

ILLUSTRATION 7.1

Basic Cover Letter Format

Your address
City, State Zip
Date

(4 SPACES)

Person's name (spelled correctly)
Title
Company
Address
City, State Zip

(2 SPACES)

Dear Mr. /Ms.:

(2 SPACES)

BODY OF LETTER

First Paragraph: Explain that you are seeking a paralegal position and have enclosed a resume for the addressee's review. Also explain how you learned about the position. If you know anything about the company, mention this in the first paragraph. Indicate if someone recommended your contacting this organization.

Second Paragraph: This is your "brag" paragraph. Relate your background to the job description. Include highlights from your experience or education that make you uniquely qualified.

Third Paragraph: Indicate that you will call about an interview. In the case of a blind ad, say that you would appreciate receiving a phone call.

(2 SPACES)

Sincerely,

Your Signature   **(4 SPACES)**

Type your name
Telephone number with area code and e-mail address

(2 SPACES)

Enclosure

ILLUSTRATION 7.2

Reply to Blind Newspaper Advertisement

123 Anywhere
Anytown, IL 22123
May 27, 2008

New York Times
PO Box 123
New York, NY 11223

Dear Sir/Madam:

I am very interested in the Legal Research Assistant position advertised in the *New York Times* on May 26, 2008. My resume is enclosed for your consideration.

Because you are seeking a person to analyze business agreements, you may find my familiarity with business procedures and contracts of particular interest. I am a recent graduate of The New Paralegal School and have an undergraduate degree in business law. I have worked for five years analyzing contracts prior to attending paralegal school.

I would like to meet with you and would be pleased to provide references and writing samples during an interview. I look forward to hearing from you soon.

Sincerely,

Susie Paralegal
(212) 333-2222

Enclosure

ILLUSTRATION 7.3

Martindale–Hubbell Mass Mailing Letter

111 Main Street, No. 3
Schooltown, MA 22222
June 23, 2008

Roberta Law, Esq.
Lawyer, Law & Attorney
555 West Lincoln Street, 43rd floor
Maytown, MA 22222

Dear Ms. Law:

I read about your firm in *Martindale-Hubbell,* and noted that you deal extensively with business litigation. With my Litigation Specialist Certificate from Schooltown University, I can be a definite asset to your firm. This program, which is ABA approved, has given me a comprehensive overview of the litigation process. Your practice offers the type of challenge that I am seeking.

As you can see from my resume, my experience has been in real estate and business. I believe that my knowledge in these areas will make an important contribution to your firm.

If you have a position for a person with my qualifications, or are anticipating one, I hope that we can meet. Please feel free to contact me at my business on weekdays at (232) 123-3456. At other times, you may reach me at my home telephone number listed below or by e-mail. I will contact you in a few days to arrange for an interview.

Sincerely,

Paul Legal Assistant
(232) 111-2222
paullegal@gmail.com

Enclosure

ILLUSTRATION 7.4

Reply to Newspaper Ad with Name of Company

111 Main Street, No. 3
Anytown, OH 33333
June 13, 2008

John Smith
Paralegal Manager
The Organization
655 Elm Street
Anytown, OH 33333

Dear Mr. Smith:

I am responding to your ad in the *Daily News* of June 12, 2008, for the position of Legal Assistant. I would like to explore the possibility of my joining an excellent company such as yours. The enclosed resume will provide information about my employment background and capabilities.

I have a paralegal certificate from Anytown Legal University, an ABA approved program. With my bachelor's degree in chemistry, I believe that my background can be of particular value in the patent litigation area, which is your specialty.

I would like to discuss how my background and experience can be of value to you. I will contact you soon to schedule an interview.

Sincerely,

Robert Paralegal
(313) 222-2222

Enclosure

ILLUSTRATION 7.5

Response to Article in Newspaper: Already Employed

567 Harvard Street
Maintown, FL 44444
October 4, 2008

Janice Smith, Esq.
Acme, Acme, & Smith
334 Rose Boulevard, Suite 444
Orlando, FL 44444

Dear Ms. Smith:

    I am interested in exploring the possibility of joining your firm as a litigation paralegal. Having followed the Acme case with great interest, I feel that my training in commercial law and personal injury litigation can be of great value to your firm.

    I have an extensive background in computerized litigation support systems and am comfortable with legal and factual research. As my resume indicates, I am currently doing my paralegal internship at a large downtown law firm specializing in litigation.

    I believe that my education and experience would be an asset to your firm. I will call you within the week to set up an appointment.

Sincerely,

Rose Litigation
(424) 444-4444

Enclosure

ILLUSTRATION 7.6

Referred by Another

321 South Street, No. 444
Dallas, TX 66766
November 23, 2008

Sarah Colleague
Smith, Martin, & Weiss
545 North Street
Dallas, TX 66766

Dear Ms. Colleague:

Ann Roberts, the paralegal recruiter at Jones & Jones, suggested that I write to you. I recently graduated with honors from Johnson Paralegal School with a certificate in corporate law. Your firm comes highly recommended to me.

The enclosed resume will demonstrate my interest in your firm's specialty area, environmental law. With my bachelor's degree in biology, I believe that I would be a definite asset to your firm.

I look forward to meeting with you soon. I will call you within the week to set up an interview.

Sincerely,

Joseph Jones
(323) 777-7777

Enclosure

ILLUSTRATION 7.7

College Graduate: No Experience

987 Flowering Street
Boomtown, CA 99789
July 1, 2008

Ms. Libby Del Monte
Paralegal Manager
Carrington & Company
1234 Maintown Boulevard, Suite 1200
Anytown, CA 99879

Dear Ms. Del Monte:

I recently saw your job advertisement in the *Boomtown Daily Journal* and immediately thought that I may be the person you are seeking. As indicated on the enclosed resume, I received my bachelor's degree from Yale University in March. I would be very interested in working with your firm.

As a legislative analyst with a lobbying firm in Washington, D.C., I have been educated about the realities of working in a large, dynamic law firm. I would enjoy the challenge of such an exciting environment.

If this position has not been filled and you believe we would work well together, I would enjoy meeting with you at your earliest convenience. I will call you within the week to schedule an interview.

Sincerely,

Betty Bates
(213) 444-5555

Enclosure

ILLUSTRATION 7.8

Response to Blind Litigation Ad

ADVERTISEMENT

High-profile downtown law firm, AV rated, is seeking an entry-level paralegal, with an ABA-approved paralegal certificate and a bachelor's degree, for a fast-paced, fast-track litigation project. Good benefits and competitive salary.
No. 2242 Local Law Journal 123 Main Street, Anytown, MA 88899

RESPONSE

546 West Fifth Street, No. 455
West Town, MA 88887
May 23, 2008

#2422 Local Law Journal
123 Main Street
Anytown, MA 88899

Dear Paralegal Director:

In response to your advertisement of May 22, 2008, in the *Local Law Journal,* enclosed please find my resume. I am interested in the entry-level litigation position.

I have recently graduated from Paralegal University, an ABA-approved program, with a certificate in litigation. I also hold a bachelor's degree from Boston University. I enjoy a fast-paced, challenging work environment and am very familiar with the local fast-track court rules.

I would appreciate the opportunity to interview with your firm. I can be reached during the day at (323) 111-1111 or at my home number below. I look forward to hearing from you soon.

Sincerely,

Joe Johnson
(323) 222-2222

Enclosure

ILLUSTRATION 7.9

Response to Corporate Ad

ADVERTISEMENT

Downtown firm seeks corporate paralegal. Requirements: bachelor's degree, information/maintenance of closely held corporations and transactional due diligence, excellent writing skills. Qualities sought include: independent judgement, attention to detail, practical focus, good sense of humor, and a professional commitment. Competitive salary and benefits commensurate with experience. Send resume to George Ball at Law & Law, PO Box 1028, Anytown, CA 90000.

RESPONSE

4365 Maple Street
Anytown, CA 90000
January 15, 2008

George Ball
Law & Law
PO Box 1028
Anytown, CA 90000

Dear Mr. Ball:

In response to your advertisement of July 14, 2008, for a corporate paralegal in the *Daily Times* I have enclosed my resume. I would enjoy working for a law firm with as sterling a reputation as yours.

I have a bachelor's degree from State University and have recently received my corporate paralegal certificate from Paralegal School. Through my course work I have learned how to maintain closely held corporations and have become familiar with transactional due diligence. I am an excellent writer, having published many short stories in my college newspaper. I also have an exceptional attention to detail and a great sense of humor.

I am positive that my skill level will meet your needs. I will be speaking with you soon to set up an interview.

Sincerely,

Allison May
(323) 555-8888

Enclosure

ILLUSTRATION 7.10

Response to Probate Paralegal Ad

ADVERTISEMENT

PARALEGAL-ESTATE PLANNING   Probate and estate planning paralegal sought for prestigious law firm in Smalltown. Preparation of probate and 706 documents, along with planning experience required. WordPerfect for Windows a plus. Send resume to: No. 4444 The Law Journal, 111 East First Street, Smalltown, NJ 11111.

RESPONSE

8764 Rose Street, No. 1
Anytown, NJ 11112
August 3, 2008

No. 4444, The Law Journal
111 East First Street
Smalltown, NJ 11111

Dear Paralegal Coordinator:

I am responding to your advertisement of August 1, 2008, which appeared in the *Law Journal*. I am very interested in the Paralegal/Estate Planning position. Enclosed please find my resume.

As my resume indicates, I have several years of experience as a trust officer with a large bank, where I gained the requisite experience in probate and 706 documents. I have just received my paralegal certificate in probate, where I acquired knowledge of estate planning. I am also proficient in WordPerfect 9.0 for Windows.

I would enjoy interviewing with your firm. I can be reached during the day at (213) 111-1111 or at my home number, which appears below. I look forward to hearing from you soon.

Sincerely,

Eric Benjamin
(211) 855-5555

Enclosure

DO'S AND DON'TS COVER LETTER CHECKLIST

DO:

➤ Write a separate cover letter for each position you are seeking, tailoring it to the specific job description.

➤ Use the same paper as your resume, with matching envelopes.

➤ Direct your letter to the hiring authority. Ask the law firm receptionist to whom you should send your resume. Be sure to get the correct job title and name spelling.

➤ Make sure that the letter is grammatically correct with no typos. It should be direct, concise, and meaningful.

➤ State that you are enclosing your resume.

➤ Remember that the first lines in the letter are vital and should appeal to the potential employer's interest.

➤ Briefly state one or two key contributions you can make; or emphasize one or two specific qualifications that fit the employer's major requisites.

➤ Request a personal interview.

➤ Type your phone number and your e-mail under the signature line, even though it appears on your resume.

➤ Mention that you are currently employed if this is the case. This will give you a boost with the potential employer. Remember the old saying that "It's easier to get a job when you've got a job."

DON'T:

➤ Cut out the ad and attach it to the letter.

➤ Use cliché, hackneyed, or silly phrases.

➤ Boast or use vulgar language. This could get you the wrong kind of attention.

➤ Refer to yourself in the third person (i.e., he or she).

➤ Try to give employers the impression that they cannot live without you.

➤ Be too aggressive, use pressure or hard-sell techniques.

➤ Use your present employer's stationery.

➤ Sign your current job title.

➤ Use cute techniques, such as writing the cover letter in the form of a pleading.

➤ Discuss salary, except for acknowledging that you would like to discuss your salary history during the interview.

➤ Say that you are "certified" if you are "certificated." (See Chapter 1 for a discussion about the difference between the two.)

8

Networking

Your Most Powerful Job Search Weapon

Networking is the single most powerful placement tool in the legal world. It consists of developing a system of contacts and resources to help you achieve your professional goals. Networking is all about people and word-of-mouth. Good networks are avenues to good jobs.

ORGANIZE YOUR JOB SEARCH

Now that you have completed your power resumes and composed your dynamic cover letters, you can start your job search. Before you begin your networking, you should organize and commit yourself to working toward your goal of getting a new job—a paralegal job.

First, set goals for yourself. These goals fall into long-term and short-term categories. Short-term goals should establish positive daily activities that can support successful attainment of long-term goals.

EXAMPLES
- ➤ Write a targeted resume.
- ➤ Contact an acquaintance for an informational interview.
- ➤ Get 20 minutes of exercise.

Long-term goals may take some time to achieve and are the lasting outcomes of short-term efforts.

EXAMPLES
- ➤ My resume will yield four job interviews.
- ➤ My informational interview will lead to a job offer.
- ➤ My daily exercise will make me look and feel fit and healthy.

Some goals should be specific, clear, and understandable so that they enable you to take concrete action. For instance:

➤ I will contact Don's friend by telephone on Monday at 10:00 A.M.

➤ I will take a computer class at the local high school to learn MS Word and Excel.

➤ I will go to the gym before Wednesday.

Other goals should be measurable with deadlines and quotas, such as

➤ On Tuesday at 10:00 A.M., I will call three people I know to find out about job prospects in their law firms.

➤ I will make five to eight cold calls this week to establish new job contacts.

I know that some of you will think this suggestion silly, but it does work. Finding a job can be very depressing. Remember to reward yourself for each goal that you meet. Too often people in a job search feel that they are not entitled to do anything nice for themselves until they land a new job. Acknowledging and rewarding each of your successes, large and small, and maintaining personal care can actually increase your productivity. Some ideas for rewards include taking a walk on the beach or hiking in a local park, going to the movies during the cheaper matinees, and visiting museums on their free days. It is important to plan some fun into your schedule so that your job search does not become a drag.

Once your goals have been set, it is time to get organized. It is important that you not only have a daily plan of action (see Illustration 8.1 for a daily work plan) but that you have a weekly one as well (see Illustration 8.2 for a weekly plan). Be sure you refer to these on a daily basis and document all of your scheduled activities. Keep records of every interaction, including the contact person, date, and type of contact—written, verbal, or personal. (See Illustration 8.4 for a record-keeping form.)

Of greatest importance is your following through. Write or call to follow up on possible positions. Always send thank-you letters promptly after every informational and regular interview. Maintain communication with your network of possible job contacts.

HOT TIP

It is also a good idea to keep a separate area in your home for your job search. This can be as large as a separate room or office or as small as a corner of your kitchen table.

ILLUSTRATION 8.1

Daily Plan

Wednesday, October 11, 2008

Time	Information
8:00	Go to the Gym
9:00	Job Search Start Time
10:00	Call Joe Smith
11:00	Informational Interview @ Law & Law
12:00	
1:00	Lunch
2:00	
3:00	Meet Jane Jones for Coffee
4:00	
5:00	Quitting Time
6:00	
7:00	Go Out and Have Some Fun

CREATE A PLACEMENT FILE

When your search starts, create a placement file and/or a notebook in which to keep all copies of correspondence with potential employers, together with a checklist of target firms, corporations, and government agencies contacted. Include contact names at each firm or corporation, along with some specific information about each person with whom you speak (e.g., personnel director at Smith, Jones, & Johnson is a former paralegal). Place all the business cards you will be collecting in the file or Rolodex. If you have completed employment applications for a government agency or other organization, be sure to keep a copy for your records.

The information stored in your placement file will help you with your correspondence. You can refer to the previous letters and/or meetings and mention the specific dates of those occurrences. This will help refresh the recipient's memory of you. Also include information from employment

ILLUSTRATION 8.2

Weekly Campaign Plan

Week of _____

A. PERSONAL CONTACT **RELEVANCE** **PHONE NUMBER**

_____ _____ _____

_____ _____ _____

B. REFERRAL CONTACTS **RELEVANCE** **PHONE NUMBER**

_____ _____ _____

_____ _____ _____

C. DIRECT LETTERS

_____

_____

D. FOLLOW-UP NOTES

_____

_____

E. SEARCH FIRMS/EMPLOYMENT AGENCIES **PHONE NUMBER**

_____ _____

_____ _____

F. MEDIA INFORMATION

_____

_____

G. WANT ADS

_____

_____

H. NEWSPAPER/PERIODICALS

_____

_____

agencies with which you have spoken in your notebook together with their literature and business cards. There are numerous legal assistant placement services in most large cities. You need to research which ones are considered the most reputable and effective; a good source for this information is your local paralegal association. (See Chapter 9 for a more detailed discussion of employment agencies.)

You should continue to update and use your placement file after you land a job. It is an excellent reference for professional contacts if you need a referral or find yourself in the job market again. This is an opportune time to start your Rolodex or other unique filing system.

HOW PEOPLE FIND JOBS

Most people find jobs through personal contact. To prove the veracity of this, conduct a survey with your paralegal classmates or among your friends. You will find that a great percentage found their most current job through contacts. But do not discount the other methods of finding work. They are discussed in greater detail later on in Chapters 9 and 10.

NETWORKING, NETWORKING, NETWORKING

Formal networks include professional organizations, such as your local paralegal associations and legal assistant alumni groups. You can usually join both as a student. Paralegal schools in the area can give students a contact person in these various organizations to call about membership. Be on the lookout for notices in your local legal newspaper about meetings of these associations and attend as many as you can. And don't forget to check their Web sites.

An informal network includes people with whom you work, classmates, friends, and acquaintances. To begin your own network, list all possible contacts that can help you gain information about the job you want. Illustration 8.3 will help you with this chore. Note if your contact has access to the people who will make the hiring decision. Even if that person does not, he or she might know someone who does.

Often the best and easiest way to get work is through personal contacts—the informal network. Over and over again, I tell new paralegals that they will get a job by using their friends. This is how I have gotten all of my jobs! Just consider all the people you know personally:

➤ Friends and acquaintances
➤ Fellow students
➤ Relatives

- ➤ Coworkers
- ➤ Customers
- ➤ Fellow professional association members

Be all-inclusive. Anyone, regardless of profession or position, has the potential to provide you with a job contact. You will be surprised at how many of these contacts know a lawyer or can recommend you to someone who knows a lawyer. I have found that professional networking with friends, even while sailing or skiing, has produced invaluable contacts.

Sue, now a corporate paralegal for a major Atlanta firm, tells how she went on her first skiing trip to Aspen. She somehow managed to sit next to two attorneys on the flight to Denver. After engaging in the usual chitchat, Sue found out that not only were they attorneys from Atlanta, but also that their paralegal had recently left to go to law school. They had not yet found anyone to replace her. Sue asked for their business cards and followed up immediately upon her return home. Sue's follow-up call, together with an informal setting and opportune moment, helped her land her first paralegal job.

Additional networking leads can be obtained from all the people you know through personal business dealings. Be sure to ask the following people if they know any attorneys or people working in law firms or corporate legal departments:

- ➤ Bankers
- ➤ Brokers
- ➤ Insurance agents
- ➤ Doctors
- ➤ Dentists
- ➤ Travel agents

You should include any other professional acquaintances whose businesses involve attorneys and legal professionals as clients. All these contacts can tell you about job openings or give you leads to people hiring paralegals.

You must be straightforward and let them know that you are job hunting. Discuss the type of position you are seeking. Send everyone a copy of your resume so they can see your qualifications. They might even pass it on to a potential employer! Even if you do not end up with an interview, you may get leads to positions, information on prospective employers, or contacts for future job openings.

It is wise to keep in touch with other paralegals that are looking for or have jobs. They are often the best source of information regarding job openings, and they can also give much needed moral support while you are hunting. Exchanging information about leads and sources is very valuable.

HOT TIP

Always carry extra copies of your resume with you. You never know when a social chat could develop into an important networking relationship or even evolve into an informal job interview. You should also carry printed business cards with your name, address, phone number, and "Paralegal or Legal Assistant" as your job title.

When you have landed your job, keep in touch with all of your contacts. They can share important information on salaries, benefits, and working conditions. If you decide to change jobs, you will be one step ahead by knowing the best places to work.

APPROACHES TO DEVELOPING A NETWORK

Joining Professional Groups or Organizations

There are many national, state, and local paralegal associations; these are rich sources of job leads. As a paralegal student, you are entitled to join almost any of the paralegal association chapters as a student member at a lower rate. If you are thinking about entering the field but are not enrolled in a paralegal school, you still may be eligible for an associate membership. This is crucial for your job search; the association members are in the best position to assist you in making contacts in the legal field. But do not just join an organization, participate in it. Volunteer to be on a committee (e.g., to arrange for a speaker). When members see how you work, you will be first in their thoughts when an opening occurs in their law firm. Several local associations have mentoring programs to help newly minted paralegals. Take advantage of these if you can.

Access to a job bank may be one of the services provided with your association membership fee. Many organizations also publish newsletters, which may contain job listings. Local law firms and corporations know that professional paralegal association job banks provide excellent candidates, especially for entry-level positions. Because the associations charge little or no fee, major firms in your area will usually list their job openings. A list of national, state, and city professional paralegal organizations appear in Appendix C.

Another excellent way to locate the groups in your area is by inquiring at the placement office of local legal assistant schools. You can also e-mail the National Federation of Paralegal Associations (NFPA) or the National Association of Legal Assistants (NALA). The Web sites for these two organizations are also given in Appendix C.

Of course, participation in the events sponsored by your local legal assistant association is a great way to start networking. You can have fun, tap into the local grapevine, and job hunt at the same time!

Over the past years, there has been a movement in a number of attorneys' professional groups to grant legal assistants formal recognition though membership. Both the American Bar Association (ABA) and the American Trial Lawyers Association (ATLA) have associate membership status for paralegals. Many local, state, and county bar organizations have followed suit.

You will need to research whether associate membership in the attorneys' groups is possible for organizations in your region. If it is available, I strongly recommend that you join. You will not only make great contacts, but you will also receive each group's publications. Most attorney association publications are excellent sources of information and timely professional articles.

Attending Seminars and Workshops

In addition to becoming active in the professional legal assistant group in your area, it is important to keep up with your profession and network at the same time. There are a number of continuing legal education (CLE) opportunities that will allow you to do this. These courses are important to know about, especially if you plan to take any of the certifying exams mentioned in Chapter 1. All require CLE courses. Area bar associations, law schools, paralegal associations, and various other organizations offer educational seminars each month or bimonthly and will frequently sponsor other legal training workshops. These are excellent places to meet people in your legal community in a professional setting, obtain information on job opportunities, and make valuable contacts.

As a new paralegal looking for your first job, you will have to pay for these seminars and workshops yourself. That's the bad news. The good news is that most organizations offer special reduced rates for students and associate members of the organizations. Once you are working in the legal field, most employers will pay for both your association dues and, frequently, seminars or workshops in your legal specialty.

Some of the most popular seminars and workshops include the following:

➤ Continuing Education of the Bar (CEB) *www.ceb.ucop.edu*

➤ American Law Institute *www.ali-aba.org*

➤ Center for Continuing Legal Education *www.abanet.org/cle*

➤ The Rutter Group *www.ruttergroup.com*

➤ Practicing Law Institute *www.pli.edu*

Attending Legal Conferences, Conventions, and Trade Shows

Below is a partial list of conventions, conferences, and trade shows that paralegals may attend. Announcements for these and other events can be found in paralegal association newsletters and in legal publications such as your state bar journal or local legal newspaper. Remember, these venues are excellent places to meet people, obtain information on job opportunities, and make valuable contacts.

Below is a list of a few conferences, conventions, and trade shows that may be worth your while to attend: (See Chapter 9 for Web site addresses.)

➤ American Bar Association (ABA)

➤ National Federation of Paralegal Associations (NFPA)

➤ National Association of Legal Assistants (NALA)

➤ Legal Tech (a convention of the latest legal technology) *www.almevents.com/r5/cob_page.asp?category_id=32941*

➤ American Association for Paralegal Education (AAfPE)

➤ International Paralegal Management Association (IPMA)

➤ Association of Legal Administrators (ALA)

➤ Local and state bar associations

➤ Local and state paralegal conventions and conferences

MAINTAINING RELATIONSHIPS WITH CLASSMATES AND FORMER EMPLOYERS

Some of the best sources of information for jobs are your peers and former employers. Because of past association with you, they will probably want to help you find your perfect paralegal job. Today's classmate or coworker may be tomorrow's reference.

During my years as a paralegal recruiter, I have seen many examples of peers helping peers. Ben and Sam went to George Washington University together. Ben went on to become a teacher and Sam went to law school. When Ben decided to change careers by becoming a paralegal, he looked up Sam, even though he had not seen him in 20 years. Sam gave Ben plenty of leads among his lawyer friends. Ben was able to use the introduction to several law firms by saying, "Sam suggested that I give you a ring." Sam's referrals led to a great job for Ben in a prestigious D.C. firm. Staying in touch helps you to grow, not just by contacts but through the benefit of accumulated group experience.

Make time for a periodic telephone call and an occasional lunch. Even if you are totally buried in work, your career is far better served by taking an hour to network rather than working that sixtieth hour at your firm. By keeping your contacts in mind, they are more likely to remember you for a pivotal career opportunity.

Joining Civic and Religious Organizations

You have come so far—do not stop now! Networking includes putting yourself in the thick of activities where attorneys search for business, including civic and religious organizations. Arts organizations in many cities have a large representation of legal professionals and company leaders; so do nonprofit sports organizations such as the Special Olympics. Sometimes, large religious organizations are another source. The Jewish Federation Council has a lawyer's division in many large cities with thousands of members. These groups help raise funds for good causes. Also consider joining the board of directors of your church, synagogue, or mosque.

You should contact the local chamber of commerce, business associations, real estate boards, and city councils to learn about energetic local groups to join. Pick your cause or activity based on what you enjoy and believe in. Get active. Who knows what "people perks" along the way may open new career opportunities for you.

Volunteering in Legal Clinics or Government Agencies

Volunteering to work for legal aid clinics, government agencies, and nonprofit programs is another good way to meet lawyers and paralegals. Most major cities have legal aid clinics that are funded by a combination of government money and support from the private sector. These clinics serve low-income citizens and are always in need of additional help.

The court system in your state may provide excellent volunteer opportunities as well. For example, the state of Minnesota has a guardian ad litem program staffed by volunteers representing the interests of minors in family court. This program is open to nonattorneys and is an invaluable source for future job contacts.

Volunteering to work in nonprofit legal programs keeps you abreast of new developments and active in the legal community. If you have no paralegal experience at all, this is a great way to gain credentials. Check with the following organizations, or look in the Yellow Pages for legal clinics and other volunteer opportunities in your city.

➤ American Civil Liberties Union (ACLU)
➤ Legal Aid Society
➤ Local feminist and civil rights organizations such as the National Organization for Women (NOW), National Association for the Advancement of Colored People (NAACP), and Mexican American Legal Defense and Education Fund (MALDEF)
➤ Law in the Public Interest
➤ Public Counsel

HOT TIP

Volunteering for Law Day, a day set aside in many communities to assist people seeking attorney referrals and free legal advice, is invaluable for making contacts. (Law Day is May 1st in most areas.) Find out if and when your community holds this type of event and sign up to answer phones or assist with questionnaires. A kind of bonding with your fellow volunteers will have happened by the end of the day. You will probably have made very good contacts that can be called on for a long time. "Volunteer, Law Day" is also a valuable addition to your resume, particularly if you have no prior legal experience.

➤ Local poverty law agencies
➤ City and state offices such as the public defender, district attorney, and county counsel

THE INFORMATIONAL INTERVIEW

Talking with attorneys, practicing paralegals, law firm managers, and others employed in the legal field is an effective way to research and gather information.

Try to set up informational interviews with people on your list of target firms and corporations. Simply call the appropriate person and ask to schedule an appointment to discuss paralegal careers. Most people will be flattered that you chose to consult with them for their expertise. Be sure to say that you are seeking an informational interview. In that way, even if there are no immediate openings, you can still set up the interview. For a script of a conversation used to set up such an interview, see Chapter 10.

One paralegal supervisor tells the story of how she ended up hiring a paralegal who had obtained her name while attending "Legal Tech." (This is an annual conference held at several locations around the country, at which new applications of technology by law firms are explored.)

"He set up an appointment with me to discuss the use of computers in the legal field. He had no real legal experience, but had just received his M.A. degree and appeared to be quite talented in the use of database programs. A month after our meeting, I realized that I had a need for just such a person. I called him up, hired him, and the rest is history."

Prepare your list of questions before the interview. You are conducting the interview and can structure it your way. Be professional and polite, and try not to take much time. Fifteen to twenty minutes should suffice. Extend the interview only if the interviewee seems interested. Always ask for the names of

HOT TIP

Informational interviews are just that—interviews for information only. These are not job interviews. If approaching the interview with an ulterior motive, you will be quickly shown the door.

additional people in the field with whom you may speak. Ask your contact to keep you in mind for future openings. Follow up by writing a thank-you letter.

Appropriate questions to ask during an informational interview include

➤ How many paralegals are employed in the firm, and what do they do?

➤ What are the salaries and benefits?

➤ Who does the interviewing and hiring?

➤ What type of on-the-job training is available?

➤ Does the firm have a paralegal program?

➤ Is there room for advancement?

➤ How did you get started in this field?

➤ What are your firm's requirements for hiring paralegals?

➤ What are the duties expected of an entry-level paralegal in a particular field?

➤ What opportunities and demand do you see for paralegals in the future?

➤ What do you look for in an entry-level paralegal?

➤ Could you examine my resume to see if my background fits your firm's expectations?

➤ Could you refer me to two or three people, or suggest an additional source of information?

With the foregoing information, you should be able to pinpoint the type of work you want, in the right setting, with good benefits and salary.

NETWORKING CHARTS HELP YOU ORGANIZE YOUR SEARCH

Name of People by Category Chart

Illustration 8.3 is a brainstorming chart. Make photocopies so that it can be used not only for this job search, but for all future job searches.

The first line of the chart includes people that you come into contact with frequently (i.e., friends, neighbors, and relatives). The next group includes

ILLUSTRATION 8.3

Name of People by Category Networking Chart

FRIENDS	NEIGHBORS	RELATIVES	GYM/HAIRDRESSER
MEDICAL	MERCHANTS	ACCTANT/BNKR†	SALESPEOPLE
COWORKERS	SUPPLIERS	COMPETITORS	FORMER EMPLOYER
PROFESSORS	FELLOW STUDENTS	SMR/WRKS/CONV*	OTHER
RELIGIOUS ORG.	TRADE ASSN.	COMMUNITY ORG.	ALUMNI ASSOC.

†Accountant/banker
*Seminars/workshops/conferences

professionals you meet in your everyday life (i.e., doctors/dentists, merchants, accountants/bankers, salespeople), as well as people you meet at the gym while working out or jogging around the track at the local high school. Also include hair dressers, manicurists, and other people who take care of you.

The next line refers to people you meet or have met on the job. It is very important when leaving a job not to burn your bridges. Keep in touch with bosses and peers from your former jobs. They are not only invaluable for references but are great resources for job opportunities. These include former employers and coworkers, suppliers, manufacturers, and customers; even competitors are great resources for jobs.

Do not forget to include your paralegal teachers, college professors, and fellow students. One of my clients went to a prestigious school for his master's degree. I asked him why he did not use his fellow classmates as a networking resource. He told me that "they were only students." It turned out that one of these "students" became very prominent in his particular field. What a lost networking opportunity!

Think of possible seminars, workshops, or conventions to attend. Finally, do not forget to join organizations, whether they are religious, community, or professionally oriented, or your local college or paralegal alumni association.

Record of Contacts Chart

Once you have completed the chart in Illustration 8.3, you are ready to fill out Illustration 8.4. Take the names from Illustration 8.3 and place them on Illustration 8.4, along with phone numbers and the places where they work, if appropriate. Organizations probably will not have contact names, but they do have addresses. It is important to follow up with all your choices.

Upon landing your job, keep track of your contacts. These groups and individuals will share important information on salaries, benefits, and working conditions. If you decide to change jobs, you will be one step ahead by knowing the best places to work.

Employer Contact Tracking System

As you complete the names on the Record of Contacts Chart (Illustration 8.4), the next step is to place hot contacts on the Employer Contact Tracking System form (Illustration 8.5). This will enable you to keep track of all advertisements responded to, all informational interviews set up, all networking contacts made regarding particular employers, and all resumes sent out. These forms should be kept in your placement notebook or cut down to fit in a placement file box. Because you will most likely be contacting several law firms or corporations, you will need to know the person spoken to and the date contacted. When you start getting those call backs, all of the pertinent information needed is right at hand.

ILLUSTRATION 8.4

Record of Contacts Chart

Date	Company Name Address Phone Number	Contact Person Title Contact Phone #	Date Resume Sent	Interview Date	Date Follow-Up Letter Sent

ILLUSTRATION 8.5

Employer Contact Tracking System

Firm/Corporation: _____

Address: _____

Phone Number: _____

Fax Number: _____

Contact & Position: _____

Position Sought: _____

Salary Information: _____

Referral Source: _____

Networking Comments: _____

* *

1. Initial contact with: _____

2. Sent resume to: _____

3. Follow-up phone call with: _____

4. First interview with: _____

5. Thank-you letter sent to: _____

6. Second interview with: _____

7. Third interview with: _____

8. Thank-you letter sent to: _____

Comments _____

NETWORKING WORKS, BUT IT TAKES TIME
• •

Even though you have cast out all your nets to the various placement services and job banks, do not depend on them to haul in a job. Start your own job search as soon as you finish writing your resume. The process is not difficult, but it is time consuming. If you are unemployed, treat your job search as a full-time job. The more time spent out in the world looking, the more contacts will be made, and the quicker that elusive first position will be found. Plan to spend at least one-half of each day on your search.

If you are employed, but wish to change positions, that kind of time may not be available. If possible, budget at least one to two hours daily, either at the beginning of the day, during the lunch hour, or at the end of the day.

Your job search is the time to lean on your classmates and friends for moral support. Ongoing emotional support is important throughout the process. Turn to your paralegal association for networking and advice. You will feel part of the legal assistant profession more quickly if you do.

Above all else during your job search, be patient and persistent. Your first job is the most difficult position to find.

9

Beginning Your Job Search

Research Sources

When looking for a new job, you should expect to spend about one month of job hunting for each $10,000 in salary for the types of positions you are seeking. For example, if the position you want pays $30,000, be prepared to spend about three months finding the right one. The job search can sometimes take longer—depending in large part on the economy in your area—so do not get discouraged.

I advise new legal assistant graduates to consider taking entry-level positions as paralegal aides, document clerks, or even receptionists or file clerks in order to get a foot in the door. Many law firms look favorably on this career move. They will be able to get to know you before committing to a legal assistant position. One woman I placed as a document clerk five years ago is now the Litigation Support Manager for a major San Francisco law firm!

Before beginning your search, make a list of the law firms and corporations you want to target. Some of these may not have openings, but an information interview can help you become familiar with and be known by the firm. (See Informational Interviews in Chapter 8.) When an opening becomes available, you will have the advantage of being familiar with that organization.

WHERE TO FIND THE STRATEGIC INFORMATION YOU NEED

As discussed in Chapter 8, your job search requires an organized and businesslike approach. Although it takes substantial effort, doing your homework up front will save time in the long run. You will be able to identify additional job opportunities and perhaps those people who can help in your search. Talk to people in the field. They will provide additional contacts.

Law Firms versus Corporate Law Departments

Expand your search beyond law firms to include corporate legal departments. These departments vary in size from one attorney to several scores. Turnover in corporations is generally not as high as in law firms. Paralegals often stay at corporations for their entire careers; frequently, there are more opportunities for promotion than in law firms. The average term of employment in a law firm appears to be two to three years.

You will encounter many issues during your search. In comparing different job opportunities, consider all the items listed below. You will find a decision will be easier to make after examining all the options.

JOB OPPORTUNITY ANALYSIS

➤ Salary—How much do you expect to be paid? How often do you expect raises or bonuses?

➤ Benefits—What level of benefits are you interested in? Are you willing to take fewer benefits if the salary is right?

➤ Duties—What level of duties do you want? What kind of variety? Do you want experience that will help you advance?

➤ Advancement—What level of advancement do you want to achieve? How important is it to advance?

➤ Responsibility—How much responsibility do you want? How important is it that responsibility increases?

➤ Firm or corporate culture—What would match with your personality? Would you prefer to work in a small or a large firm or corporation?

➤ Attorney attitudes toward paralegal utilization—Are you looking for firms or corporations with strong utilization of paralegals? Do you want to be the trailblazer?

➤ Work categories—What practice areas interest you? Do you plan to specialize?

➤ Location—How important is the physical location? Is paid parking available?

➤ Job setting—Are you looking for traditional, conservative settings or something more modern? Is it important to have a private office?

Analyze how you feel about each of these issues before looking for a job. This will help you focus your search in the right places and make suitable choices. Your classmates, professional associates, and personal friends in the legal field are usually the best sources of information on the issues outlined above (see Chapter 8).

HOT TIP

Very few paralegal positions are advertised openly. Law firms and corporations frequently rely on "blind" resumes in their files. Therefore, it is to your advantage to send out your resume as often as possible. Actively network with other paralegals and law firm personnel. People already employed in law firms may let you know about potential openings and act as personal references.

Paralegal Employer Reference Books

Martindale–Hubbell Law Directory

Martindale–Hubbell Directory (martindale.com) lists law firms and lawyers throughout the country. Law firms pay a fee to be listed, and nearly all major firms are included. A few hours browsing through a copy of *Martindale* at your local library or online is time well spent. Each volume is organized alphabetically by state and then by city. Individual law firm listings include information about the following topics:

- ➤ Firm name
- ➤ Address, telephone number, fax number, e-mail, and/or Web site
- ➤ All branch offices, both U.S. and worldwide
- ➤ All practice areas, in order of importance
- ➤ Representative clients
- ➤ Firm profile (not always)
- ➤ All lawyers in the firm, organized by partner or associate status, stating each attorney's
  - ❑ Name
  - ❑ Birthplace
  - ❑ Date admitted to bar and in which states
  - ❑ Education
  - ❑ Honors
  - ❑ Legal resume
  - ❑ Local bar memberships
  - ❑ Legal works published
  - ❑ Languages
  - ❑ Practice areas

Online, you can find out about the company, the personnel, and locations. What is good about the online method is that you can choose law firms by

HOT TIP

If you want to find a local attorney, most bar associations have published their own association directory, so refer to one.

specialty. So if you are interested in Family Law or Corporate, you can click on that category, then click on your state and city and you will get all of the law firms in your area that practice the kind of law that interests you.

Other Law Firm Directories

Periodically review all state and local bar association journals, which are usually published monthly, as well as local legal newspapers, most of which are published daily. These publications almost always carry classified advertising for various positions, including ads for paralegal openings. They will also feature articles and information about what various law firms are doing and cases they are trying.

The books and directories listed below are invaluable for finding out about law firms. In my experience, most librarians are happy to assist in finding more local reference resources. Do not hesitate to ask. In addition, check to see if a local or state law firm directory is published through your local legal newspaper, bar association, or other resource.

➤ *The American Bar*
➤ *American Bar Association Directory*
   ❑ Directory of individuals in leadership positions within the association and related organizations
➤ *Attorneys and Agents Registered to Practice before the United States Patent and Trademark Office*
   ❑ Listed alphabetically by state
➤ *Best Lawyers in America*
➤ *Best's Directory of Recommended Insurance Attorneys*
   ❑ National directory; good reference for those who know in which field of law they want to practice
➤ *Canada Bonded Attorney Legal Directory*
➤ *Directory of Bar Associations*
➤ *Directory of the Legal Profession: Major Firms and Corporate Legal Departments*
➤ *Directory of Opportunities in International Law*
➤ *Fisher's Probate Law Directory*
➤ *The Insurance Bar*

❏ Directory of eminent lawyers and the selective digest of insurance and related topics

➤ *International Directory of Intellectual Property Law Firms*

➤ *Kime's International Law Directory*

➤ *Law and Legal Information Directory*

❏ Guide to more than 19,500 national and international legal institutions, services, and facilities

➤ *Law Firm Yellow Book*

❏ Who's who in the management of leading U.S. law firms

➤ *The Lawyer's Director by the Sharp and Alleman Company*

➤ *Lawyer's Register International by Specialties and Fields of Law Including a Directory of Corporate Counsel*

❏ International directory of lawyers and their firms, identified as specializing, concentrating, or practicing in a specific field of law; also included are in-house lawyers and the staff of U.S. and international corporations, along with their chief counsel, areas of practice, and law schools attended

➤ *Martindale–Hubbell Bar Register of Pre-eminent Lawyers*

➤ *Martindale–Hubbell International Law Directory*

❏ Contains lists of Canadian and international lawyers

➤ *National Directory of Legal Employers*

➤ *The Official Guide to Legal Specialties: National Association for Law Placement*

➤ *Presumed Equal: What America's Top Women Lawyers Really Think about Their Firms*

➤ *Que's Official Internet Yellow Pages*

➤ *Who's Who in American Law*

➤ *Women in Law*

➤ *World Legal Directory*

➤ *Yellow Pages* (local editions)

❏ Look for "Attorney" listings; lawyers are usually listed according to areas of specialty at the end of the main alphabetical section

HOT TIP

Smaller firms often do not list themselves in *Martindale–Hubbell*. To find them, use the Yellow Pages; they are especially helpful in locating smaller firms in specific geographic areas.

Legal Aid Organizations

If your interest lies with nonprofit organizations instead of private law firms, the sources listed below should provide a good start. I also recommend checking with your local library to determine which nonprofit organizations can be found in your area.

> ➤ *Arco 100 Best Non-Profits to Work For*
> ➤ *Directory of Legal Aid and Advice Facilities Available throughout the World*
> ➤ *Directory of Legal Aid and Defender Offices in the United States*
> ➤ *Directory of Legal Aid and Defender Services*
> ➤ *Directory of Non-Governmental Organizations and Drug Abuse Prevention, Treatment and Rehabilitation*
> ➤ *Global Non-Profit Organizations' Directory*
> ➤ *National Directory of Nonprofit Organizations*
>> ❏ Includes every type of organization found among hundreds of thousands of nonprofit organizations in the United States, with names of officers and directors
> ➤ *Public Interest Group Profiles*
> ➤ *Pursuing the Public Interest: A Handbook for Legal Professionals*

Corporate Law Departments

If you are seeking a position in a corporation, *Martindale–Hubbell* also contains a corporate legal department section, located in the last volume of the series. These listings are organized alphabetically by company name.

You can also use *Standard & Poor's Register of Corporations, Directors, and Executives*, a roster of over 37,000 U.S. publicly held corporations, listed alphabetically by company. It includes a description of the company as well as the names of its corporate officers and general counsel. The lead attorney in the corporation could be either the General Counsel or the Secretary of the Corporation. You may address your letter to this person.

Check your local business directory for corporations in your area; before tackling *Standard & Poor's*, make a "hit" list of companies where you would like to work. The following publications also have listings of corporations and other nonlaw firm entities.

> ➤ *The Almanac of American Employers: The Only Complete Guide to America's hottest, fastest-growing corporate employers*
> ➤ *The American Almanac of Jobs and Salaries*
> ➤ *Aspen Law and Business Directory of Corporate Counsel, Corporations and Public Utilities*
> ➤ *The Big Book Of Jobs*

- *Corptech Directory of Technology Companies*
  - ❑ Lists more than 400,000 companies with profits and company rankings given under each industry
- *Corporate Directory of United States Public Companies*
- *Corporate Report Card*
  - ❑ A rating of 250 U.S. corporations for the socially responsible investor
- *Corporate Yellow Book*
  - ❑ Who's who at the leading U.S. companies
- *Directory of American Firms Operating in Foreign Countries*
  - ❑ Volume one is in alphabetical order by corporate name; volumes two and three are alphabetized by country
- *Directory of Corporate Counsel*
- *Dun and Bradstreet Business Rankings*
  - ❑ List of companies, products, services, and activities; compiled from a variety of published sources
- *Dun and Bradstreet Million Dollar Directory: America's Leading Public and Private Companies*
  - ❑ List of leading U.S. public and private companies
- *Hoover's Handbook of American Businesses*
- *Hoover's Handbook of Emerging Companies*
- *Martindale–Hubbell Corporate Law Directory*
- *Reader's Guide to Periodical Literature*
  - ❑ Current articles on different companies, organized by subject matter or proper name
- *Ward's Business Directory of Private and Public Companies*
  - ❑ Listed both geographically and alphabetically; includes corporate officers
- *US Private Companies*

Public-Sector Jobs

You can obtain more detailed information regarding federal careers by going to the Web site of the

Office of Personnel Management (OPM)   *www.opm.gov*

OPM publishes a variety of materials. I recommend that you ask for "Job Family Position Classification." *www.opm.gov/fedclass/gs0900c.pdf* lists the qualifications for paralegals in the federal government.

The following directories and books will help you figure out which jobs are available in the public sector and how to apply for them.

➤   *Bna's Directory of State and Federal Courts, Judges and Clerks: By State and Federal Listing*

➤   *The Book of U.S. Government Jobs: Where They Are, What's Available and How to Get One*

➤   *Federal Civil Service Jobs*

➤   *Federal Jobs: the Ultimate guide*

➤   *Federal Jobs Digest:* Lists over 20,000 international and national federal jobs in each issue

➤   *Federal Yellow Book, Who's Who in Federal Departments and Agencies*

➤   *Guide to America's Federal Jobs: A Complete Directory of Federal Career Opportunities*

➤   *Judicial Staff Directory: Federal and State Courts, Judges, Staffs, Biographies*

➤   *The Students Federal Career Guide: 10 Steps to Find and Win Top Government Jobs and Internships*

➤   *Ten Steps to a Federal Job: Navigating the Federal Job System, Writing Federal Resumes, KSAs and cover letters with a mission*

➤   *Washington Job Source*

➤   *Working for Your Uncle:* A complete guide to landing a job with the federal government

As you compile your list of employers, try to locate the names of the people to contact for each organization. Although the names of many of your contacts are listed, it would be a good idea to call the organization and confirm that this person is still the correct one to receive the resume. You can also phone the company or agency and ask the receptionist for the name of the person in charge of paralegals. Be sure to get the full name with correct spelling and specific title. Do not be put off by curt receptionists; they can be circumvented by calling at another time or asking for the legal or paralegal department.

THE INTERNET—A VALUABLE RESEARCH TOOL

The Internet is another resource that should not be underutilized. It is one step in your job search. This dynamic medium is a necessary tool for finding work in the twenty-first century. Having a computer and being hooked up to the Internet is as vital a job search tool as having a cell phone or voice mail. One of the conveniences of being online is that you can e-mail your resume to an employer immediately. It will arrive long before a fax or mailed letter can get to the same destination.

When sending your resume over the Net, you can use either the chronological or functional format found in Chapter 4 and Chapter 5. You can send your resume and cover letter as an attachment or attach the text to the body of the e-mail. Send a follow-up e-mail asking if your resume was received. Sometimes employers may have difficulty opening an attachment.

Currently, there are many Web sites that post legal job listings and accept resumes. I have listed several found while surfing the Web. By the time this book is published there will be many more, and those that I have indicated below may be gone. I have also included a number of useful sites that may be helpful to you for legal or factual research or for general legal information.

LEGAL JOB SEARCH SITES

➤ *http://legalemploy.com* lists WWW sites that deal strictly with legally related employment.

➤ *http://legal.monster.com/articles/paralegal* Monsterboard, one of the largest job search sites, is easier to search. There is a separate legal section that allows you to search for paralegal jobs.

➤ *http://www.ihirelegal.com/*dedicated to legal jobs only.

➤ *http://www.job-hunt.org/law* a list of Web sites that specialize in jobs for attorneys, legal assistants, paralegals, legal secretaries, and others in law-related professions.

➤ *www.aila.org* a professional organization for immigration attorneys, has paralegal job listings.

➤ *www.careers.findlaw.com* not only is job opportunities listed, but this site is a good resource for legal research.

➤ *www.counsel.net* has a few paralegal jobs and chat rooms for legal professionals.

➤ *www.hg.org/employment* legal research center—has many job listings and other legal information.

➤ *www.idealist.org* you can search here for jobs in the nonprofit sector.

➤ *www.jobs.lawinfo.com* you can post your resume, which will be seen by anyone who logs onto this site.

➤ *www.lawyersweeklyjobs.com* job openings and legal news.

➤ *www.legalstaff.com* delivers the tools and services needed to help bring legal professionals and employers together. Reaches the combined resources of over 89 Legal Career Centers across the nation.

➤ *www.paralegaljobs.com* a database of jobs listing for paralegals and legal assistants. There are jobs for those with years of experience or just out of college.

➤ *www.paralegals.org* NFPA's Web site has many paralegal job listings around the country with legally related jobs and agency openings.

➤ *www.salary.com* a site where you can find job search links as well as salary information.

➤ *www.vault.com* has many paralegal job listings nationwide in a special law section.

➤ Check out *craigslist.org* for jobs in your part of the country. Each city is listed individually.

FEDERAL JOB SITES

➤ *http://www.usajobs.opm.gov/* is the official job site of the United States Federal Government. It's your one-stop source for Federal jobs and employment information.

➤ *http://www.lib.lsu.edu/gov/fedgov.html* LSU Libraries Federal agencies directory.

➤ *http://www.jobsfed.com* America's Federal employment newspaper.

➤ *http://www.sec.gov/jobs* for jobs with the Securities and Exchange Commission.

➤ *http://www.fcc.gov/jobs/* for jobs with the Federal Communications Commission.

➤ *http://www.govtjob.net* online source of jobs available in state and local government. Sponsored by the Local Government Institute.

NATIONAL ORGANIZATIONS

➤ *www.abanet.org* site for the American Bar Association

➤ *www.paralegals.org* National Federation of Paralegal Associations

➤ *www.nala.org* National Association of Legal Assistants

➤ *www.nationalparalegal.org* National Paralegal Association

➤ *www.paralegamanagement.org* International Paralegal Management Association

➤ *www.aapipara.org* American Alliance of Paralegals

➤ *www.nals.org* National Association of Legal Professionals

The following sites are a selection of associations representing specific areas of the law. You may also find similar legal associations linked to the American Bar Association site: *www.abanet.org.*

➤ *www.afda.org* American Federation of Defense Attorneys.

➤ *www.aipla.org* American Intellectual Property Law Association.

➤ *www.healthlawyers.org* American Health Lawyers Association.

LARGE JOB SEARCH SITES

There are many paralegal job opportunities listed in these megajob banks. Most of these services have a separate paralegal section.

➤ *www.americasjobbank.com* (America's Job Bank) This site from the U.S. Department of Labor is linked to 1,800 state employment services offices throughout the country, with over 250,000 job listings.

➤ *www.careermag.com* this is a good resource for paralegal job listings. Out of all the giant databases, this site seems to have the most paralegal listings.

➤ *www.nationjob.com* not many paralegal jobs.

➤ *www.jobgusher.com* has some paralegal jobs.

OTHER SITES OF INTEREST

➤ *www.westlaw.com* use this address for legal research online.

➤ *www.ilrg.com* (Internet Legal Research Guide) is a categorized index of more than 4,000 selected Web sites concerning the law and the legal profession. It includes information about lawyers from the *West Legal Directory* and the *Martindale–Hubbell Lawyer Locator.*

➤ *http://www.bls.gov/oco/ocos114.htm* for job description of Paralegals and Legal Assistants.

➤ *http://www.soyouwanna.com/site/syws/paralegal/paralegal.html* general information about the profession.

➤ *www.alllaw.com* a wide variety of legal information

➤ *www.lawguru.com* a wide variety of legal information including paralegal job leads.

➤ *www.paralegalgateway.com* Where Paralegals Connect. Offers career tools specifically for the paralegal profession along with chat rooms, message boards, etc. to interact with paralegals around the world!

The Internet is an incredible resource. Soon it may be the only source of networking and legal research. If you haven't become familiar with the resources of the Web, I suggest that you get online and start surfing!

SEARCH ORGANIZATIONS CAN HELP

If you are graduating from a paralegal program, your school may have a job placement service. Many of the best firms in the nation place requests at the top schools for entry-level legal assistants. They know that they will get high-quality candidates without having to pay an expensive search fee. These placement services, along with paralegal association job banks, are the best sources of outside assistance for the beginning paralegal. In addition, they cost you nothing.

A paralegal search company may be another excellent source of outside help with your search. Most large urban areas have one or more search firms working primarily with legal assistant placements. Some of these are national in scope. If you live in Houston but want to move to Denver, a national search firm from Los Angeles may be able to place you. In this particular example, you would also check with Denver paralegal associations for job banks, as well as with Denver area placement companies. Going online is also a must for your search.

Search firms are able to offer superior job placement possibilities, as they have built strong, trusting relationships with law firms and corporate clientele. Many law firms place exclusive job orders that never hit the papers, thus eliminating the need to screen hundreds of resumes. The law firm or corporate client really wants to see only the top two or three candidates.

To find placement companies, look in the telephone book under "Employment." You can also call your local legal assistant school and association for referrals. Most associations can recommend well-connected placement companies. The Web is also a good source of connections as indicated in the above Internet Web site listings.

When scheduling interviews with paralegal placement companies, be sure to distinguish between "search" firms, "employer-retained" agencies, and "applicant fee-paid" agencies. The search and employer-retained agencies are full-fee paid by the employer and cost you nothing. On the other hand, you must pay the applicant fee-paid agency's fee—a cost that few starting paralegals can afford.

When calling an agency, ask what types of positions they have available. If there are many secretarial and clerical positions but only one paralegal job, you are probably in the wrong agency. You may have to take certain tests, whether written or on the computer. If these tests are too clerical in nature, the company does not understand the paralegal profession. Paralegals should not have to perform secretarial duties unless the position is a secretarial/paralegal job. Paralegals may use a computer to input their own documents, but they rarely perform clerical duties. Use your network to determine which are the best placement agencies.

Some agencies are reluctant to represent entry-level paralegals, because the law firms will not pay a fee for novice legal assistants. Many law firms feel that they can get qualified recent graduates from reputable paralegal schools at no cost. Some agencies do offer temporary assignments for "rookie" paralegals. If you are able to work on a temporary basis, it is wise to apply. Temporary paralegal services often look for paralegals to handle some of the "paying your dues" work. The types of tasks at this level include document coding, organizing, photocopying, and/or summarizing documents. These jobs at least provide some legal experience and a foot in the door. Temporary positions may lead to permanent jobs. Do not rely entirely on search firms to do your job search for you. They will be only one part of your job search plan which should include several of the ideas presented in Chapter 10.

10

Effective Job Search Strategies

Additional Methods for Finding a Job

In addition to networking and informational interviews, there are several other effective methods for landing a job. Some of the tools utilized for these methods are similar to those you have developed for networking. As I have mentioned earlier however, no one method will prove to be "magical." Try a variety, to see which are most comfortable; find out what works best for you.

HOW COMPANIES FIND APPLICANTS

Before I begin discussing alternative methods for finding work, it may be beneficial for you to find out how companies hire their employees.

- ➤ Internal Job Posting—If you know people at other companies who could bring you a job posting, that will often provide a direct line to the hiring authority. If you do not know someone, often you can call and request the posting, or go to the main office and pick one up. This is particularly true for major corporations.

- ➤ Employee Referral—Many companies have a formal referral program that encourages employees to refer qualified acquaintances for employment. Often, the employee receives a monetary bonus for a successful hire.

- ➤ Professional/Trade Associations—Companies will list their openings with professional associations, who publicize these opportunities through meetings, newsletters, job banks, or hotlines.

- ➤ Local Colleges and Universities—Companies will frequently list their openings at the career centers of major area schools or with alumni associations. You do not always have to be a graduate of the school to use their services. However, most paralegal school placement offices require your being a student or graduate of their program.

➤ Advertising—Most companies use a small percentage of their budget for employment advertising. The type and level of position will dictate the size and placement of the ad. In general, companies prefer to use the previous methods before paying for advertising. That is why it is imperative to tap into the hidden job market.

MASS MAILINGS

A mass mailing is an effective way of getting your resume into the hands of as many employers as possible. E-mail or send your resume and an effective cover letter, printed or neatly typed on the same quality paper, and placed in a matching envelope. Be sure that your letter and envelope are addressed to the name of the hiring authority, not just to the personnel department or office manager, or "To whom it may concern." Send out at least five to ten resumes per week.

A director of administration at a major law firm tells the story of receiving a cover letter and resume from an aspiring legal assistant. The applicant was so confident of her abilities that she stated in her letter that she would make herself available to work on a temporary basis for one week, just so the firm could see that her claims were justified. The director was so impressed by her undaunted assurance that he forwarded her resume to the firm's legal assistant manager for special attention.

It is not unheard of to send or e-mail over 200 resumes each time you look for a job, so be prepared. Now is the time to start keeping accurate notes in your placement file. Nothing is worse than bombarding a prospective employer with five or six resumes in that many weeks.

You do not want your resume to end up in "resume heaven"; follow up your letter with a follow-up e-mail or better yet, a phone call. (See scripts of effective telephone calls in the following section, Telephone Solicitations.) Now is the time to overcome any telephone phobias you may have. Be businesslike and direct. You will probably have to go through a secretary or leave a message on voice mail before actually speaking to the hiring authority. You may feel put off, but be friendly and persistent.

If you have to leave a message, ask if your resume was received. You may not get a call back, but at least your name will be before the hiring authority. If you do get to speak to someone, ask if you could make an appointment for an interview. If there are no openings, ask when would be a good time to call back

HOT TIP

Always be friendly to the secretary. If the secretary becomes your ally, you will have easier access to the boss.

HOT TIP

As stated before, make sure that your e-mail address is professional in nature. Also when sending any correspondence by e-mail, make sure that you don't use cute abbreviations. Use a formal style and be professional. Check your grammar and spelling before hitting the "send" button.

or when new openings are anticipated. Make sure to put the date into your weekly calendar as a reminder to call back. Law firms will usually keep your resume on file for up to six months. It is wise to resubmit your resume, if necessary, every four to six months.

Occasionally, you may receive a rejection letter. This can be viewed as an invitation to keep the lines of communication open, as most firms do not feel obligated to respond to every resume they receive. Also, the letter will provide the name of a person to call. Of course, be guided by the language of the letter. If it is noncommittal in tone, call the firm the following month to inquire if any positions have become available.

TELEPHONE SOLICITATIONS

While gathering the information about your target employers, the receptionist may offer to connect you directly to the hiring authority. This is an excellent opportunity to preface the mailing of your resume. Remember, each exposure to your name will make you more memorable. Be direct when talking with the person. Get straight to the point; do not waste his or her time. A good example of how to handle this type of call is as follows:

> Hello, my name is _____. I am very interested in working for your firm as a paralegal. I just graduated from Paralegal University, an ABA-approved program, and I would like to set up an interview if possible. . . . Oh, you don't have any openings.
>
> In that case, I would like to send you my resume in the event that a position opens up. I'll call sometime next week to see if you've received it. Thank you for your time.

Even if the firms you reach by telephone do not wish to see you, send them your resume for future reference. The fact that you spoke to someone will trigger recognition when your resume and cover letter arrive. As a result, the firm will be more apt to remember you when a job opens up. Make sure to mention in your cover letter the name of the person to whom you originally spoke.

HOT TIP

If you have trouble getting past the secretary, try calling early in the morning or after office hours. Frequently, the hiring authorities and attorneys are in the office before and after the support staff. You may get right through to the proper person if you call at these times.

SETTING UP AN INFORMATIONAL INTERVIEW

As discussed earlier, an informational interview is a good way to gather data about your new career. Upon gaining access to the appropriate person in the corporation or law firm, ask if you could schedule an appointment to discuss the paralegal career. Outlined below is a good way to handle this request. Remember, this is not a job interview . . . you are only looking for information.

Paralegal:	Hello, could you please tell me the name of the person who is responsible for hiring paralegals?
Receptionist:	That would be Ann Jones.
Paralegal:	What is Ms. Jones' title?
Receptionist:	She is our paralegal manager.
Paralegal:	Could you please connect me with her office?
Secretary:	Ms. Jones' office.
Paralegal:	Is Ms. Jones in, please?
Secretary:	May I tell her who is calling?
Paralegal:	Yes, this is Bob Smith.

Do not, at this point, tell the secretary why you are calling; the secretary may put you right through.

Secretary:	May I tell Ms. Jones the nature of your call?
Paralegal:	Yes. I am conducting research for a project for my paralegal class.
Manager:	This is Ms. Jones.
Paralegal:	Hello, Ms. Jones. My name is Bob Smith. I am a student at Paralegal University and I am hoping that you can help me. I am trying to obtain information to take back to my paralegal class about job-searching techniques . . . how to get a job, what top employers look for, and what constitutes a great candidate. Is it possible to take 15 to 20 minutes of your time next Tuesday afternoon?
Manager:	Why yes, Bob, I would be happy to help.

> **HOT TIP**
>
> In regards to information interviews, by stating that you only want 15 to 20 minutes for the interview, you will get his or her attention. During the interview, try not to take more than the time you set, unless the person with whom you are speaking wants to extend the conversation. (See Informational Interview in Chapter 8 for additional ideas.)

Following Up on Mailed Resumes

Always follow up on resumes you have mailed, by telephoning the person to whom the resume was sent; unless of course, it went to a blind ad, fax number, or e-mail. Remember to review your placement file and information tracking chart before calling. You may need to refer to exact dates, job title of the person to whom your resume was sent, or something specific about the firm's practice.

Paralegal: Good morning, Ms. Jones. My name is Brad Thomas. I am following up on the resume I sent you last week. Have you had a chance to review it?

Manager: Yes, Brad. However, we are really looking for someone with more experience.

Paralegal: I can appreciate that. Training entry-level paralegals does take time. I'd really appreciate it though if I could take only 20 minutes of your time to meet with you to find out what top firms, such as yours, look for in its candidates. I also may be able to share with you my expertise and how it relates to this particular position. I believe my medical background, although not in the legal field, is particularly relevant to the personal injury cases your firm handles. I noticed in *Martindale–Hubbell* that you also represent hospitals. My history as a physical therapist can probably be of some use to you.

Manager: You know, you may have something there. How about meeting next Tuesday at 1:00?

Even if you do not get past the hiring authority's secretary, you can still make an impression and perhaps even an ally in your job search.

Secretary: Ms. Jones' Office.

Paralegal: Hello, this is Nancy Martin calling for Ms. Jones.

Secretary: May I tell Ms. Jones the nature of your call?

Paralegal: Yes, I am following up on a resume I sent to her last week.

Secretary:	Nancy, she'll have to get back to you. Ms. Jones is not taking any calls at this time regarding positions.
Paralegal:	I can appreciate that. Can you tell me your name, please?
Secretary:	I'm Viola Johnson, Ms. Jones' secretary.
Paralegal:	Ms. Johnson, I was curious to know if there are any particular qualities that this firm looks for in a paralegal position. I am new to the field and need all the information I can gather. Can you help me out for just a moment?
Secretary:	Well, Nancy, this firm always wants people who can write well. That's the first thing they look for.
Paralegal:	Great, Ms. Johnson. If I send Ms. Jones a writing sample, even though I generally give this to the interviewer at the interview, could you see that she gets it?
Secretary:	Sure, Nancy, I'll be happy to help you out.

Sometimes you will be granted an interview, even if no position is open. Use this opportunity as an informational interview to meet the person in charge of hiring and to gather more data about the firm. It will also provide interviewing experience, putting you more at ease in the future.

TRACKING LAWSUITS

Many firms hire additional paralegals for large litigation cases. Entry-level paralegals interested in litigation have a number of options for tracking such cases. Remember, cases like antitrust or complex litigation are usually very document-intensive. Those are the types of cases for which firms might hire several additional paralegals or document clerks.

Look for articles in local legal newspapers or the *National Law Journal* about law firms and attorneys working on any large litigation matter. If you find a case that interests you, contact the attorneys (or hiring authority) at that firm and ask about employment opportunities.

Review current federal and state case law reporter advance sheets (the most recently published court opinions) for courts located in your part of the

HOT TIP

Avoid using the phrase, "I was wondering if . . ." This is too tentative and sounds as though you did not have anything better to do that day. Use a more positive approach, such as: "I am seeking a position with your firm and would like to set up an interview."

HOT TIP

While studying local law journals and legal newspapers, look for firms hiring associates. Check out the "Attorneys Wanted" classified advertisements. If the organization appears to be expanding, it is more than likely that they will also need paralegals. Suggest this in your cover letter.

country. At the beginning of each opinion, there is a list of attorneys who represented the parties in that case. If the opinion is in an area of law in which you have an interest, call or send your resume to that attorney. Talk about and ask questions regarding the case in your cover letter or on the phone. Then inquire about employment opportunities for paralegals in that area of law. (Review the informational interview techniques in Chapter 8.)

TRACKING OTHER AREAS OF THE LAW

Start reviewing the articles in your local bar journal or magazine. These can routinely be found in a law library or on line. The articles and comments are usually written by local attorneys and will cover most practice areas. These articles are then indexed by subject matter in the publication's reference guide. If an area interests you, call or write the author. (You can obtain the telephone number and address from your state's attorney directory, *Martindale–Hubbell*, the phone book, or the Internet.) Ask a question or two about the topic of the article and the area of law involved. Then ask about employment opportunities for paralegals in that area of law.

Your state bar association is another excellent source of information about specific practice areas. These associations typically establish specialty committees for each practice area. As an associate member, you can attend the committee meetings of your choice and get to know people working in that area of law. Frequently, the activities of these committees are also reported in the bar association journals. Call the attorneys mentioned to see if you can arrange an informational interview.

Legal Publications to Review for Law Firm Information

There are many legal publications, both local and national, that should be quite helpful in gathering information about the activities of law firms and corporate legal departments. Although most of these publications do not contain specific job listings for paralegals, some do, and you can gain tremendous insight and knowledge of current events in the legal field by reviewing them periodically. You may find mention of some exciting litigation matter being handled by a major firm in your area, and as a result, will know that now is the time to send that resume! Some are daily, weekly, or monthly. To find out more about local legal publications talk to your instructors or administration at your paralegal school or ask your local paralegal association for help. You can also find this information on the Internet by "googling" legal publications.

DOOR-TO-DOOR CONTACTS

Going door-to-door is another way to contact employers. This method is not popular in some cities but is thought to be more effective in smaller towns. Before you try it, find out what your city's firms think of this technique.

Law firms are frequently clustered in the skyscraper section of town. Visit these buildings and make a list of all the firms. Then call each firm to ask who hires the paralegals. When you return to the buildings—in your "dressed for success" clothes (see Chapter 11)—go to each office and ask to see this person.

Always indicate a willingness to return at a later time if it would be more convenient. If you are asked to return, leave a copy of your resume with a note stating why you would like to speak to the person who hires paralegals. If you are able to get an interview on the spot, be prepared to state why you requested it and what you are seeking. Since you initiated the meeting, you must be ready to get the ball rolling.

Keep in mind that most prospective employers will be unable to see you without an appointment. The strategy behind the door-to-door approach is getting your name in front of the hiring authority. By all means, follow up with a phone call.

Below is a list of the largest 25 law firms in the United States, which you may want to target in your door-to-door search. The list was compiled from the *National Law Journal*'s 250 compiled in 2006 and can be found at *www.law.com*. In order to get the list, you have to sign up for a free subscription. The city listed is the headquarters for the law firm. Branches in other cities and countries may also exist. Check *Martindale–Hubbell* for additional information.

1. Baker & McKenzie, Chicago
2. DLA Piper, Chicago
3. Jones Day, Cleveland
4. Latham & Watkins, Los Angeles
5. Skadden, Arps, Slate, Meagher & Flom, New York
6. White & Case, New York

7. Sidley & Austin, Chicago
8. Greenberg Traurig, Miami
9. Mayer, Brown, Rowe & Maw, Chicago
10. Morgan, Lewis & Bockius, Philadelphia
11. Kirkland & Ellis, Chicago
12. Wilmer Cutler Pickering Hale & Dorr, Washington
13. Weil, Gotshal & Manges, New York
14. Holland & Knight, New York
15. Paul, Hastings, Janofsky & Walker, Los Angeles
16. Morrison & Foerster, San Francisco
17. McDermott, Will & Emery, Chicago
18. Hogan & Hartson, Washington
19. O'Melveny & Myers, Los Angeles
20. Reed Smith, Pittsburgh
21. Dechert, Philadelphia
22. Foley & Lardner, Milwaukee
23. Kirkpatrick & Lockhart, Nicholson Graham, Pittsburgh
24. Fulbright & Jaworski, Houston
25. Akin, Gump, Strauss, Hauer & Feld, Washington

SELF-ADVERTISING

Advertising yourself in local legal journals is an unorthodox but sometimes effective way to find a job. Place a brief advertisement in the classified "services available" section. Your ad should simply state that you are an entry-level paralegal (with a specialty, if applicable) and that you are available to work in a particular area of town. Be sure to state where you attended school and that your salary is negotiable.

Believe it or not, this method has worked for several new paralegals. It is one more idea to use in a competitive job market. You may be offered a temporary or part-time position from a firm that does not use formal hiring channels. The following ad copy is an appropriate approach.

> Entry-level paralegal is seeking a litigation position with a respected downtown law firm. I have a B.A. degree in history from State University, as well as a paralegal certificate from Paralegal School, which is ABA-approved. I am well organized and understand the litigation process. My salary is negotiable and I am available immediately. Please call Jane Hoskins at (333) 444–5555 for an interview.

A MENTOR CAN BE YOUR BEST ALLY

Many successful people have started their careers by finding a mentor, someone who has expertise in the field you wish to enter and takes a personal interest in your career. A mentor can ease your way into the job market. This person must care about your success and be in a position to give you good advice.

You may meet your mentor at paralegal functions, alumni meetings, or at formal interviews. A mentor could be a teacher you had in paralegal school, a recruiter you found during your job search, or someone you met during an informational interview. One of the best mentors to have is an experienced paralegal, willing to commit the time necessary to help with your career development. Similarly, someone who has been a paralegal but has moved into other arenas of the legal field such as management recruiting or education can provide that much needed support and guidance. Nurture such relationships and value them highly. Be careful, however, to avoid taking undue advantage of your mentor's time and contacts.

Once you have been hired, try to find a person in your law firm (or corporation) who will help you through the maze of office politics and personalities. Sometimes, with just a minimum of inside knowledge, you can avoid certain difficulties. Unfortunately, not everyone is lucky enough to find such a person. If you do, you will find that having an experienced guide can be of enormous value to your career at the firm.

11

After You Get Through the Door

Ensuring a Successful Interview

Up to this point, your entire job search—research, networking, resume, cover letter—has focused on one goal, getting an interview. Now you are there. You have pulled away from the pack, and the prospective employer wants to talk with you in person. The interviewer is looking for the answer to a single question: "Why should I hire you?"

HOW TO APPROACH THE INTERVIEW

The interview enables you to enhance your resume, to shine, to be the one person they want to hire. You can discuss your applicable skills and abilities in more detail, describing how you will use them in your new position. You can show your enthusiasm and desire. The prospective employer can see you as a poised professional who will be an asset to the firm.

Getting a job is like getting married. You will be with your colleagues for at least eight hours a day if not longer. It is imperative to ask questions that will reveal whether this is a place where you will be happy. The interview gives you the opportunity to learn about the firm.

Over the years as a recruiter, I have interviewed all types—from outstanding candidates with an excellent professional demeanor, to those chewing gum or wearing what seemed like a bottle of perfume. In this chapter I discuss the do's and don'ts for interviewing. Two basic rules apply to all legal interviewing. First, dress conservatively. Even if your personal style is hip-hop or punk, if you want a job in the legal industry, you must dress in traditional business attire—no heavy makeup, outlandish hairstyles, or casual clothes. You must be neat, clean, and professional in appearance.

Second, you must have good verbal communication skills. The resume demonstrates your writing abilities; the interview demonstrates your speaking talent. Therefore, it is extremely important to prepare your questions and to rehearse answers to those questions that you believe will be asked. Be friendly and positive. Do not malign a previous employer or become arrogant toward the interviewer. Once, a woman actually swore at me when I told her we had no immediate job openings. She had an excellent educational background, and although she may have just been having a bad day (as everyone does), her resume was filed away permanently, never to see sunlight again.

Legal and professional interviews are usually comprised of at least two sessions: the initial interview and a call-back second (or even third) interview if the firm is considering making you an offer or narrowing the field of candidates. This chapter provides an overview of the interview process so you will know what to expect at each stage.

Sometimes candidates will jump the gun by asking questions that are appropriate only in the second interview. An initial interview usually reviews the basic information presented in your resume:

➤ Background
➤ Education
➤ Work experience
➤ Interests
➤ Skills
➤ Abilities

When asked back for a second (or third) interview, you will probably discuss some of these same areas with the various people involved in the hiring decision. However, you will also discuss salary, benefits, and working conditions with the legal assistant manager (or other hiring authority). It is certainly appropriate at this point to bring up the types of questions discussed in Questions to Ask the Interviewer in Chapter 12. Being asked back for further interviews indicates that the firm is definitely interested in you and is now willing to address financial concerns (see Chapter 13).

BEING PREPARED WILL BUILD YOUR CONFIDENCE

The initial phone call requesting your coming in for an interview is probably the first time that the employer is contacting you. Therefore, the call should actually be considered part of the interview. Obviously, you do not want to miss any calls. If you do not have an answering machine, voice mail, cell phone, or BlackBerry, buy or sign up for one now.

If you are not able to receive calls from potential employers, consider the impression made by the outgoing message on your cell phone or voice mail. It should not be cute, clever, or have loud music in the background. Leave out the barking dogs, limericks, and singing children. Your outgoing message should be

HOT TIP

Your answering machine or voice mail may be the very first impression the potential employer has of you, after your resume. Create a message that sounds as if the potential employer has called your home office.

straightforward and businesslike, asking for the caller's name and telephone number and assuring that the call will be returned. Even if someone is home all the time, unless he or she is a professional receptionist, let the machine take the messages. Consider getting a BlackBerry or a cell phone. No calls will be missed, and you will be the first to respond to an opening.

When called for an interview by a law firm or corporation, be sure to get all of the necessary information. Write down the following:

- ➤ Name of company or firm
- ➤ Address
- ➤ Room, suite, or floor number
- ➤ City
- ➤ Phone number and extension
- ➤ Name of person(s) (and their titles) you will be seeing (write the names phonetically, to be sure of the pronunciation)
- ➤ Time of the interview
- ➤ Directions and where to park (if applicable)

If you do not know the location of the firm, call the receptionist for directions. If that doesn't work, look up the address on one of the many maps sites on the Internet. If possible, take a trip to the firm before the scheduled interview to find out how much time is needed to arrive. During this trip you can also discover the best place to park. If taking public transportation, familiarize yourself with the schedule so that you arrive on time. If you are more than just a little bit late, the interview will be over before it even begins. Do not be late! If an unforeseen problem such as car trouble stalls you, call the interviewer and explain the situation.

HOT TIP

Never ask the firm if they will pay for parking. Take along extra money, just in case they do not!

Learn as much as possible about the people and organization with whom you are interviewing. An interviewer will be impressed with your taking time to research this information. In your earlier research targeting the companies to which you are attracted, you should have become familiar with the *Martindale–Hubbell Directory* and *Standard & Poor's Register of Corporations, Directors, and Executives.* These directories are excellent sources of basic information. Check the *Readers' Guide to Periodical Literature* or an Internet search engine like Yahoo or Google for recent articles and information about the company or law firm. You can also ask a corporation to send an annual report. Because many law firms publish quarterly newsletters for their clients, ask for a copy. Inquire if the firm has a brochure—these typically discuss their history, representative clients, and practice groups. Also, get their Web site address. Valuable information can be gleaned from the site.

When called for your interview, clarify the position for which you will be interviewing. Knowing which position is open will help to determine beforehand what the interviewer will be looking for, as well as what will be expected, as an employee of the firm. Use your judgment about when and how to ask appropriate questions of the interviewer, a list of which appears in Chapter 12.

Know the information on your resume thoroughly and highlight it during the interview. Be prepared to discuss and describe any relevant prior work experience, both paid and volunteer. In lieu of work experience, paralegals who have just completed school can describe course work, research papers, and projects that have relevance to the legal field.

Know how to describe yourself. Prepare a thumbnail sketch that should be no more than three minutes in length, including your education and relevant work experience. The personal aspects of your life are private and should not be included, unless you choose to reveal them. Sometimes, sharing your personal interests is a good strategy. Outside activities such as hobbies and sports can make you more memorable to the interviewer. However, you may always choose not to share this information.

SAMPLE SELF-DESCRIPTION (THUMBNAIL SKETCH)

I am a recent graduate of Paralegal University, having completed my litigation certificate with honors. Some of the courses I took were: legal research, writing, and litigation procedures, including the discovery process and various pleadings. My

HOT TIP

To get an annual report or brochure from a law firm or a corporation, inform the receptionist of your interest in investing or becoming a client, and that the information is needed to make an informed choice. You should get the brochure within a couple of days.

bachelor's degree is from State College, where I also received a teaching credential. I taught English (my college major) for three years at the high school level. Toward the end of my tenure, I was elected chair of the English department. One of my primary responsibilities was curriculum development.

CHECKLIST: WHAT TO BRING TO THE INTERVIEW

➤ Copies of your resume (even if you have already supplied copies to the firm)

➤ List of references

➤ Reference letters (if available)

➤ List of questions you want to ask

➤ Writing samples

➤ Legal writing sample portfolio

➤ Money for parking and/or transportation

➤ Directions to the firm

Make enough copies of your printed materials so that at least two additional sets can be given to the interviewer. They might be needed for that second interview!

REHEARSALS HELP YOU GET IT RIGHT

An experienced interviewer will ordinarily make rapid assessments of potential employees. Knowing this, you should be as thoroughly prepared for the interview as possible. It may sound silly to rehearse, but it works. Rehearse for the interview by using questions you believe will be asked. This is a necessity if you want to appear calm and poised, with well-thought-out answers. Some questions are easy. For example, "What was your major in college?" does not take too much thought. On the other hand, "What are your weaknesses?" is difficult to answer. Be honest, of course, but frame your response in a positive light. For example, if you work slowly, it is because you are thorough. How do you know what questions will be asked? Most interviewers ask similar questions, and a list of the most common ones can be found in Chapter 12.

If you have left a job and are unemployed, the question "Why?" will invariably be asked. Do not just blurt out "The company is a sweatshop" or "My job was boring." Plan your answer; make it as positive as possible. It is much more effective to say, "I am taking time off to enhance my career." You can also frame your answer around the features sought in your new career. You may be looking for a firm that offers paralegal training, a new area of law, or a firm that combines your past experience with the paralegal field. Emphasize these points if they fit your interviewer's profile.

HOT TIP

Employers are "put on alert" when they receive the following responses to questions:

- I am willing to take a pay cut.
- I left for personal reasons.
- I am looking for a greater challenge.
- I did not see eye-to-eye with my employer.
- There was a personality conflict with my coworkers and/or supervisor.
- I was fired.

By carefully planning what to say, you will present yourself as an intelligent and polished candidate. Go through the questions on the list. Find the ones that are difficult or require a negative answer. Prepare positive answers and rehearse them.

Consider audio- or videotaping your answers to hear and/or see how they appear. To check your body language, practice in front of a mirror. Watch your facial expressions. Avoid frowning or looking gloomy. Look yourself directly in the eye. There is nothing more distracting or uncomfortable than a candidate who looks everywhere but directly at the interviewer.

Through practice, you will develop self-confidence. You will radiate your feelings by the way in which you walk, sit, and speak. Employers are impressed by candidates who present themselves positively.

Interview Rehearsal Checklist

DO:

➤ Think about what you will wear (see the next section).

➤ Practice positive answers about your past employer even if you were fired or forced to quit.

➤ Practice establishing eye contact.

➤ Practice a firm handshake with family members and friends.

➤ Time your trip to the interview location, allowing for traffic and parking.

➤ Review questions you will ask the employer.

DON'T:

➤ Decide that you do not need to interview.

➤ Assume that you know all about the job.

➤   Adopt a passive or indifferent attitude.

➤   Have a know-it-all attitude (even if you attended law or graduate school).

➤   Embarrass the interviewer

Use positive, powerful action words (see Chapter 6, Illustration 6.7) to describe what you have accomplished and want to achieve. The word list found in Chapter 6 will provide some ideas. Choose words that will enhance your image but with which you feel comfortable.

"SUIT" YOURSELF—IT'S YOUR APPEARANCE

Your appearance is of the utmost importance. First impressions are crucial; you do not get a second chance. The legal world is usually very conservative; traditional professional attire is expected at the interview. It is as inappropriate to wear casual clothing to your interview, as it would be for a lawyer to wear jeans and a T-shirt to court. The lawyer will not win; neither will you.

Sometimes we are unaware of the impact made by our choice of clothing. I will never forget the "Lady in Black," a candidate of mine I had briefly coached on how to "dress for success." Unfortunately, I had assumed that she knew what was meant by "dressing conservatively." Immediately after her interview, I received a call from the paralegal administrator I had referred her to. "I want you to know," she said, "that I just saw your candidate, and I really appreciate your sense of humor." I wondered what she could possibly be talking about. "Oh, you know," said the administrator, "that gag of sending her wearing a black suit, black blouse, black shoes, and black stockings . . . even a black hat and black gloves." Uh oh.

Appropriate Attire for Women

The best choice for women is a business suit in conservative colors, such as navy, blue, gray, or beige. The suit fabric should be appropriate for the season: wool for winter, linen or a light summer fabric of good quality for summer. A combination of fibers is acceptable. The blouse should be simple, in white or a pale color, to complement the suit. Do not wear a low-cut or V-neck blouse or dress, or one that is too bright, has too many ruffles, or is too sheer. Having at least two outfits, one for each interview, is a necessity. If there is a third interview, mix and match the previous outfits.

HOT TIP

Dress as though you are applying for the interviewer's position.

If choosing to wear a dress, it must be in a tasteful print or color that is flattering to you, preferably of silk or a good-quality fiber mix. Avoid cotton, as it has a more casual look. Wear a blazer over your dress to make you look more professional. A sweater is not appropriate, though a cashmere sweater set may do even though it is less formal.

Skin-toned pantyhose are the best bet. Also acceptable are dark-toned hose (off-black) for winter and a pale tone (off-white) for summer. The color of your hose should never be darker than the hem of your skirt. If wearing a red skirt, never wear black pantyhose.

Shoes should be a closed-toe pump with a moderate-height heel (less than 2 inches is preferred), or flats in a color that coordinates with the outfit. Do not wear black leather shoes with a brown or navy suit. Similarly, do not wear white shoes with anything other than a white suit. The color of the shoes should never be darker than the hem of your skirt.

Never wear black pantyhose with white or light-colored shoes. If you usually wear tennis shoes when leaving your office, make sure to have pumps with you on the day of your interview.

Jewelry must be kept simple and conservative. Do not wear jingly, noisy jewelry, long or dangling earrings, or anything that indicates a religious, fraternal, or political affiliation. You want the interviewer to concentrate on you, not be mesmerized by your jewelry. If you have any pierced parts of you body that the interviewer can see, such as eyebrow or nose pierces, it is a good idea to remove the jewelry for the interview. Likewise if you have any tattoos, make sure that they are covered. If you are planning to get a tattoo, make sure that it isn't visible when you put on your interview clothes.

Do not wear perfume to the interview, as many people today are sensitive to overriding odors. In addition, your fragrance should not remain after you have left the room.

Makeup should be minimal and conservative; do not pile it on. You are interviewing for a legal position, not auditioning for a play. Your hair must be neat and clean. Long hair should be pulled back, away from your face. Go easy on the hair spray and mousse.

Take a good-quality briefcase or portfolio, in lieu of a handbag, to the interview. It should open from the top, not "suitcase style" with latches. Taking both a handbag and a portfolio can be cumbersome. When sitting down for the interview, you will first have to place the briefcase on the floor, followed by your purse. Inevitably, because of your nervousness, one or the other may be forgotten.

HOT TIP

Never wear white shoes before Memorial Day or after Labor Day, even in California or Florida.

> ### HOT TIP
> ···················
> You may want to seek the advice of an image consultant, or take advantage of a personal shopper, if at all unsure of your appearance. These consultants can usually be found at larger department stores.

If you decide to carry a handbag, make sure that it complements your outfit. You may then choose to bring a leather-covered notebook in which to carry your resume. Include the following items in your portfolio: copies of your resume (at least five), your list of references, writing samples, the questions you have prepared for the interviewer, a legal pad for notes (if necessary), pens, car keys, wallet, brush, and makeup. See Illustration 11.2 for a picture of how to dress.

Appropriate Attire for Men

Think Brooks Brothers, not Armani. Wear a two-piece business suit or sport jacket and slacks. Wool is the best fabric, as it holds its shape the longest. The lapel should not be too wide or narrow but a classic width that can last many seasons. Colors should be muted in gray or navy; never brown or black, unless you want a position as a mortician or chauffeur. Do not wear a sweater, except as a vest underneath a sports coat. Slacks should be long enough to just break over the tops of your shoes.

Wear a white shirt with a conservative tie. Make sure that all the shirt buttons close when you sit! Ties must blend well with the ensemble; they must not be too wide, too narrow, or too wild.

Always wear dark socks, preferably knee-highs that match your pants. Never wear white socks. Socks should be long enough so that no skin on your legs shows when sitting down. Avoid the "no sock" look, no matter what fashion dictates. Shoes should have tied laces or be loafer style; never wear boots. Their color should be black or brown, to complement the outfit.

Jewelry should be kept to a minimum—only a watch (not a Rolex or something too ostentatious) and a maximum of one ring on each hand. If you usually wear an earring—don't! Nor should you wear after-shave or cologne for the same reasons as those given above for women. If you are following the recent trend and getting tattoos, try to place them where they won't be seen when wearing business clothing. If this is not possible, wear clothing that will minimize their effect. The same goes for piercings. Take out the hardware or hide it under your clothing. If you have a tongue piercing, take it out. There is nothing more distracting than having someone speak to you with a piece of metal in his/her tongue.

Hair should be cut neatly in a conservative style. If it is long and you refuse to get it cut, pull it back into a neat ponytail. If you have a mustache or beard, make sure that they are neatly trimmed. Men should carry a high-quality brief-case or portfolio. See Illustration 11.1 for a picture of how to dress.

ILLUSTRATION 11.1
Dressing for Success—Men

Men's
Suit – Dark 3 button solid color suit Navy or charcoal
Shirt – Pressed long sleeve cotton dress shirt in white.
Tie – small print that coordinates with suit
Shoes – wing tip
Socks – match suit

Dressing on the Job

Once hired for the job, you can change the way you dress to fit your own style, provided that it fits in with the firm's typical dress standards or culture, this includes whether or not you can expose your tattoos or piercings. Observe how other members of the firm dress. However, always present yourself in a businesslike manner. Dressing appropriately on the job will help to ensure that you are treated as a professional.

ILLUSTRATION 11.2

Dressing for Success—Women

Women's

Suit – Dark 2 piece skirt suit Navy or charcoal
Blouse – White or off-white (cream color) long sleeve blouse
Shoes – updated dark color pump with 1–1½ inch heel
Hose – neutral color

THE INTERVIEWING PROCESS

Arrival

Arrive at least 10 minutes early for your interview. You may need the time to fill out an application (see Illustration 11.3 to see how to do this). This will also allow some time to use the rest room to make sure that you look your best. If your hands are sweaty, wash them and use a little talcum powder to keep them dry. If you arrive too early, drive around the block a few times or take a short walk. If you are going to be late—even by five minutes—call to let the interviewer know your approximate arrival time.

Do not take anyone else with you. If driven to the interview by someone else, have your friend wait in the car or go for a cup of coffee. Do not bring your children. You should have received enough notice to arrange for adequate day care. If unable to find day care, reschedule the interview. If you are ill, reschedule your appointment for another time. You want to present yourself in the best possible light.

The Firm's Personality and Culture

Another reason to arrive early for the interview is to get a feeling about the firm. You can absorb the atmosphere of the office. Is it too quiet or too noisy? How is the receptionist treated? Your first impression will provide an idea as to whether this is the place for you, as each firm has its own personality, its own culture.

The reception lobby may be an indicator of the company's personality. For example, a dark-paneled lobby with English antiques and oriental rugs could indicate that the firm is very conservative. A high-tech lobby with splashy modern art or a neoclassical look could indicate the firm's progressive or forward-thinking attitude. However, generalizations do not always hold true. One of my candidates talks about how she almost did not go through with an interview, after going through the doors of one firm:

> The lobby was paneled in dark mahogany, and decorated with those English hunting prints, rich oriental carpets and antiques. Although it was quite impressive, my first thought was, "Oh no, this is going to be one of those really stuffy firms." For once, however, appearances were deceiving. The firm turned out to be very modern, open-minded, and liberal, with many fast-track and entertainment clients. I am glad that I took the time to find out what the firm was really like.

Pay attention to other clues. How prosperous does the firm feel? Do the phones ring often? Is there a busy hum to the office? Do you feel comfortable? If something feels wrong about the place, respect your intuition and think twice before accepting an offer.

> **HOT TIP**
>
> Choose a straight-backed chair to sit in while waiting. If sitting on a cushiony, low couch or chair, chances are that you will be forced to extricate yourself awkwardly just as the interviewer walks up to greet you. Bad impression!

Completing the Application

Be prepared to fill out a job application. Do not get upset about this requirement or feel that the firm is treating you as clerical help. In today's job market, which is governed by so many regulations, some firms even require attorneys to complete the forms. It is just part of the game. Fill out the form as quickly as possible. For information reflected on your resume, such as education and work history, write "See Resume." Ask the receptionist first if this is an accepted practice. Some companies want you to fill out the entire application and then may ask you to attach your resume. Be truthful, especially about dates and past salaries. (See Illustration 11.3 below.)

Your job search should have provided information about starting salaries in your region. If there is a question about salary requirements on the application form, leave it blank. Also, do not write "negotiable." If you do write a salary range, it is more than likely that the lower figure will be given if a job offer is extended. See Chapter 13 for more techniques on salary negotiations.

Getting Acquainted

Introduce yourself to the interviewer and offer to shake hands. Do not forget to shake hands after the interview, as well. First impressions are the most important. Many employers make their decisions in the first few seconds. The rest of the interview will only add to, or detract from, their initial impression of you.

When you enter the interviewer's office, sit in the chair offered. I was once interviewing a candidate who sat in my chair by accident. The person was very embarrassed and did not get the job—not for that reason alone, but the interview did get off to a bad start.

> **HOT TIP**
>
> Some firms actually note how long it takes to fill out an application, as an indication of how quickly you might complete you work. Try to take no more than 10 minutes to fill in the blanks. It would be a good idea to have a sample application already prepared to take with you.

ILLUSTRATION 11.3

Employment Application
Sample

Date: May 20, 2008   **Position Desired:** Litigation Paralegal

Date Available: As soon as possible   **Minimum Salary:** $33,000/year

Personal Data

Last Name: Doe   **First Name:** Jane   **Middle Name:** NMI   **Phone:** (213) 555-1111

Street Address: 1234 North Maple Street   **City:** Anytown   **State:** MI   **Zip:** 64518

Are you above the minimum working age? Yes _X_ No ___

Have you the legal right to work in the United States: Yes _X_ No ___
(Verification will be required upon employment).

Have you ever been convicted of a crime within the last 7 years? Yes _____ No X

If yes, please give details and dates: _____
(This will not necessarily disqualify you from employment).

How were you referred to this company? Employee_Employment Ad ___ X ___
Employment Agency ___ **Other** _____

Please specify source: _____

Skills: Please specify computer, word processing, language, office equipment, or other skills that may be relevant to employment with our company.

Knowledge of MS Office suite and various deposition software. Fluent in French, both

written and spoken.

Employment History: List the most recent employment first. (Present employer will not be contacted without your consent.)

Company Name Jones, Smith et al.   **Job Title** Legal Intern

Street Address 123 B Street   **From** 1-2008 **To** 3-2008

City Los Angeles   **State** CA   **Zip** 90008   **Salary** no salary

Supervisor Steven Jones   **Other Comp.** School Credit

Phone Number (213) 553-2222   **Reason for Leaving** Semester

Position Description Organized Documents   ended

Company Name LAUSD   **Job Title** Substitute Teacher

Street Address 1234 Main Street   **From** 9-2004 **To** 6-2006

City Los Angeles   **State** CA   **Zip** 90010   **Salary** $29,000/year

Supervisor Brian Smith   **Other Comp.** None

Phone Number (213) 456-7890   **Reason for Leaving** went to

Position Description Subbed for High School   Paralegal School

Education: High School

School Name Central High School   **Address** 456 Adams Street

City Plano   **State** TX   **Zip** 45678

Graduate? Yes **Degree/Diploma** Diploma   **Major** General Course work

College

School Name UC Berkeley   **Address** University Avenue

City Berkeley   **State** CA   **Zip** 95032

Graduate? Yes **Degree/Diploma** B.A.   **Major** History/Cum Laude

Graduate School or Other

School Name Univ. of Para. Studies   **Address** 145 3rd Street

City Fremont   **State** CA   **Zip** 95145

Graduate? Yes **Degree/Diploma** Cert   **Major** Litigation

Certification: I certify that the statements made by me in answer to the questions asked on this application are true and correct. I understand that any false, misleading, or incomplete statements made by me will be grounds for rejection of my application and termination of employment. Furthermore, I understand that any offer of employment is contingent upon a satisfactory review of my references and a satisfactory background check.

Signature Jane Doe   **Date** 5-20-08

Place your briefcase on the floor beside you, not on the desk. It is important to respect other people's space. Sit straight and lean a little forward during the interview; do not slump or get too comfortable. Never lean over the interviewer's desk, put your elbows on the desk, or grab your resume back to clarify something. Try to sit with your feet together or crossed at the ankles. Never sit with your arms crossed; this action closes you up and also indicates some hostility on your part. It is saying, "Do not get close to me."

CREATING A STANDOUT IMPRESSION

Create a positive and professional attitude. Always maintain eye contact and speak clearly, showing interest and enthusiasm. Employers are not only trying to determine if you will fit in, they are also trying to gauge how you will appear to others. If hired, you will be representing the firm whenever working with clients, other law firms or corporations, judges, and juries. The firm must feel comfortable with the image that you project to these significant people.

Use the interview to enhance the employer's impression of you. Demonstrate self-confidence about your skills, interests, and achievements. Concentrate on giving clear and concise responses to the questions asked. Responding with vague generalities shows that you have not given much thought to the interview.

Express yourself as clearly as possible. Use correct grammar. Listen to your rehearsal tape recording. Notice if you say "um" or "uh" frequently. Eliminate such sentence fillers as "you know," "like," and "I mean." These speech patterns make you appear hesitant, and as a result, will weaken your presentation. It is acceptable to make "agreeing" noises and to laugh or smile at the appropriate time. This demonstrates that you are listening and are a friendly person.

Do not be afraid to stress your attributes. It is appropriate to sell yourself in order to get the job. It cannot hurt to emphasize those skills or qualities that make you particularly well-suited to the job. This is the information the interviewer needs. On the other hand, avoid appearing boastful, overbearing, or conceited.

Be careful about criticizing or belittling the paralegal profession. When a candidate confides to me that "I'm only doing this until I find a real job," the interview might as well be over. I have already determined from this comment that the candidate is not willing to make a real commitment to a paralegal career.

If you do not know the answer to one of the interviewer's questions, say so. You are not expected to know everything, particularly if the subject relates to an area of substantive law that has not been studied. If asked a question requiring experience that you do not have, be honest about it. If you have related experience, point that out. This allows the interviewer to know that you have made the connection between the topic of the question and the experiences you do possess.

INTERVIEW PREPARATION CHECKLIST

➤ Getting Ready
  ❑ Write resume
  ❑ Make contacts
  ❑ Network
  ❑ Make appointments from mass mailings, telephone solicitations, and network contacts
➤ Before the Interview
  ❑ Know your resume
  ❑ Be familiar with a typical application form
  ❑ Know something about the company or firm; check the *Martindale–Hubbell* or *Standard & Poor* directories

❑ Have a list of good questions to ask the interviewer, and know when to ask them

❑ Rehearse your answers, then rehearse again

❑ Plan a thumbnail sketch of yourself

❑ Know the location of the interview site and where to park, or become familiar with the public transportation schedule

❑ Be at least 10 minutes early

❑ Go alone

❑ Bring copies of your resume, list of references, and writing samples and or a writing portfolio (see Chapter 4 for details on how to prepare this) in a briefcase or portfolio

➤ The Introduction

❑ Dress the part (review "Suit Yourself" above)

❑ Do not smoke, eat, chew gum, or drink coffee

❑ Maintain good eye contact and good posture

❑ Shake hands firmly

❑ Establish rapport and be cordial without being overly familiar

❑ Be positive—convert negatives to positives

❑ Remember that first impressions are lasting impressions

➤ The Interview

❑ Be sure to supply all important information about yourself

❑ Sell yourself—no one else will

❑ Use correct grammar

❑ Do not be afraid to say "I do not know"

❑ Find out about the next interview or contact

❑ Try to anticipate problem areas, such as inexperience or gaps in your work history

❑ Be prepared to handle difficult questions, and know how to overcome objections

❑ Find out when a decision will be made

❑ Do not answer questions about age, religion, marital status, or children unless you wish to

❑ Shake hands at the end of the interview

➤ After the Interview

❑ Immediately document the interview in your placement file

❑ Send thank-you letters

❑ Call to follow up

12

Successfully Handling the Job Interview

Selling Yourself and Gathering the Information You Need

Not too long ago, another placement counselor told me about one particularly unusual job interview. The paralegal assistant candidate was interviewing with a law firm partner who apparently did not like his new phone system. During the interview, a call transferred to him was botched. He became so angry that he ripped the phone jack out of the wall and threw the phone across the room! He repeated this performance with his secretary's phone and then resumed the interview. The legal assistant applicant—showing great presence of mind—carried on as though nothing had happened. She now has an excellent paralegal position with that firm.

In this chapter I present many situations that you might find yourself in during a job interview. However, each interview is unique. If the interviewer surprises you, do not get flustered. Prepare, rehearse, and expect the unexpected.

STRUCTURE OF A TYPICAL INTERVIEW

There is a fairly well-established pattern for job interviews, such as the one discussed below. Nearly all interviews consist of the same components, although sometimes in a different order.

Small Talk and Introduction

The interview will open with a "warm-up," consisting of some small talk about weather, traffic, or finding the building. Always answer positively. Tell your interviewer "I love the rain" or "Your directions were perfect" (even if they were not!).

HOT TIP

Always turn off your cell phone, BlackBerry, pager, or whatever new technology has been invented since the publishing of this edition of my book, before you enter the law firm lobby. There is nothing ruder than having your interview interrupted by a ringing cell phone!

Comment on the firm's lovely offices or excellent view of the city. Never challenge or disagree with a statement the interviewer makes. Remember, you want to impress, not antagonize, the interviewer. The chat at the beginning of the interview should relax you and put both you and the interviewer at ease. Do not accept anything to eat or drink. You do not want to be embarrassed by spilling something or dropping crumbs on yourself.

Purpose of the Interview

The interviewer should tell you some details about the job and what should be accomplished during the interview. Ask about the general procedures for this interview. Is this a screening interview? Will you meet the attorneys or legal assistants with whom you might be working? Will you be expected to come back for more interviews?

Background Information

At this point the interviewer will explore the background information presented on your resume. There will definitely be questions about your education and work experience. These questions might be presented as follows:

➤ Why did you choose the paralegal field?

➤ Why did you leave your last job?

➤ What skills do you have that relate to the position we are offering?

There are many other possible questions on this issue. See the section "Questions You Might Be Asked" later in this chapter.

General Information

You will be asked questions that test your ability to reason, your philosophy, and your personality. These areas are frequently tested by asking how a hypothetical situation might be handled. Topics will include your strengths and weaknesses. You might also be asked your opinions on various subjects, perhaps about a new U.S. Supreme Court nominee, or some other current event topic.

Your Questions

Prepare and rehearse questions about the firm and the duties of the particular position. The more pertinent questions you ask the more thoughtful and prepared you will appear. If all of your questions have been answered, try to think of something else. A list of appropriate questions to ask the interviewer appears later in this chapter.

Never ask about money—salary or benefits—in the initial interview unless the interviewer brings up the subject or if this is your only interview before the company decides on the appropriate candidate. If the latter is the case, the question of salary could be brought up toward the end of the interview.

Salary negotiations generally take place at the end of the interview, or during the second interview. Information about benefits (health insurance, vacation policy, etc.) is usually provided by the interviewer toward the end of the first interview. Do not be surprised if a second—or even third—interview is required. Most law firms conduct the interviewing process in stages, usually involving the attorneys at the final interview only.

Closing

Before leaving the interview, be sure you understand the details of the position. Do not drag out the interview, however. If there are further questions, ask them in your follow-up letter. Clarify the question of when you can expect to hear back from the employer. Shake hands as a final closing, and always thank the interviewer for his or her time.

QUESTIONS YOU MIGHT BE ASKED

This section is divided into topics, for ease in selecting those questions that most affect you. During your preparation for the interview, make an honest assessment of yourself, frame your answer, and then rehearse it. It is a good idea to role-play with a friend as interviewer to test your answers.

EXPERIENCE AND SKILLS
➤ How soon will it be before you are contributing to this firm?
➤ What are the most important accomplishments thus far in your career?
➤ How did you get along with your last supervisor?
➤ Did you enjoy working for your last employer? Explain.
➤ How will your major strengths help in this job?
➤ In what way do you feel you can make the greatest contribution to this firm?
➤ Why are you leaving (or why have you left) your present company?

➤ Does your present company know that you are planning to leave?

➤ What did you like best about your last job?

➤ What qualifications do you have that make you successful in this field?

➤ What is your experience?

➤ If you could have made improvements in your last job, what would they have been?

➤ Describe some emergencies in prior jobs when you had to quickly "think on your feet."

➤ Tell me about the last time that you had to make a quick decision.

➤ Tell me about the best and worst supervisors you ever had.

➤ Can you describe your typical workday?

➤ If you ran into a certain situation (make one up for rehearsal), how would you handle it?

➤ How could you make our company more successful?

➤ What risks did you take in your last few jobs; what were the results of taking them?

➤ What are your qualifications as a paralegal?

➤ What does a paralegal do?

➤ Why did you specialize in this particular area of law?

➤ What are your computer skills?

➤ Describe your last two positions.

BEHAVIOR AND ATTITUDE

➤ Which is more important to you, salary or the job itself?

➤ Describe the best person with whom you ever worked.

➤ What do you think determines a person's progress in any firm?

➤ What do you generally find to criticize in most people?

➤ If you could tailor-make a job for yourself, what elements would it include?

➤ Have you every thought about becoming an independent paralegal or starting your own company?

➤ Describe a time when you were able to have a positive influence on others.

PERSONALITY

➤ Can you tell me something about yourself?

➤ What magazines do you read?

➤ Who in history do you most admire?

➤ Do you work well under pressure?

➤ Do you consider yourself a competitive person?

➤ What hobbies do you enjoy?

➤ What kinds of books do you read and how much time do you spend reading?

➤ What kinds of people attract you?

➤ What kinds of people annoy you?

➤ Who or what influenced you most in your career?

➤ How flexible are you?

➤ If you were starting all over, what career would you enter?

➤ How do you spend your spare time?

➤ If you could go back to a place in history, where would it be?

EDUCATION

➤ Tell me about your education. Which courses did you like the best?

➤ What was your college major?

➤ What were your extracurricular activities at school?

➤ How did you spend your summers while in college?

➤ Do you think your school grades reflect your true abilities?

➤ How did you happen to get into the paralegal field?

➤ Why did you choose this particular college?

➤ Do you plan to complete your bachelor's degree?

➤ Why did you choose this particular paralegal school?

➤ What did you study in your paralegal program?

➤ Are you planning to go to law school? If yes, why? If no, why not?

PERSONAL PHILOSOPHY

➤ Do you prefer working alone or with others?

➤ What do you think are the most serious problems facing law firms today?

➤ What motivates you?

➤ What are your short-term goals?

➤ What are your long-term goals?

➤ What is your greatest strength?

➤ What is your greatest weakness?

➤ Are you creative? Give an example.

➤ Are you analytical? Give an example.

➤ How intuitive are you?

➤ How do you handle conflict?

➤ What is your philosophy of life?

➤ Everyone has pet peeves. What are yours?

COMPENSATION

➤ What do you feel this position should pay?

➤ What was your previous salary?

➤ What is your current salary?

➤ What salary are you worth?

➤ How much would you like to be earning in five years?

GENERAL

➤ What sort of job would you really like?

➤ How can you justify our hiring you?

➤ Why have you changed jobs frequently?

➤ Are you willing to relocate?

➤ How long would you stay with us?

➤ What are you looking for in a job?

➤ Why do you want to work for us?

➤ Why do you want this job?

➤ Why did you want to interview with this firm?

➤ How do you know about this firm?

➤ What is the most fulfilling part of your career?

➤ What are the disadvantages associated with the paralegal career?

➤ How would you like our firm to assist you if you join us?

➤ Can you take instructions without becoming upset?

➤ Are you considering any other positions at this time?

➤ What kind of references will your previous employer give about you?

➤ Can you work overtime? Are you willing to travel?

➤ If you could have any position in this firm, what would it be?

➤ With your background, we believe you are over/underqualified for this position.

➤ Have you ever been fired from any job?

➤ Why have you been unemployed for so long?

➤ Why do you have gaps in your resume?

➤ Why has it taken so long to find a job?

HANDLING INAPPROPRIATE QUESTIONS

The interviewer may ask inappropriate questions or questions that you are not required to answer. In fact, asking some types of questions violates federal and state laws against discrimination. If prepared in advance for this possibility, you can refuse to answer gracefully. Such questions may deal with your age, marital status, family planning, or anything else having no relevance to your ability to work effectively.

Most interviewers are aware that these questions are inappropriate and will not ask them. Even if these questions are asked, the interviewer will most likely refrain from pursuing the matter if you indicate an unwillingness to answer.

RESPONSES TO INAPPROPRIATE QUESTIONS

I have found three ways of answering these questions. One of them should be appropriate in most situations. First, if asked whether anything would prevent your working overtime, a good answer is: "Everything in my home life is supportive of my career efforts." Nothing else need be said.

Second, if you feel comfortable answering the questions, do so with just a short answer. Do not elaborate. For instance, if you are asked your age, simply state: "I am 30 years old" and say nothing else.

Third, try to determine what the interviewer is really asking. If asked the age question, you may respond: "If what you are asking is whether I have the energy required for this type of job, the answer is 'Yes.' "

Illegal Questions

Title VII of the Civil Rights Act is a comprehensive, antidiscrimination federal law enacted in 1964. This law prohibits pre-employment inquiries that either directly or indirectly solicit information that may be used for discriminatory purposes. Most states also prohibit inquiries on job applications concerning race, color, religion, sex, or national origin, unless that employer is seeking such information in order to implement affirmative action programs.

The following are topics about which employers may not inquire:

AGE

Any inquiry suggesting a preference for persons less than 40 years of age. This includes asking about your date of high school or college graduation, whether it is orally or on the application.

ARREST

Any inquiries relating to arrests not accompanied by conviction.

CITIZENSHIP

Any inquiry about citizenship status must be limited to requirements for completing the Federal I-9 citizenship veri fication form.

CONVICTIONS

Questions about convictions that seek to solicit information not related to one's fitness to perform a particular job. Questions related solely to convictions or prison releases more than seven years old are not permitted.

FAMILY

Questions tailored to specifically elicit information about your spouse, spouse's employment or salary, children or child care arrangements, and whether you have any other dependents.

DISABILITIES

Inquiries that are so general as to reveal handicaps or health conditions not related directly to the applicant's fitness to perform the job.

HEIGHT/WEIGHT

Questions not based on actual job requirements.

MARITAL STATUS

Anything related to an applicant's marital status. This includes checklists that ask applicant to indicate a category: Mr./Mrs./Miss/Ms.

MILITARY SERVICE

Inquiries asking about discharge or request for discharge papers.

NAME

Questions about a name or its origin, which if answered, would divulge marital status, lineage, ancestry, national origin, or religion.

NATIONALITY

Questions relating to lineage, ancestry, national origin, descent, birthplace, native language; or any similar inquiries about your spouse.

ORGANIZATIONS

Any requirement that asks an applicant to list all memberships in organizations, clubs, societies, or similar groups.

PHOTOGRAPHS

Any request for your photo, prior to hire.

PREGNANCY

Inquiries regarding pregnancy, medical history, or family planning issues.

RACE

Questions regarding race or skin color.

RELATIVES

Any inquiries about names and addresses of relatives that might reveal discriminatory information.

RELIGION

Questions about religious choices, including holidays.

RESIDENCE

Any inquiry about names or relationships of person with whom you reside, or any questions about home ownership.

SEX

Any question regarding sex, gender, or sexual preferences or orientation.

HOW TO ANSWER DIFFICULT QUESTIONS

The following difficult questions may be asked by the interviewer. I have listed some suggested and wrong answers.

1. I see you have not worked in a while. Why is that?
   a. I was continuing my education and will receive my degree/certificate in a few months/soon.
   b. I took some personal time that does not relate to my paralegal work.
   c. I have been working in another field, but would like to get back into legal work.
   d. I realize that I have not worked in a while. However, as you can see from my resume, I have been taking continuing education courses to hone my legal skills.
   e. *Wrong Answer:* I was so stressed out from my last job, I wanted to recuperate.

2. You do not have any legal background. Why should I hire you?
   a. My background lends itself nicely to this entry-level position. My organizational skills and attention to detail are excellent.
   b. You will notice that in my previous positions, I organized documents, reviewed contracts, and/or did the corporate minutes (list whatever skills you possess that are applicable). I believe that all of these skills are transferable to the paralegal field.
   c. *Wrong Answer:* I do have legal background. I organized my own divorce/criminal/traffic court trial.

3. This position requires somewhat more experience than you have.
   a. If you will notice my years in the business world, I believe that will translate to the experience level you are seeking.
   b. Because of my excellent legal education and internship, I know that I can handle the position.
   c. *Wrong Answer:* Can you explain then, why you called me for an interview?

4. Why don't you have any computer skills?

   a. I am currently taking a WordPerfect course at the local college.

   b. In two weeks, my paralegal school will be offering a course in computerized litigation support. I am planning to take it.

   c. I am working hard on my computer at home.

   d. *Wrong Answer:* I am computerphobic and refuse to learn how to use one.

5. Your specialty is in corporate law. This is a real estate position.

   a. Corporate and real estate are very similar at the entry level. I have learned about corporate acquisitions, utilizing skills similar to those required for a real estate specialty, namely UCC searches and dealing with banks.

   b. I am very interested in the real estate field. I am currently working on receiving my broker's license.

   c. *Wrong Answer:* My resume doesn't indicate that I have real estate experience.

6. Your grades are not really good enough for this firm.

   a. If you will notice, I did exceptionally well in paralegal school.

   b. I realize that my undergraduate grades were not exceptional because I

      1. had a family crisis during my senior year;

      2. worked full time while going to school;

      3. supported a family while attending college.

      (Fill in the appropriate reason, but stick with the truth.)

   c. You are entirely correct. However, you will notice that I have excelled in my work history.

   d. *Wrong Answer:* Well, my college was a party school. I goofed off in my last year.

7. We cannot train you. Will that be a problem?

   a. As I belong to the local paralegal organization, I have a vast resource of qualified paralegals that will be happy to answer any questions I may have.

   b. I learn very quickly, and see no problem with that.

   c. *Wrong Answer:* Yes, I don't know how I can be expected to learn the job without training.

8. You do not have a B.A., and/or a certificate from an ABA-approved school.

   a. My lack of education has been compensated for through my work experience.

   b. I realize that my certificate is not from an ABA-approved school, which is a hiring requirement of this firm. However, I feel that

I went through a very substantial program, which followed the ABA guidelines. I am confident that my performance will be excellent.

   c. *Wrong Answer:* I really do not feel that I need the extra education. I have gotten this far without it.

9. This is not a legal secretarial position.

   a. I am making the transition to paralegal, and feel that my extensive background as a litigation legal secretary, along with my paralegal certificate, qualifies me for this position.

   b. I realize that my previous experience as a legal secretary is not applicable to this position, but my five years' work in real estate has provided me with a hands-on view of the practice.

   c. *Wrong Answer:* Good, I do not want to type anymore.

10. Why were you fired?

   a. Economic conditions were not very good at the time, and unfortunately, I was let go when my firm downsized.

   b. My position with the firm was eliminated when several of my cases were nearing an end; the firm found it more economical not to use paralegals at that point.

   c. *Wrong Answer:* It was the worst place in the world to work. It's really a revolving door over there.

11. Why have you changed jobs so often?

   a. My previous positions were problematic because

     1. The firm folded/relocated/dissolved my particular division.

     2. Financial constraints made it necessary to seek higher compensation.

     3. I have always tried to increase my responsibilities.

   b. I have been searching for a career that would satisfy my needs. I have now found it with the paralegal profession.

   c. *Wrong Answer:* I always seem to have personality conflicts with my supervisors. I was never happy at the last several places where I worked.

12. Why have you been looking for work for so long?

   a. I am very selective. I would like to stay at my next position for a long period of time.

   b. I am looking for exactly the right opportunity.

   c. *Wrong Answer:* It's the economy's fault.

13. Why are your earnings so low?

   a. I was hired at a low starting salary, in order to gain the experience necessary to do a great job.

b. Now that I have experience, I am worth and expect to receive greater compensation.

c. *Wrong Answer:* My employers were really cheap.

OVERCOMING OBJECTIONS

Objections to your being hired are bound to occur. Do not allow them to throw you. They will most likely be raised regarding your lack of legal expertise, salary expectations, or that your prior work experience does not relate to the job for which you are applying. Some key phrases to effectively counter these objections follow:

➤ Let's look at a different perspective on that . . .

➤ One alternative solution may be . . .

➤ It's certainly understandable how you have reached that conclusion. A different interpretation of that date may be . . .

➤ I am open to any suggestion you may have to overcome that problem.

Whatever phrasing you choose to use, do not issue ultimatums. These will immediately designate you as an adversary. Your approach should be that of a team player; this is a quality that law firms in particular seek in those people filling paralegal positions.

QUESTIONS TO ASK THE INTERVIEWER

During the interview, you should ask some of the following questions tactfully and at the appropriate time. Some of the questions might be omitted, or reserved for the final interview, depending on the circumstances. Remember that the firm is not only interviewing you; you are also interviewing the firm. If hired, you will be spending more time with these people than with your significant other. So be very careful about choosing the right environment. By asking the right questions, you can make the right decision.

Interviewers are also wary of candidates who have no questions. It is not a possibility that the interviewer will answer all of your questions, if you do not ask them. So be prepared. Note that this list does not include questions about salary. The topic of salary negotiations is covered in Chapter 13.

JOB DUTIES

➤ Will I be expected to travel?

➤ Will I have an expense account?

➤ Will I be required to perform any clerical or secretarial duties?

➤ Will I be expected to travel locally on court runs or other errands? If so, will I use my own car? Will I be reimbursed for gas and/or mileage?

➤ Will I be required to do any kind of investigative work?

➤ Will I be expected to relocate?

➤ Am I replacing a paralegal or is this a newly created position?

➤ Why is this position open?

➤ What characteristics do you most desire in the person who will fill this position?

➤ Would you describe the job duties for me?

➤ What do you consider the ideal experience for this job?

➤ I have read about this firm's involvement with _____ (fill in the appropriate information). Will I have a chance to work on that case/deal/matter?

➤ On what types of cases will I be working?

➤ To whom will I be reporting? Who is in charge of giving me work?

➤ What are the negatives about this job? The positives?

➤ Will I have my own computer?

FIRM STRUCTURE

➤ Do you have a structured paralegal program?

➤ Will I be expected to obtain additional education and/or training?

➤ Will I be trained on the job?

➤ Is there a paralegal career path? What are the prerequisites required of a senior legal assistant?

➤ Does the firm require a specific minimum number of billable hours? How many?

➤ What is the average tenure of your paralegals? What is the turnover rate?

➤ What exactly would I be expected to accomplish in the next two years?

➤ With regard to this firm, where can I expect to be next year?

BENEFITS

➤ What will be my regular work hours?

➤ What benefits are offered by the company?

➤ What holidays does the firm provide?

➤ What vacation time is available?

➤ Will the firm pay for continuing education?

➤ Does the firm pay for professional organizations?

➤ Will paid parking be provided?

QUESTIONS YOU SHOULD NOT ASK AT THE FIRST INTERVIEW

➤ Will I have to work much overtime?

➤ What happened to the person who had this job before me? (It is okay to ask why this position is available.)

➤ What are the office politics like here?

➤ What is the salary?

➤ Do you pay overtime?

➤ What kind of bonuses do you offer?

TIPS FOR THE SECOND (AND THIRD) INTERVIEW

If you are called back for a second interview, chances are the firm is seriously considering making you an offer, or at least narrowing the scope of possible candidates. Approach this next stage as not only another chance to sell yourself, but to determine whether, if offered the position, you want to work at this particular firm.

Meeting the Lawyers

Most of the lawyers for whom you will be working will want to meet and talk with you. Paralegals usually work for more that one attorney. Therefore, a third interview may be necessary to schedule meetings with all of the attorneys. Ask to meet everyone with whom you will be working, including the elusive senior partner.

For the second (or third) interview, draft and rehearse additional, more substantive questions to ask the lawyer(s). Concentrate several of these questions in your areas of law. For example, you may want to ask how a certain procedure in litigation is handled at the firm. Put the research you have done on the firm to work, asking questions about favorable articles that you have read concerning the firm.

How an attorney responds to your questions is as important as the content of the responses. Believe me; you do not want to end up working for an ogre. How can you tell in advance if the attorney you are meeting for the first time will be tough to work for? The best advice I can give is to ask the person to describe his or her approach to working with legal assistants. You will be able to glean good clues from their answers. For example, responses such as, "I give a person one chance and one chance only," "I do not like a lot of questions," or "I tell a person once what I want and expect them to get it," are dead giveaways that this person will not be an easy employer. Do not be shy. You are entitled to know about this person's working persona before accepting the offer.

HOT TIP

Do not take out your list of questions during the interview; memorize them instead. Also, do not start taking voluminous notes. This may appear threatening to a lawyer or other members of the firm. Ask permission before beginning to take any notes.

Meeting the Paralegals

Try to meet as many paralegals as possible. At your second interview, you may be questioned by the senior paralegal in the department considering your employment. Be sure to clarify the relationship. This person may become your immediate supervisor. The chemistry established with the senior paralegal is crucial to your success in first getting the offer, and later on the job itself.

Ask if you can meet other legal assistants in the department, to discuss what they do and how they like their jobs. Do not suggest that you want to "grill" them about the firm. Suggest a social setting such as a lunch meeting. If the firm will not arrange a meeting with their legal assistants, try to get in touch with them through your network. Your local paralegal association's membership book will identify the firm where each member is employed. Accepting a job is a serious decision, and merits the time taken researching it.

Touring the Firm's Offices

Request a tour of the offices. See where your office will be located. It may be important to you to have a window office. If the firm only provides cubicles, or has legal assistants sharing offices, this will be a problem. If you are shown the firm's law library, observe the level of resources offered, and if it is computerized. Ask to see other important parts of the firm, including the file and copying rooms.

Meet with your prospective secretary, because this is a crucial professional relationship. The legal team is composed of the lawyer, paralegal, and legal secretary; though not necessarily listed in order of real importance. Ask to meet the word processing staff, if that department will be doing a lot of your work.

Find out what technical tools you will have. The firm may have the latest computer equipment and resources, or lag behind in the development of this area. A variety of technical support tools may be necessary, depending upon your area of law. If you specialize in litigation, does the firm have a good document search and retrieval database system in place? If working in real estate or probate law, will you have document assembly software to assist with drafting? If necessary, review the computer courses you have taken in order to prepare pertinent questions concerning this issue.

REVIEW OF INTERVIEW DO'S AND DON'TS

DO:

➤ Dress conservatively, neatly, and carefully

➤ Plan to arrive at least 10 minutes early

➤ Announce yourself properly to the receptionist or secretary by stating your name and the name of the person you will be seeing

➤ Complete application forms neatly, completely, and quickly

➤ Have a good, firm handshake

➤ Sit up straight

➤ Look the interviewer in the eye

➤ Make sure the interviewer knows your name, its pronunciation, and the job you are applying for

➤ Ask if the interviewer has your resume; if not, supply another copy

➤ Use positive responses to break the ice

➤ Be prepared to overcome negative responses

➤ Be prepared to answer typical, difficult, and illegal questions

➤ Be positive and assertive

➤ Conduct yourself as if you are determined to get the job . . . Sell yourself!

➤ Ask for the next interview

➤ Shake hands firmly at the end of the interview

DON'T:

➤ Wear heavy makeup, exaggerated hair or clothing styles, or any cologne or perfume

➤ Be late; there is no excuse for this!

➤ Drink coffee or eat anything; politely refuse, if offered

➤ Chew gum

➤ Smoke, even if offered a cigarette

➤ Be overly aggressive, boastful, flippant, or boisterous

➤ Be meek or mild

➤ Be negative about your previous or present employer

➤ Answer only with a "yes" or "no"

➤ Be a motor mouth

➤ Use incorrect English or offensive language

➤ Ask about salary, vacation, or retirement until the interviewer indicates that it is acceptable to do so

➤ Attempt to prolong the interview after the interviewer concludes

➤ Start adding new thoughts or qualifications as you are walking toward the door

13

Getting Paid What You Are Worth

Salary Negotiation Strategies

This can be one of the most difficult segments of your job search, if you are unprepared. The good news about entry-level paralegal positions is that starting salaries are usually higher than other entry-level occupations. The bad news for career changers is that initially, you might have to take a cut in pay. However, remember that in this field, you are generally recognized as a "senior" after three to five years of experience. Many senior legal assistants make well over $60,000 per year. Some paralegals with management responsibilities or high-level specialties earn $80,000 or higher annually. I even know of several paralegals that are well into the six figures, not including bonuses.

Law firms are known to increase starting salaries at a very rapid pace, particularly in the early stages of your career. This is because the steep learning curve is recognized and rewarded. In addition, law firms have historically raised legal assistants' compensation more rapidly than typical cost-of-living increases.

WHERE TO FIND OUT HOW MUCH YOU WILL EARN

Your research into starting salaries begins at the local paralegal association. Ask about prevailing salary levels in your area. Most state and local paralegal associations conduct salary surveys that are made available to their members. NFPA, NALA, and *Legal Assistant Today* magazine conduct periodic national surveys. Your paralegal school may also have information on local salaries as well.

Bear in mind, however, that some national salary surveys do not break down the information gathered according to each region of the country or level of experience. Looking at national averages alone can give a skewed picture of prevailing regional averages. For instance, if most of the respondents in a national survey work in large cities, there will usually be higher average salary figures than those prevailing in smaller towns. To obtain the most accurate picture, review both regional and local surveys.

Most surveys are generally broken down by experience level and area of law. For example, you can find information on what corporate paralegals with two to five years' experience are generally paid. In addition to salary, overtime, and bonuses, other compensation issues such as fringe benefits are also addressed. The Bureau of Labor Statistics Web site regarding paralegals has general wage information as well (*www.bls.gov/oes/current/oes232011*).

Federal Salary Schedules

If you are looking into a federal job, paralegals are usually paid according to the Federal Employer's Pay Schedule. Each general rating schedule under that system has 10 levels of pay, termed "GS levels." (GS stands for general schedule.) Entry-level paralegals typically begin their careers with the federal government at a pay scale classified as "GS-5" or above. The pay scales change yearly. Check with your local Office of Personnel Management for the latest schedule (*www.opm.gov/oca/07tables/pdf/gs.pdf*).

WHEN TO DISCUSS SALARY

An experienced interviewer will generally plan for the discussion on salary to occur at the end of the first interview, or at some point during the second interview. Allow the interviewer to bring up the subject first. Be careful not to jump the gun. Position yourself to appear primarily concerned with the work, level of assignments, and the corporation itself. Your emphasis should be on how your skills, abilities, and determination to succeed will benefit the firm. If overly anxious to discuss salary or benefits, you will appear—to paraphrase John F. Kennedy—as more interested in what the firm can do for you, rather than what you can do for the firm.

Find out what the interview process will be. If you are going to have only one interview, it is acceptable to discuss salary toward the end of the meeting. If more than one interview is planned, salary should be discussed during the last interview, be it the second or third.

HOW TO NEGOTIATE

Law firms are populated with master negotiators. Attorneys spend years in law school learning the latest techniques. Nonattorney staff members also learn to be equally skilled at negotiating, simply by being in the environment. If you have not had any prior negotiating experience, this game can still be skillfully played by understanding your opponent and knowing

- ➤ what you want
- ➤ what you will settle for (but do not sell yourself short)
- ➤ what the potential is of the job (growth, more money?)
- ➤ the firm's history regarding its use of paralegals (talk to former employees)
- ➤ who you are negotiating with, and what kind of power they have to get you what you want
- ➤ if the firm pays a year-end or merit bonus (benefits, other perks?)
- ➤ when the next raises are scheduled
- ➤ whether the firm pays overtime

Before you start the negotiations, check with your network and your paralegal association to find out if any of them have any information about the law firm and what its compensation package entails.

The overtime issue is critical in your negotiations. You can easily earn an extra $2,000 to $10,000 per year in overtime alone. On the other hand, if the firm is known for generous year-end or merit bonuses, this might outweigh your getting paid overtime even though, according to the latest in federal wage and hour rules, paralegals should be paid overtime.

Skilled interviewers will put the ball in your court by first asking, "What kind of salary are you looking for?" Having conducted your prenegotiating research, you will already have a general idea about the salaries paid by firms in your area to entry-level paralegals. The natural tendency is to throw the ball back into the interviewer's court by asking, "What does the position pay?" Some interviewers may respond to your question; others will indicate that your response is required first.

Let's say you have conducted your research, and determined that a good starting salary in your region is between $24,000 and $26,000 per year. Hopefully, you have tapped into your paralegal network, school, or placement agency to gain inside information. First determine whether

- ➤ this level of starting salary is applicable to the firm/corporation with whom you are interviewing
- ➤ you can accept this salary
- ➤ you are flexible with respect to the exact amount of salary you will accept
- ➤ you can demand a higher salary than the norm, because of your transferable skills, education, certification (CLA, RP), etc.

You can answer the question, "What kind of salary are you looking for?" in several ways:

- ➤ I am looking to be paid at the market rate.
- ➤ My salary requirements are in the mid-20s.

➤ My salary range is between $23,000 and $26,000 per year.

➤ I understand the going rate for paralegals at this level of experience is between $25,000 and $30,000 per year.

If choosing to respond with a salary range, be aware that by doing so, you are giving the interviewer permission to offer the lower salary. It is unlikely that an employer will offer the higher end of the range, as you have already stated that the lower amount is acceptable. Therefore, it is a wise idea to increase the lower end of your range by approximately $2,000 above the salary actually sought. It is common for many employers to offer less than the stated range; therefore, if your bottom line is $24,000, ask for a range of $26,000 to $28,000 per year.

Never set a specific inflexible dollar amount, as this leaves no room for negotiation with the interviewer. Always ask for more than your minimum, so that you have room to negotiate.

You may be asked about the amount of your present salary. If changing careers, your current salary may be higher than that normally paid to an entry-level paralegal. There are several answers you may give to the present salary question:

> I know that I may have to take a cut in salary in starting my new career. However, working for your firm is exactly what I would like to do. Therefore, my salary range would be between $ _____ and _____. I realize that my current salary is higher than what an entry-level paralegal may expect, but with my background in _____, I feel that I should be worth somewhere in the mid-_____s to your firm.

If you are a career-changer whose present profession relates specifically to this paralegal position, you may say

> My current salary as an RN is $35,000 per year. Given that the medical malpractice position you are offering utilizes most of my current skills, I would be willing to make a lateral move at that salary.

If your current salary is lower than the norm, do not inflate it. Your interviewer can easily verify the amount. Simply mention that you are being paid below market value, and you expect between $ _____ and _____, which is what entry-level paralegals are being paid. Quote the most recent survey by name. Law firms are used to documentation and should not be offended when you substantiate your information.

IF THE OFFER IS LESS THAN YOU EXPECTED

If the offer is less that you expected, go ahead and negotiate! Do not be intimidated. Lawyers love to argue. It is what they do best! Some effective answers to lower-than-expected salary offers are

➤ I am worth more because of my education and prior experience.

➤ The current salary survey states that entry-level paralegals make
$ _____.

➤ My _____ background relates well to the paralegal field. It
will not cost the firm as much to train me.

Also, don't think that the first offer from the employer is his/her best offer.
Continue the discussion. Bring up perquisites that you may want to include in
the offer (see below). But don't give up until you have exhausted all of the suggestions in this chapter.

Negotiate for Perquisites

You can also negotiate further benefits and perquisites (or perks) which translate
into more dollars. In your negotiating, it is imperative to convince the interviewer of the value of the firm's bestowing these items upon you. Some of these
perks (and their selling points) include the following:

➤ **Continuing Education**

By granting you a continuing education allowance, the firm will gain a
more valuable employee who will quickly learn the position. You can even
offer a cost-cutting benefit! Upon returning to the firm, you can educate
other paralegals on the subjects learned, thus saving the firm the cost of
sending everyone. You may also want to include future training and review
courses for your CLA, CLAS, RP, or other certification programs.

➤ **Law or Graduate School Tuition**

Some firms will grant paralegals law school or graduate school tuition,
if they agree to remain for an extended period, utilizing their education.
For example, once the paralegal passes the bar exam, he or she agrees to
remain with the firm for at least two or three years as an associate. Firms
that have paid for undergraduate or graduate degrees obtain similar com-
mitments for positions such as specialty paralegals. One firm I know of paid
for a portion of a paralegal's MBA degree, and then asked that person to
stay on as the Director of Administration.

➤ **Association Dues**

When asked, many firms do not hesitate to pay association dues for
their professional staff. It is worth requesting, and will indeed be a benefit
for you.

➤ **Health and Dental Benefits**

If receiving health or dental benefits through your spouse's employer,
you might ask the firm if they could rebate their costs of these benefits

directly to you. They would not be paying for benefits that you do not need, and it will be less expensive to the firm in the long run as these costs tend to increase over time.

➤ Vacation, Sick Leave, and Personal Leave

If your salary offer is below the average, and the firm simply will not negotiate, ask to receive one more week of vacation, or additional sick or personal days.

➤ Bonuses

You can also use exempt status (no overtime pay) and a bonus as negotiation issues. Find out if the firm gives bonuses to legal assistants at the end of the fiscal year. If they do not have an established paralegal policy, or you will be the only paralegal, it may be possible to negotiate a bonus for yourself. I know of a paralegal that successfully negotiated a six-month review bonus for himself, in lieu of a salary review at that time.

OTHER NEGOTIATING OPTIONS

➤ Early Salary Review

If you feel strongly about the job, but the salary is just too low, ask for a salary review in three to six months instead of the customary one year. Of course, that raise must be earned. Merely having your salary reviewed at this time does not mean that a raise will automatically be given if your performance does not warrant one. However, if you knock their socks off, a substantial increase can be achieved.

On my advice, a legal assistant I know successfully negotiated for an early salary review. At the end of her first six months with the firm, she was given a 16 percent increase over her starting salary!

Be sure to ask for a salary review, not a performance review. A performance review may only result in a "you're doing great" pat on the back, with no increase in salary. Request the promise of a salary review in writing, because law firm management personnel do change. A new manager may not honor your original request.

➤ Hiring Bonus

A hiring bonus is often used to attract associates. This is a one-time bonus given at hiring. If the objection is voiced that "this is the maximum salary our budget will allow," and you are bringing an extra-special talent, educational background, or certification to this position, the firm may be willing to grant this one-time bonus. The firm benefits, because if amortized over a one-year period, the hiring bonus is a trivial dollar amount. In addition, they can probably fund the bonus from a different part of their budget, and still remain within their compensation guidelines for paralegals. They will pay if they really want you!

➤ **Other Ideas**

Other negotiating points may include a more prestigious job title, or challenging duties or responsibilities. These may be negotiated in lieu of salary. If the law firm sees that you are doing a credible job with increased responsibilities or duties, negotiate a timetable for an increase in salary.

IF YOU ARE USING A PLACEMENT AGENCY TO NEGOTIATE FOR YOU

If using a good agency, their representative should be able to negotiate the best possible compensation package for you. Your agency should be aware of starting salaries, hiring practices, benefits, frequency of raises, continuing education policies, and history of the firm's utilization of paralegals. However, even if the representative relates all of the above data to you, it is far more advantageous to learn this information during your own job interviews. A skilled recruiter will relay all offers, and let you know if they believe that the firm will offer a higher salary. It is entirely up to you to accept or reject the offer. Recruiters can only relay your specific instructions to the prospective employer; they cannot decide for you.

WHAT SHOULD NOT BE USED AS NEGOTIATION TECHNIQUES

The fastest way to terminate a salary negotiation is by appealing to the interviewer's emotions. Anything that is unrelated to specific expectations of job performance is irrelevant and not negotiable. Below are some obvious ways to guarantee an unfavorable end to your salary negotiations:

➤ I cannot believe this amount.
➤ My friend got $ _____ and that is what I want.
➤ I want more money because I have to travel farther to get here.
➤ Whatever you give me is fine.
➤ I am a little older than most of the people here and therefore worth more.
➤ I have two children at home and need more.
➤ I have a better office where I am now.
➤ Parking is more expensive here.
➤ I need to buy new clothes to work here.
➤ I want more because I feel that I will do a better job than anyone else.

A law firm does not care what salary you can live on. They are far more concerned with their bottom line. Citing a friend's salary is not quoting an official source of information. It is much more difficult for the firm to debate your worth when you have a salary survey in hand.

DEADLINES FOR NEGOTIATIONS

According to experts, conclusions to negotiations will occur as close to the deadline as possible. Therefore, you must establish a date for resolution of the issue. Ask the interviewer when the firm will make its decision. Do not hesitate to call on that date to ask how the decision-making process is proceeding. Ask if any further information about yourself can be offered, or if anyone at the firm would like to see you again.

If the firm indicates that the decision is between you and one or two other candidates, let them know that you would appreciate knowing by a certain date, as you have other offers to consider. Do not, however, push yourself out the door by being overbearing or insisting that the firm react to your deadlines. Be flexible and accommodating. Many firms make decisions by committee, which is not always a quick process.

If you are made an offer, do not accept immediately, even though you are dying to accept. It is alright to think about the offer overnight or over the weekend. Do not let the employer know that you have to ask your spouse or your mother for advice. This shows weakness. Let them know that you will be able to get back to them on "Wednesday at 10 A.M." or "Monday at 2 P.M." Be very specific as to the time. You must call back then. If not, the offer may disappear.

TAKING AN ACTIVE ROLE

Take an active role in the negotiations concerning your salary. You are entering a profession whose members earn their livelihoods through the negotiation process. Practice negotiation with a friend so that you sound confident and self-assured, even if you are very anxious. Stay realistic about your salary expectations and, above all, have fun.

14

Wrapping Things Up
The Importance of Interview Notes and Follow-Up Letters

EVALUATING THE INTERVIEW

Evaluating your interview will assist you in making a decision about accepting a job. It will also help you to recognize different ways to improve future interviews.

Make notes immediately after each interview. These notes should be specific, containing information about the organization of the firm or company, description of job responsibilities, paralegal program structure, career growth opportunities, and benefits and compensation packages. List the clerical and technical support that will be available. Also include your impressions of the firm's culture, working environment, and physical facilities. Refer to Illustration 14.1. This form should help in organizing your thoughts and impressions.

File your notes in your placement file for future reference. They will refresh your memory if participating in numerous interviews. If you receive more than one job offer, these notes will be invaluable in helping to choose a firm, as most of the important issues will have been considered.

Once you have accepted a position, you are in. Your hard work and patience will have paid off. Do not discard your placement file; the interview evaluation notes will be helpful if you decide to seek another position a few years down the road.

THANK-YOU LETTERS ARE OPPORTUNITIES FOR MARKETING YOURSELF

After an interview, write a thank-you letter to everyone you met. This letter reminds the employer who you are and can serve as another writing sample. It can also be used to furnish references, or any other information that may have been forgotten or requested during your interview. This letter is your last effort to sell yourself.

ILLUSTRATION 14.1

Interview Evaluation and Review

Firm/Company: _____

Address: _____

Date of Interview: _____

Interviewed with: _____

Title: _____

Position: _____

Thank-you letter sent (date): _____

1. My initial reaction was: _____

2. I enjoyed meeting the interviewer: _____

3. The interviewer was clear and concise regarding the responsibilities of this position: _____

4. To what extent will this position meet my goals? _____

5. I think I understand the firm's/company's culture and attitudes toward employees: _____

6. The salary meets my requirements: _____

7. The salary is not what I am seeking. However, the firm/company offers other advantages: _____

8. I understand clearly what the perks and benefits are and I am excited by what is offered: _____

9. I need another interview to clarify: _____

10. Areas to negotiate: _____

11. I would like the following from this position: _____

12. The following excites me about this position: _____

13. The following concerns me about this position: _____

14. I have discussed this position with my network, colleagues, mentor, or board of advisors: _____

15. I would like to pursue this position: _____

HOT TIP

Always try to relate something that was discussed in the interview to how it matches with your skills. This is generally accomplished in the second paragraph.

HOT TIP

To be sure of the names and titles of the people with whom you interviewed, ask for their business cards before leaving their office.

The letter should be professional in tone, and typewritten on stationery that matches your resume. It is wise to use full names in any correspondence, even if you were asked to address the person who interviewed you by their first name. Call the receptionist for clarification if unsure of the spelling or title of anyone with whom you interviewed.

The letter allows the employer to know that you are interested in the position, and encourages the firm to seriously consider you. It is also appropriate to make a follow-up telephone call within a week or so after mailing your thank-you letters, if interested in the position and not as yet contacted. Remember that law firms are somewhat slower than other organizations in making hiring decisions; it may take some time before hearing the final results. See Illustrations 14.2 through 14.4 for sample thank-you letters.

HOT TIP

The situation may arise in which you have interviewed for a position, which for various reasons did not appeal to you. Always write a follow-up letter to the employer explaining why you are not interested. This will leave a favorable impression with the interviewer, who is potentially a valuable contact for future positions.

ILLUSTRATION 14.2

Thank-You Letter

123 North Main Street
Anytown, RI 33332
June 4, 2006

Larry Lawyer, Esq.
Law & Law, Inc.
111 Elm Street
Anytown, RI 22221

Dear Mr. Lawyer:

Thank you for meeting with me last week. The interview and tour of your offices were most informative. I remain very interested in joining Law and Law.

I would also like to emphasize that my experience as a teacher has helped in developing skills that transfer well to paralegal work, such as writing and supervising.

If there is any further information needed before your recruitment committee reaches a decision, please let me know. I would be more than willing to meet with you again. As requested, I will be calling next week, to see if you have reached a decision.

Sincerely,

Sally Teacher
(333) 333-3333

ILLUSTRATION 14.3

Thank-You Letter

123 Small Street
Small, CA 99999
July 12, 2006

Lee Kramer, Esq.
Kramer, Cramer & Chramer
222 Main Street
Small, CA 99999

Dear Mr. Kramer:

Thank you for an enlightening interview yesterday, regarding the paralegal position with your firm. I was very impressed by everyone I met.

The new law regarding product liability for automobile seat belts is a hot issue in the state legislature. I understand your firm's concern regarding such cases. As we discussed, my background as a researcher fits in well with the new cases your firm is handling.

I look forward to hearing from you soon regarding this position. I would appreciate the opportunity to demonstrate my abilities at Kramer, Cramer, and Chramer. I will call next week to see if you have made a decision.

Sincerely,

Joan Jackson
(333) 222-9999

ILLUSTRATION 14.4

"Not Interested" Thank-You Letter

444 Any Street
Anytown, NJ 11111
July 3, 2006

Joe Lawyer, Esq.
Lawyer & Lawyer
3456 Mail Street, Suite 444
Anytown, NJ 11111

Dear Mr. Lawyer:

Thank you for taking the time to meet with me on June 1st, 2006. I thoroughly enjoyed speaking with you and your colleagues at Lawyer & Lawyer.

Your presentation of the litigation position was exciting; however, (choose one of the following phrases that fits or make up your own)
1. I have decided to accept another position.
2. I am sincerely trying to land a corporate paralegal position.
3. The hour and one-half commute to your offices unfortunately prevents me from accepting an offer at this time.
I appreciate your time and thank you once again for the opportunity to meet with you.

Sincerely,

Polly Paralegal
(444) 444-4444

15

Congratulations! You Are Hired

It is the first day on the job and you are excited. You probably want to start right in and go to work, but first it is necessary to learn the physical layout of the firm, find out who the important players are, and what procedures are peculiar to the firm.

GETTING YOUR BEARINGS

During your initial orientation, find out who should be spoken to for work assignments, payroll, and office services; and who to consult with when problems arise. Find out the firm's history, office procedures, and billing requirements. It is very important to understand how things are done. Thoroughly read through the employee handbook and ask questions about office policies and procedures. An office manager of a large firm told me that there were two things she looked for in a good employee: solid legal skills and an ability to follow office procedures. The firm's legal secretaries and other members of the support staff can be your best allies in the law firm maze. They are good sources for learning how the office really works.

In addition, during your orientation, ask about the attorneys with whom you will be working. Later, locate their offices and take the time to introduce yourself. Learn where to find the office supply room, copying center, and central files department. (Do not forget to find the lunch room and bathroom!) Get acquainted with the office layout so you will not get lost.

After the orientation, take your own tour of the office space. Introduce yourself to the support staff, even if you have met them before. Some firms are large enough to require a staff telephone list or map of the office. If you carry these items while on your tour, you can put names with faces.

Ask what is appropriate regarding the office technology. Many employers do not encourage surfing the Web during company hours or replying to your personal e-mail or text-messaging. Be sure you turn off your cell phone. It could be very embarrassing if, during a discussion with an attorney in your office, your cell phone rings. Make sure that you also have the appropriate signature block for your outgoing e-mails. Most law firms require disclaimers so that only the person who is to receive an e-mail receives it. Remember that voice-mail, e-mail, and all technology in the office are the property of that office. If you are found to be looking for inappropriate information on the Internet, sending off-color e-mails or leaving voice messages that could be construed as sexist, racist, etc., you could be terminated. Sometimes we forget that the office is a professional organization and not our playground.

WORKING WITH LEGAL SECRETARIES AND SUPPORT STAFF

It is important, when dealing with the firm's support staff, to be clear and concise in giving directions. If your secretary is working on a project that requires following a certain court rule, make sure to know that rule and communicate what is needed. If unfamiliar with the rule, ask your secretary to assist you. He or she probably has more experience with it. If you are unsure, do not bluff.

Assure your secretary that you want to make the best use of his or her time; this is vital for a smooth-running operation. Structure the relationship with your secretary as one built upon teamwork. If you are smart enough to realize how much an experienced legal secretary can help, you are on the right track.

Respecting the support staff is not only polite, but shows that you are considerate of others' feelings. If sharing your secretary with other paralegals and lawyers, cooperate with the team to be certain that everyone's priorities and deadlines can be met. Avoid constantly requesting that your secretary do work at the last minute. Use the phrase, "This is a rush," sparingly, and only when it is honestly a "rush" project. Try to work with your secretary, making the best use of his or her time.

ASSERTIVENESS TRAINING HELPS

As a paralegal, you will be interacting with professional and clerical personnel, who for the most part are thorough and exacting. To effectively communicate with these people, you must learn to be assertive. This means learning how to handle difficult, stressful situations, and asking for the support you need.

Attorneys prefer working with paralegals that are not reticent about speaking up. If you are not assertive, attorneys will lose confidence in you.

You may find yourself burdened with excessive or tedious work assignments. Paralegals who hesitate to assert themselves are frequently stuck with low pay, poor working conditions, and monotonous situations.

In order to have a manageable workload, learn how and when to say "No" tactfully, but firmly. By grudgingly accepting each new assignment because of a fear of refusing it, or of offending the attorneys, you will soon become disgruntled and resentful of the situation. However, by informing the attorney that the new assignment will conflict with your other priorities, you will avoid overburdening yourself. Be certain that the person understands that you are not trying to avoid doing the work:

> Paralegal: I would like to do the research project for you, Mr. Jones, but I have to draft a complaint for Mr. Smith that must be filed today. I will not be able to do your research today, but I would be happy to do it tomorrow. Will that be O.K.?

You might even suggest someone else to do the project, if, in fact, the attorney needs it immediately.

If you are asked to complete an unfamiliar task, do not agree and then do it poorly. Ask questions about the project and write down the instructions. It is quite acceptable to say that you have not completed this type of assignment previously, but that you are willing to try. An attorney may not be aware of precisely what you do not know. However, do not accept a project unless you are willing and able to handle it.

Many employees are afraid to assert themselves because of irrational fears of someone's disliking them. If constantly seeking approval from others, you will find yourself intimidated and unable to do your best work. This is especially true in law firms, where praise for a job well done is sometimes hard to find.

Learning to assert yourself takes time and practice. There is no question that attorneys can indeed be intimidating. Remember, as long as you have all of the work that can honestly be handled, you have a right to refuse additional assignments.

KNOW WHAT IS EXPECTED

It is very important to find out exactly what is expected of you on the job. For example, if hired as a document clerk, you will probably be organizing documents on large litigation cases; that is the extent of what you will be doing. If, however, you were hired as an entry-level paralegal and your work assignment is limited to number-stamping documents, you may be able to expand your horizons. Complete the present assignment to the very best of your ability. Then, if the next assignment is a repetition of the first, speak to your supervisor about increasing your responsibilities.

Be forewarned that your first assignments will not be researching a Supreme Court brief or drafting a multimillion dollar deal. You will probably be organizing boxes of documents or assembling closing binders. Do these projects well and maintain a positive attitude. Remember, attorneys are ultimately responsible for your work. You must first earn their trust before they feel comfortable with delegating significant work to you. If you consistently do well, the attorneys will realize that they can trust you with advanced assignments. If you are pleasant and persistent, I guarantee that you will get the kind of work you know how to do.

A LAST WORD OF ADVICE

Welcome to the world of paralegals! It is a profession that is constantly growing and changing, offering new challenges and opportunities. Remember, starting at the beginning is starting at the beginning. It takes hard work and perseverance to reach the top.

I am glad that you have chosen this career. You are certain to have exciting and challenging experiences, allowing you to maximize your potential. A legal assistant is a great career choice.

From an "old" paralegal to a "new" paralegal, I wish you outrageous success!

appendix A

Buzzwords

Terms You Will Hear in the Legal Community

Have you ever been caught in a conversation where discussions about working in a law firm are flying around, and because you do not know some of the terminology, you cannot contribute? What follows is a listing of some of these commonly used terms, along with definitions.

This is not meant to replace legal dictionaries. Instead it is intended to define some of the common terms used in talking about the business of practicing law.

AAfPE   American Association for Paralegal Educators Association made up of administrators of ABA-approved and other paralegal schools.

ABA   American Bar Association.

ABA approved   Designation awarded by the American Bar Association to paralegal schools and programs that meet stringent requirements for scholastic excellence and thorough coverage of subject matter.

abstract   In some practice areas, this term has a very specialized usage, such as in "abstract of title." Generally, however, it means a brief précis or overview of a document, highlighting only the key elements.

In litigation, abstracts of documents are frequently computerized for easy retrieval. Sometimes, deposition summaries that focus only on key issues or words are called abstracts of the deposition.

affidavit   Written statement of facts sworn by the maker, taken before an official of the court, notary public, or other authorized person.

appellant   Party bringing the appeal.

appellee   The party against whom the appeal is brought.

arbitration   Referral of a dispute to a third party (chosen by the opposing parties) rather than a court. By prior agreement of the parties, the decision of the arbitrator may be binding. This procedure is often handled through the American Arbitration Association.

associate   Title usually given to a full-time attorney member of a law firm who has not yet been elevated to partner. The associate is salaried, whereas the partners share in the profits of the firm.

attorney–client privilege   Confidential statements made by a client to an attorney may not be disclosed to others by the attorney without the client's permission, including court proceedings. Staffs of law firms, including paralegals, enjoy this privilege and must scrupulously avoid breaking client confidentiality. This privilege is for the benefit and protection of the client.

audit letters   Information requested from law firms representing corporations to complete statements of liabilities required in annual statements and by other Securities and Exchange Commission (SEC) regulations.

Bates stamping   Method of numbering documents sequentially by utilizing a small hand-held numbering device manufactured by the Bates Company. The purpose is to have a unique identifier for each page of each document. These processes can also be accomplished by certain specialized copying machines.

billable hours   Any legal service performed in an hour for which a firm's clients can be charged. Most firms have a minimum billable hour requirements for the time keeper, attorneys, and legal assistants alike, and compensation above base levels frequently depends heavily on whether these requirements are exceeded.

Blue Sky Laws   Popular name for state statutes covering the regulation of securities offerings and sales.

Bluebook   Shorthand term for *A Uniform System of Citation*, a spiral-bound book published by the Harvard Law Review Association. Named for its historic and distinctive blue cover, the Bluebook is a well-accepted guide for the citation of all types of legal authorities.

boilerplate   Used to describe documents (or portions of documents) containing standard verbiage, such that very little, if any, modification is required to tailor the document to specific situations. For example, most contracts, real estate documents, and some pleading forms contain boilerplate language that can be used over and over again.

bonus   Perquisite given to attorneys, paralegals, and sometimes other staff members, usually at year end, to reward merit, tenure at the firm, billable hours, or other significant performance-based criteria. Bonuses can be given more often than just at year end.

boutique law firm   Small, highly specialized law firm that focuses on a particular area of law or on a particular type of client (i.e., entertainment law or computer companies).

brief 1) Written statement prepared by the counsel arguing a case in court, usually including a summary of facts of the case and the pertinent law, and an argument of how the law applies to the facts supporting counsel's position.

2) Summary of a case picking out pertinent facts, identifying the issues involved, determining the holding (or decision), and defining the reason behind the court's decision. In most paralegal schools, students are taught to brief cases in order to understand the legal reasoning process.

bylaws Rules and regulations adopted by a corporation or association for its own governance.

calendar Used both as a noun—in referring to a firm's calendar (or docket) of upcoming events—and a verb—the act of placing events on the firm's docket. The act of calendaring involves reviewing incoming and outgoing pleadings and correspondence for important dates, and recording such dates in either a manual or computerized tickler or reminder system. A firm's calendar can be specific to attorneys or departments, or apply generally to everyone in the firm.

case management Approaching the management of a litigation matter as a project needing input from many people and various support departments of a firm, in addition to outside vendors.

certificated Paralegal possessing a certificate from a paralegal institution . . . not to be confused with the following, "certified."

certified State-recognized or organization-recognized designation usually given upon the successful completion of a complex examination. NALA offers the CLA designation, which refers to the Certified Legal Assistant.

cite checking Involves checking all citations to legal authorities that might be found in a legal document to confirm that they are still "good law." That is, all citations must be "Shepardized" to make sure that there are no superseding statutes or overruling cases that would undermine the authority of the materials cited.

It also involves confirming that all legal authorities are properly cited, according to the Bluebook standards. In addition, all jump cites (point pages) must be checked to confirm that the quote (or other material) cited is actually found on that page. Finally, all direct quotes must be checked to make sure they are quoted accurately.

CLA Certified Legal Assistant is the designation offered through NALA upon successful completion of a two and one-half day examination.

CLE Acronym for continuing legal education, now required by most state bar and paralegal accrediting organizations.

coding Refers to abstracting pertinent pieces of information from each document for indexing in a document retrieval database. Used in large, complex litigation cases.

complaint   Plaintiff's initial pleading.

complex litigation   Large-scale litigation, defined by a number of different situations. Usually refers to a large document case (500,000 or more). Can also refer to multidistrict litigation, class-action lawsuit, multiparty actions, cases with a number of cross claims, or many technical, factual, or legal issues.

conflict of interest   Can arise in a number of situations. The most common is when a law firm accepts a new client that would put the firm in conflict with an already existing client. Another common situation arises if a firm hires an attorney or paralegal that has had close involvement in a matter opposing a firm's existing client. The firm could possibly be disqualified from continuing to represent its client in that matter. Checking for conflicts when hiring attorneys or paralegals is mandatory. If the conflict is too direct or there is no efficient way to alleviate the conflict, the legal professional cannot be hired.

In some cases, an ethical wall (sometimes called a "Chinese wall" or a "cone of silence") can be erected around the person with the conflict, allowing the firm to hire that person. The person with the conflict is then diligently screened from all conversation, documentation, and knowledge about the matter involved in the conflict. The person behind the "Chinese wall" must also be very diligent in reminding others not to discuss the matter whenever he or she is around.

corporate maintenance   Duties of a corporate paralegal that include updating corporate minute books, preparing minutes of board meetings, and ensuring that the corporation files are timely documents.

counsel   Attorney or lawyer. A corporation's general counsel is its principal lawyer.

defendant   Person against whom a civil or criminal action is brought.

depo   Abbreviation for deposition.

deposition   Discovery device by which a transcript is made of testimony of a witness taken under oath but not before a judge.

deposition summarizing or digesting   Being able to accurately summarize requires sensitivity to the nuances of language, knowledge of evidence rules, and a thorough understanding of the issues involved in the particular litigation. Methods vary widely from handwriting, dictating, or inputting the summary directly into the computer. The degree of summarization depends on how it will be used.

discovery   Pretrial procedures by which the parties to an action "discover" facts and other relevant information about the case from the opposing party in order to prepare for trial. Discovery tools in civil actions include depositions, interrogatories, and requests for production of documents.

document assembly programs   Computer programs used for customizing standardized legal documents.

document clerk   Support position to paralegals, sometimes called a paralegal assistant or case clerk. A document clerk ordinarily handles the more routine and clerical tasks of a law suit, such as organizing, filing, numbering, and indexing documents.

document control   Various methods of identifying rooms, files, file drawers, file folders that must be reviewed for possible production during discovery; marking the documents selected with a unique identifier for later identification; and establishing a document archive system either through a master document set or by some file or image system for later retrieval.

document production   Can refer solely to a specific response to a "demand to produce documents" in a litigation matter as part of the discovery process. On a broader scale, document production refers to the technique of establishing document control and managing an organized production (or receipt) of documents.

due process of law   Administration of law according to established rules and practices for the enforcement and protection of individual rights.

estate planning   Associated with the drafting of wills and trusts before the person dies.

evidence   Any type of proof of an issue, legally presented at trial by the parties through witnesses, records, documents, etc.

exempt   Employees who are determined to be exempt from federal (and/or state) overtime laws because of their professional status, specialized training, or executive level administrative responsibilities. Some law firms classify all legal assistants as exempt employees, while other firms reserve that status for senior paralegals only. New laws indicate paralegals should be nonexempt.

expert witness   Person with expertise in any field who may be needed to testify about certain aspects of a matter involving his or her expertise.

felony   Serious crime, usually punishable by more than a year in prison.

form files   Refers to files of court-mandated or other types of forms. Particularly necessary in jurisdictions in which litigation is form-driven. Also important in real estate and corporate practices. Can be a manual or computer file.

freelance or contract paralegal   Paralegal who works as an independent contractor rather than as an employee, but who still works under the supervision of an attorney.

IPMA   International Paralegal Management Association, an organization open only to paralegal managers. IPMA sponsors an annual conference, collects data for and publishes an authoritative salary survey, and also publishes a newsletter. The national organization sponsors and provides support to local chapters.

intake   Process of interviewing potential clients to determine if their needs match the services provided by the firm. Also describes initial interviews of clients to determine the pertinent facts of the case.

intellectual property   Category of law that covers patents, copyrights, and trademarks.

interrogatories   Discovery tool consisting of a set of written questions propounded to a party or a witness.

issue coding   Process of picking out pertinent issues designated by an attorney from depositions, documents, or other sources. Can also refer to picking out certain subject matters and placing such information in a document retrieval database.

LEXIS   Database developed to provide easy access to legal reference materials. The database makes available all legal authority—both case law and statutes.

license   Permit issued by a government agency that permits a person with certain qualifications to engage in a specific occupation (i.e., lawyers and beauticians have licenses).

limited licensure   Permit issued by a government agency that permits a person with certain qualifications to engage in limited activities within a specific occupation.

malpractice   Professional misconduct; the failure of one who offers professional services to exercise those skills in a manner generally held to be prudent, with resulting injury or damage to the recipient.

misdemeanor   Offense less serious than a felony.

motion   Written or oral request made to a judge to obtain a ruling on any issue arising during a lawsuit; for example, motions to compel discovery, dismiss a complaint, or obtain a summary judgment.

NALA   National Association of Legal Assistants, which is an umbrella organization for regional and/or specialty paralegal associations as well as individuals.

NFPA   National Federation of Paralegal Associations, many regional or specialty paralegal organizations belong to this national umbrella organization.

nonexempt   Employees who, because of their classification primarily as support staff, are entitled to payment of overtime. Persons in these positions are considered not to be exempted from federal (and state) overtime laws, because the jobs do not ordinarily and primarily require the exercise of independent judgment and initiative.

of counsel   Attorney associated with a law firm who is neither an employee nor a partner. Frequently, an "of counsel's" compensation is geared to his or her own client base, and is not dependent on, or part of, the firm's general compensation system.

outside counsel   Used by members of corporate legal department to describe attorneys associated with a law firm that handles all or part of the corporation's legal business.

PACE   Paralegal Advanced Competency Exam was developed by NFPA for the experienced paralegal.

paralegal program   The paralegal department in a law firm or corporation. Most paralegal programs offer a vertical career path and are fairly specialized. It can also refer to a program of study to learn the paralegal profession.

P.I.   Abbreviation for personal injury.

plaintiff   Person who brings a civil lawsuit against another.

plea bargaining   One accused of a crime can bargain though his or her attorney with the prosecutor. The trade usually involves an agreement by the accused to plead guilty rather than not guilty, in return for which the prosecutor agrees to charge the accused with a lesser crime. The court may enter a written agreement to this effect, though the rules vary by state.

pleadings   Formal allegations of the parties' claims and defenses.

pro bono   Community service work done without cost by the lawyer or law firm.

probate   Procedures that are followed in the administration of estates, trusts, wills, and guardianships after a client is deceased.

proprietary school   Business or trade school that is run for profit.

rainmaker   Attorney in a law firm who has great skill at attracting, soliciting, and keeping clients.

redact   To delete text from a document by either covering up the text with self-adhesive corrective tape or by marking over the text with a black marking pen. The purpose of redacting is to delete material that is privileged or otherwise exempted from production during discovery.

redlining   Highlighting the changes in different versions of the same document by underlining all changed words, sentences, paragraphs, etc. Frequently used to track changes in drafts of contracts, real estate offerings, and other complicated documents.

reporter   Collection of written opinions by a court which are reported via publication in book form. There are numerous reporters for state and federal courts.

request for admission   Written statement of fact submitted by one party to the other to admit or deny; these facts admitted are deemed proven without the need for a trial.

RP   Designation given to a person who has passed the PACE Exam from NFPA (Registered Paralegal).

Shepardizing   The trademark property of Shepard's Citations, Inc. The term describes the general use of its publications. Sometimes used colloquially to mean tracing both the prior and subsequent history of a decision and determining the treatment of that decision by others who have cited it as authority.

statue of limitations   Nearly all civil and criminal actions have time limits for which suits must be filed. These are spelled out in state and federal statutes and vary from one action to another and from state to state. An attorney who neglects to file an action within the time period has committed a serious mistake that may be grounds for a malpractice suit.

subpoena   Court or administrative agency order compelling a witness to appear and testify in a certain proceeding. A subpoena *duces tecum* requires the witness also to bring specified documents with him or her.

summary judgment   Court's decision, in response to a motion by a party before trial, that there is no genuine issue of material fact and that the party is entitled to prevail as a matter of law.

tickler file   Manual calendaring and docketing system. Such files frequently consist of numerous multipart forms, containing certain date deadlines, along with client/case information. These forms are filed in date order and then pulled as the date for the reminder approaches.

transactional work   Legal work involving "deals" or transactions such as those found in real estate, entertainment, or corporate practice.

trial prep (preparation)   Phase before trial that may include putting together witness notebooks; preparing witnesses to testify; collecting key pleadings, depositions summaries, and other key documents for trial notebooks; finalizing the exhibit list and putting together the exhibit documents into notebooks; and designing and producing graphic exhibits such as charts.

vendor   Company, organization, or person who sells services to a law firm (i.e., photocopying service, stationery store, temporary paralegal service, etc.).

Westlaw   Online research database built by West Publishing Company. Features "InstaCite" function for quick cite checking.

Legal Assistant and Paralegal Schools List

If you are considering attending a legal assistant school or paralegal program, consult the list below which is separated by states. The list has been compiled from the American Association for Paralegal Education and the American Bar Association.

Only schools that appear on these lists are included. There many other programs offering paralegal studies that are not included because they are not ABA approved or are not members of AAfPE. Any school not on the list is invited to contact the author for inclusion in the next edition of this book.

This list is for informational purposes only, and is not intended as an endorsement of any particular program. Those schools marked with an "A" have been approved by the American Bar Association. Those schools marked with an "E" are members of the American Association for Paralegal Education.

For updated information on schools, you may search the following Internet sites:

American Association for   *www.aafpe.org*
Paralegal Education

American Bar Association   *www.abanet.org*

A = ABA approved, E = Member of AAfPE

ALABAMA

[AE]   Auburn University, Montgomery
       Department of Justice & Public
         Safety
       PO Box 244023
       7601 Senators Drive
       Montgomery, AL 36124-4023
       www.aum.edu/jps

[A]   Community College of the Air
         Force
       Paralegal Program
       Air Force Judge Advocate General
         School
       150 Chennault Circle
       Maxwell Air Force Base
       Montgomery, AL 36112-6418
       *www.maxwell.af.mil/au/cpd/
         jagschool/*

[AE]   Faulkner University
       Legal Studies
       5345 Atlanta Hwy.
       Montgomery, AL 36109
       www.faulkner.edu

[AE]   Gadsden Community College
       PO Box 227
       Gadsden, AL 35902-0227
       www.gadsdenstate.edu

[AE]   Samford University
       Box 2200
       Birmingham, AL 35229-0001
       www.samford.edu

[AE]   South University—Montgomery
       5355 Vaughn Rd.
       Montgomery, AL 36116-1120
       www.southuniversity.edu

[E]   Virginia College at Birmingham
       PO Box 19249
       Birmingham, AL 35219-9249
       www.vc.edu

[E]   Wallace State Community
         College
       PO Box 2000
       Hanceville, AL 35077-2000
       www.wallacestate.edu

ALASKA

[AE]   University of Alaska, Anchorage
       Justice Center
       3211 Providence Dr.
       Anchorage, AK 99508
       www.uaa.alaska.edu/just

[AE]   University of Alaska, Fairbanks
       Tanana Valley Campus Center
       604 Barnette St., Room 103
       Fairbanks, AK 99701
       www.uaf.edu/tvc

[E]   University of Alaska Southeast
       11120 Glacier Hwy.
       Juneau, AK 99801
       www.jun.alakska.edu

ARIZONA

[AE]   Everest College
       10400 N. 25th Ave., Ste. 190
       Phoenix, AZ 85021-1641
       www.everest-college.com

[E]   Everest College
       10924 E. Boston Street
       Apache Junction, AZ 85220
       Theresa_Prater@rmetro.com

[AE]   Lamson College
       Legal Assisting Program
       1126 N. Scottsdale Rd., Ste. 17
       Tempe, AZ 85281-1700
       www.lamsoncollege.com

[A]   Long Technical College
       13450 N. Black Canyon Highway
       Phoenix, AZ 85029

[E]   Long Technical College—
         East Valley
       4646 D. Van Buren Street E350
       Phoenix, AZ 85008
       www.longtechnicalcollege.com

[E]   Mohave Community College
       Legal Assistant Studies
       1971 Jagerson Ave.
       Kingman, AZ 86401
       www.mohave.edu

[AE] Phoenix College
Legal Studies Program
1202 West Thomas Road
Phoenix, AZ 85013-4234
www.phoenixcollege.edu/legalstudies

[AE] Pima Community College
Legal Assistant Program
Downtown Campus
1255 N. Stone Ave.
Tucson, AZ 85709-3030
www.dtc.pima.edu/legal

[AE] Yavapai College
Paralegal Studies Program
1100 East Sheldon St.
Prescott, AZ 86301
*www.yavapai.us/ychrome.nsf/pages/
home*

ARKANSAS

[E] Northwest Arkansas Community
College
One College Drive, Burns 1441
Bentonville, AR 72712
www.nwacc.edu

[E] Pulaski Technical College
3000 West Scnnic Drive
North Little Rock,
AR 82118-3347
cunderwood@pulaskitech.edu

[AE] University of Arkansas-Fort Smith
5210 Grand Ave.
Ft. Smith, AR 72913-3649
www.uafortsmith.edu

CALIFORNIA

[E] Argosy University-Orange County
3501 West Sunflower Avenue,
Ste. 110
Santa Ana, CA 92704
rlondon@argosyu.edu

[E] Braham's College
1431 Carley Creek Drive
Patterson, CA 95363-8764
Fredf134@hotmail.com

[E] California Polytechnic State
University, San Luis Obispo
Extended Education Department
1 Grand Ave.
San Luis Obispo, CA 93407-9750
www.calpoly.edu

[AE] California State University, East Bay
Paralegal Studies and Legal Nurse
Consultant Programs
Extension Division
25800 Carlos Bee Blvd.
Warren Hall, Room 804
Hayward, CA 94542-3012
www.extensoncsuhayward.edu

[AE] California State University, Los
Angeles
Certificate Program in Paralegal
Studies
Continuing Education
5151 State University Dr.
Los Angeles, CA 90032-8919
*www.calstatela.edu/exed/certificate/
paralegs*

[AE] Cerritos College
Paralegal Program
11110 East Alondra Blvd.
Norwalk, CA 90650
www.cerritos.edu

[E] City College of San Francisco
Business Department
50 Phelan Ave., C106
San Francisco, CA 94112
www.ccsf.edu.legal

[AE] Coastline Community College
Legal Assistant Program
11460 Warner Ave.
Fountain Valley, CA 92708
www.coastline.cccd.edu

[E] College of the Canyons
26455 Rockwell Canyon Road,
C-309
Santa Clarita, CA 91355-1803
Patricia.robinson@canyons.edu

[E] College of the Sequoias
Paralegal Program
915 South Mooney Blvd.
Visalia, CA 93227
www.sequoias.cc.ca.us

[AE] Cuyamaca College
Paralegal Studies Program
900 Rancho San Diego Pkwy.
El Cajon, CA 92019-4303
www.cuyamaca.net

[AE] De Anza College
Paralegal Program
21250 Stevens Creek Blvd.
Cupertino, CA 95014
www.deanza.fhda.edu

[AE] El Camino College
Legal Assistant Program
16007 Crenshaw Blvd.
Torrance, CA 90506
www.elcamino.cc.ca.us/paralegal

[E] Empire College
3035 Cleveland Avenue
Santa Rosa, CA 95403
mickey@empirecollege.com

[E] Fresno City College
Business Education Div.
1101 E. University Ave.
Fresno, CA 93741
www.fresnocitycollege.com

[AE] Fullerton College
Paralegal Studies Program
321 E. Chapman Ave.
Fullerton, CA 92832-2093
www.fulcoll.edu

[E] Humphreys College
6650 Inglewood Dr.
Stockton, CA 92507

[E] John F. Kennedy University
100 Ellinwood Way
Pleasant Hill, CA 94523-4817
som@jfku.edu

[E] Los Angeles City College
Legal Assistant

855 North Vermont Ave.
Los Angeles, CA 90029
www.lacc.cc.ca.us

[E] Los Angeles Mission College
Professional Studies Program
Interdisciplinary Studies Center
13356 Eldridge Ave.
Sylmar, CA 91342
http://Lamission.edu/las

[AE] Mt. San Antonio College
Paralegal Program, Business
Administration Department
1100 N. Grand Ave.
Walnut, CA 91784
www.paralegal.mtsac.edu

[A] MTI College
Paralegal Studies
5221 Madison Avenue
Sacramento, CA 95841
www.mticollege.edu

[E] Palomar College
Paralegal Studies
1140 W. Mission Rd.
San Marcos, CA 92069
acorpora@palomar.edu

[AE] Pasadena City College
Legal Assisting Program
Business Education Division
1570 E. Colorado Blvd.
Pasadena, CA 91106-2003
ckellogg@paccd.cc.ca.us

[E] Platt College
Paralegal Studies Program
3700 Inland Empire Boulevard
Ontario, CA 91764
www.plattcollege.com

[E] Riverside Community College
4800 Magnolia Avenue
Riverside, CA 91764
www.rccd.cc.ca.us

[A] Saint Mary's College of California
Paralegal and Law Studies Program
375 Rheem Blvd.

Moraga, CA 94556
www.stmarys-ca.edu

[E]   Salt Lake Valley College
        1111 Bayside Drive, Suite 111
        Corona del Mar, CA 92625

[AE]   San Diego Miramar College
        10440 Black Mountain Road
        San Diego, CA 92126
        www.miramarcollege.net

[AE]   San Francisco State University
        Paralegal Studies Program
        College of Extended Learning
        425 Market St.
        SFSU Downtown Center
        San Francisco, CA 94105
        www.cel.sfsu.edu

[E]   San Joaquin College of Law
        Paralegal Program
        901 5th St.
        Clovis, CA 93612
        www.sjcl.org

[AE]   Santa Ana College
        Legal Assistant Program
        1530 W. 17th St.
        Santa Ana, CA 92706
        www.rsccd.org

[E]   Santa Barbara Business College
        4839 Market Street
        Ventura, CA 93003-8053
        judithm@sbbcollee.edu

[E]   Sonoma State University
        Extended Education
        1801 E. Cotati Ave.
        Rohnert Park, CA 94928
        www.sonoma.edu/exed/certificates/
            aa/attindex

[E]   Southwestern Community
            College
        Paralegal Studies Program
        900 Otay Lakes Rd.
        Chula Vista, CA 91910

[AE]   University of California, Irvine
        Paralegal Certificate Program

University Extension
PO Box 6050
Irvine, CA 92716-6050
www.unex.uci.edu.~unex

[AE]   University of California, Los
            Angeles
        Attorney Assistant Training
            Program
        10995 Le Conte Ave., Ste. 517
        Los Angeles, CA 90024
        www.uclaextension.edu/attp

[A]   University of California, Riverside
        Extension & Summer Session
        Legal Assistantship Certificate
            Program
        11200 University Ave.
        Riverside, CA 92507-4596

[AE]   University of California,
            San Diego
        Legal Assistant Training Program
        UCSD Extension
        9500 Gilman Dr.
        La Jolla, CA 92093
        www.paralegal.uscd.edu

[AE]   University of California, Santa
            Barbara
        Paralegal Professional Certificate
            Program
        6950 Hollister Ave., Suite 102
        Goleta, CA 93117
        www.extension.ucsb.edu

[AE]   University of La Verne
        Legal Studies Program
        1950 Third St.
        La Verne, CA 91750
        www.ulv.edu

[AE]   University of San Diego
        Paralegal Program
        Graduate Career Programs
        5998 Alcala Park AW1-204
        San Diego, CA 92110
        www.acusd.edu/paralegal

[AE]   West Los Angeles College
        Business/Paralegal Studies Dept.

9000 Overland Ave.
Culver City, CA 90230-3000
www.wlac.cc.ca.us/paralegal

[AE]   West Valley College
Paralegal Program
14000 Fruitvale Ave.
Saratoga, CA 95070-5640
www.westvalley.edu

[AE]   Western College
10900 E. 183rd St. #290
Cerritos, CA 90703-5342
www.westerncollegesocal.com

[E]   Witkin Legal Institute
425 Market Street, 4th Floor
San Francisco, CA 94105
John.hanft@thomson.com

COLORADO

[AE]   Arapahoe Community College
Paralegal Department
5900 South Sante Fe Dr.
PO Box 9002
Littleton, CO 80120
*www.arapahoe.edu/programs/
paralegal*

[AE]   Community College of Aurora
Paralegal Program
Business & Public Service
Division
16000 E. Centre Tech. Pkwy.,
C308
Aurora, CO 80011-9036
www.ccaurora.edu

[AE]   Denver Career College
Legal Assistant Program
500 East 84th Street, Suite W-200.
Thornton, CO 80229
mdemarest@denvercareercollege.com

[E]   Parks Junior College
Paralegal Studies Dept.
9065 Grant St.
Denver, CO 80229-4339

[AE]   Pikes Peak Community College
Legal Assistant Program
100 West Pikes Peak Avenue
Colorado Springs, CO 80903
Rich.kellholtz@ppcc.edu

CONNECTICUT

[AE]   Briarwood College
Legal Assistant/Paralegal Program
2279 Mount Vernon Rd.
Southington, CT 06489
www.briarwoodcollege.com

[AE]   Manchester Community College
Legal Assistant Program
Great Path
PO Box 1046 MS17
Manchester, CT 06045-1046
www.mcc.commnet.edu/staff

[E]   Naugatuck Valley Community
Technical College
Legal Assistant Program
750 Chase Pkwy.
Waterbury, CT 06708
www.nvcc.commnet.edu

[AE]   Norwalk Community College
Legal Assistant Program
188 Richards Avenue West
Campus
Norwalk, CT 06854
www.ncc.commnet.edu

[AE]   Quinnipiac College
Legal Studies Department
275 Mount Carmel Ave. Cl-AC1
Hamden, CT 06518
www.quinnipiac.edu

[AE]   University of Hartford
HCW Legal Studies Program
200 Bloomfield Avenue
Hartford, CT 06117
*www.admissions.hartford.edu/
legalstudies*

[E]   University of New Haven
Paralegal Studies

300 Orange Ave.
West Haven, CT 06516
www.newhaven.edu

DELAWARE
....

[AE] Wesley College
Paralegal Studies Program
120 N. State St.
Dover, DE 19901
www.wesley.edu

[AE] Widener University Law Center
Paralegal Studies Department
4601 Concord Pike
Wilmington, DE 19803
www.widner.edu

[E] Wilmington College
320 N. DuPont Highway
New Castle, DE 19720
Amy.l.feeney@wilmcoll.edu

DISTRICT OF COLUMBIA
....

[E] George Washington University
Paralegal Studies Program
2101 F street NW Suite 100
Washington, D.C. 20052
www.nearyou.gwu.edu/plx

[AE] Georgetown University
Legal Assistant Program
1437-37th St. NW
Poulton Hall, 2nd Fl.
Washington D.C. 20057-1007
www.georgetown.edu/ssce/pdp/lap

FLORIDA
....

[E] Barry University
Legal Assistant Institute
11300 NE Second Ave.
Miami Shores, FL 33161-6695
*www.barry.edu/ace/programs/
certificte.asp*

[AE] Broward Community College
Legal Assistant Program
7200 Hollywood/Pines Blvd.
Building 71
Pembroke Pines, FL 33024
www.broward.edu

[AE] Edison Community College
Paralegal Studies Program
8099 College Pkwy. SW
Ft. Myers, FL 33906-6210
www.edison.edu

[AE] Florida Community College at
jacksonville
Legal Assistant Program
3939 Roosevelt Rd.
Jacksonville, FL 32205-8999
www.fccj.org

[E] Florida Gulf Coast University
Legal Studies
10501 FGCU Blvd. S.
Fort Myers, FL 33965-6565
www.cps.fgcu.edu/cj/ls

[E] Florida International University
Legal Studies Institute
University Park-GL-120
Miami, FL 33199
www.flu.edu

[E] Hillsborough Community College
2112 North 15th Street
Tampa, FL 33605
www.hccfl.edu/ybor/paralegal

[E] International College
Paralegal Program
2655 Northbrooke Drive
Naples, FL 34119-7932
www.internationalcollege.edu

[E] Jones College
5353 Arlington Expressway
Jacksonville, FL 32211-5540
mbrasca@jones.edu

[E] Kaplan University
166 Catania Way
Royal Palm Beach, FL 33411-4314
www.kaplan.edu

[E] Kaplan University
     1944 Discovery Circle East
     Deerfield Beach, FL 33442
     Newyen1@yahoo.com

[E] Kaplan University
     10840 NW 10th Street
     Plantation FL 33322-7812
     Sandro67@gmail.com

[E] Kaplan University
     School of Paralegal Studies
     8305 South Military Trail
     Boynton Beach, FL 33436
     teethnlaw@hotmail.com

[E] Manatee Junior College
     Legal Assistant Program
     PO Box 1849
     Bradenton, FL 34206-7046
     www.mcc.cc.fl.us

[E] Miami-Dade Community College
     Legal Assistant Program
     341 SW 28th Road
     Miami, FL 33132
     jpowel@bilzin.com

[AE] Miami-Dade Community College
     300 NE 2nd Ave., Room 3506-12
     Miami, FL 33132
     www.mdcc.edu

[AE] Nova Southeastern University
     Paralegal Studies Program
     Department of Behavioral Sciences
     370 Parker Building
     3301 College Ave.
     Ft. Lauderdale, FL 33314
     www.nova.edu

[E] Palm Beach Community College
     Legal Assisting Program
     3160 PGA Blvd.
     Palm Beach Gardens, FL 33410
     www.pbcc.edu

[E] Pensacola Junior College
     Legal Assistant Program
     418 W. Garden St.
     Pensacola, FL 32501
     www.pjc.cc.fl.us

[E] Santa Fe Community College
     Legal Assistant Program
     3000 NW 83rd St.
     Gainesville, FL 32605
     www.santefe.cc.fl.us

[AE] Seminole Community College
     Legal Assistant Program
     100 Weldon Blvd.
     Sanford, FL 32773-6199
     www.scc-fl.edu

[AE] St. Petersburg College
     2465 Drew Street
     Clearwater, FL 33765-2816
     Demers.susan@spcollege.edu

[AE] South University-West Palm
         Beach
     Paralegal Studies/Legal Studies
     1760 N. Congress Ave.
     W. Palm Beach, FL 33409
     www.southuniversity.edu

[E] University of Central Florida
     Criminal Justice Department
     PO Box 161600
     Orlando, FL 32816-1600
     www.ucf.edu

[E] University of North Florida
     Legal Studies Institute
     12000 Alumni Dr.
     Jacksonville, FL 32224-2678
     www.unf.edu

[E] University of West Florida
     Legal Studies
     11000 University Pkwy.
     Building 85, Room 159
     Pensacola, FL 32514-5751
     www.uwf.edu/justice

[AE] Valencia Community College
     Legal Assistant Program
     701 N. Econlockhatchee Trail
     Mail Code 3-25
     Orlando, FL 32802
     *http://valenciacc.edu/departments/
         east/business/paralegal*

GEORGIA

[AE] Athens Technical College
Paralegal Studies Program
800 U.S. Highway 29 North
Athens, GA 30601-1500
www.athenstech.edu

[E] Brenau University
Conflict Resolution and Legal
Studies
One Centennial Cir. Box 18
Gainesville, GA 30501
www.brenau.edu

[E] Clayton College & State
University
Legal Assistant Program
5900 N. Lee St.
Morrow, GA 30260
www.tech.clayton.edu

[E] Darton College
2400 Gillionville Road
Albany, GA 31707
Heather.perfetti@darton.edu

[AE] Gainesville College
Legal Assistant Program
PO Box 1358
Gainesville, GA 30503
www.gsc.edu

[E] Griffin Technical College
Paralegal Studies Program
501 Varsity Drive
Griffin, GA 30220
ssilvis@griffintech.edu

[E] Kennesaw State University
1000 Chastain Road, #3301
Kennesaw, GA 30144
pbarnes@kennesaw.edu

[AE] South University-Savanah
Paralegal Studies Program
709 Mall Blvd.
Savannah, GA 31406
*www.southuniversity.com/camput/
savanah*

HAWAII

[AE] Kapi'olani Community College
Legal Assistant Program
4303 Diamond Head Rd.
Honolulu, HI 96816
www.kee.hawaii.edu

IDAHO

[AE] Boise State University
Legal Assistant Program
1910 University Dr. HRS
Room 109
Boise, ID 83725
www.boisestate.edu

[E] Eastern Idaho Technical College
1600 S. 25th E.
Idaho Falls, ID 83404
www.eitc.edu

[E] Idaho State University
Campus Box 8380
Pocatello, ID 83209-8380
www.isu.edu

[E] Lewis-Clark State College
500 8th Avenue
Lewiston, ID 83501-2466
imccann@lcsc.edu

ILLINOIS

[E] American Institute for Paralegal
Studies
Paralegal/Legal Assistant
2777 Finley Road, Suite 11
Downers Grove, IL 60515
www.americanparalegal.edu

[E] College of Lake County
19351 West Washington Street
Grayslake, IL 60030-1148
gmiller@clcillinois.edu

[AE] Elgin Community College
Paralegal Program, Business
Division

1700 Spartan Dr.
Elgin, IL 60123
www.elgin.cc.il.us

[AE]   Illinois Central College
Paralegal Program
Thomas K. Thomas Building
201 South West Adams Street
Peoria, IL 61635
http://iccparalegal.com

[E]   Illinois State University
Legal Studies Program
4600 Dept. of Politics &
Government
Normal, IL 61790-4600
www.ilstu.edu/dep/polisci/legs

[AE]   Kankakee Community College
Paralegal/Legal Assistant Studies
Program
100 College Drive
Kankakee, IL 60901
www.kcc.edu

[AE]   Loyola University Chicago
820 North Michigan Avenue
Chicago, IL 60611
www.luc.edu/depts/paralegal

[E]   MacCormac Junior College
29 East Madison Avenue
Chicago, IL 60602-4405
www.maccormac.edu

[AE]   Northwestern Business College
Paralegal Program
4829 North Lipps Ave.
Chicago, IL 60630
www.northwesternbc.edu

[A]   Robert Morris College-Chicago
Paralegal Studies Program
401 South State Street
Chicago, IL 60605
www.robertmorris.edu

[A]   Robert Morris College-Springfield
Paralegal Studies Program
3101 Montvale
Springfield, IL 62704
http://www.robertmorris.edu

[E]   Rockford Business College
Paralegal-Legal Office Assistant
Program
730 N. Church St.
Rockford, IL 61103
www.rbcsuccess.com

[AE]   Roosevelt University
Lawyer's Assistant Program
430 S. Michigan Ave.
Chicago, IL 60605
www.roosevelt.edu/paralegal

[AE]   South Suburban College
Paralegal/Legal Assistant Program
15800 S. State St.
South Holland, IL 60473
www.ssc.cc.il.us

[AE]   Southern Illinois University
Paralegal Studies Program
SIU Mail code 4540
Carbondale, IL 62901-4540
www.siu.edu/~para

[E]   Southwestern Illinois College
Paralegal Studies
2500 Carlyle Ave.
Belleville, IL 62221
www.southwestern.cc.il.us

[AE]   William Rainey Harper College
Paralegal Studies
1200 W. Algonquin Rd.
Palatine, IL 60067
*www.harpercollege.edu/catalogu/
career/para*

INDIANA

[AE]   Ball State University
Legal Assistant Studies
Muncie, IN 47306
www.bsu.edu/csh/poli-sci/legal

[E]   Calumet College of St. Joseph
2400 New York Ave.
Whiting, IN 46394
www.ccsj.edu

[E]   Indiana University
Certificate in Paralegal Studies
425 University Blvd.
Cavanaugh Hall, Room 504J
Indianapolis, IN 46202
www.lupui.edu

[E]   Indiana University at South Bend
Paralegal Studies Certificate
1700 Mishawaka Ave.
PO Box 7111
South Bend, IN 46634-7111
www.lusb.edu/~cted

[E]   Ivy Tech State College
Paralegal Program
3800 N. Anthony Blvd.
Fort Wayne, IN 46805
www.ivy.tec.in.us

[E]   Ivy Tech State College, Region 6
Paralegal Regional Program
4301 S. Cowan Rd.
Muncie, IN 47302
www.ivy.tec.in.us

[E]   Ivy Tech Community College
of Indiana
Central Indiana
50 Fall Creek Parkway North Drive
Indianapolis, In 46208-5752
saltman@ivytech.edu

[E]   Ivy Tech Community College
of Indiana
Region 4
3101 South Creasy Lane
Lafayette, IN 47905-5241
wmarion@ivytech.edu

[E]   St. Mary of the Woods College
Paralegal Studies Program
Guerin Hall
St. Mary of the Woods, IN 47876
www.smwd.edu

[E]   University of Evansville
Legal Studies Program
School of Business
1800 Lincoln Ave.
Evansville, IN 47722
www/cedar/Evansville.edu/~db4

[AE]   Vincennes University
Paralegal Program, 1002 N. 1st St.
Vincennes, IN 47591
www.vinu.edu

IOWA

[AE]   Des Moines Area Community
College
Legal Assistant Program
1100 7th St.
Des Moines, IA 50314
www.dmacc.cc.ia.us

[E]   Kaplan University
23420 200th Avenue
Davenport, IA 52804
mconnor@kaplan.edu

[AE]   Kirkwood Community College
Legal Assistant Program
PO Box 2068
Cedar Rapids, IA 52406
www.kirkwood.cc.ia.us

KANSAS

[AE]   Johnson County Community
College
Paralegal Program
12345 College Boulevard
Overland Park, KS 66210
www.johnco.cc.ks.us/acad/paralegal

[E]   National American University
Overland Park, 10310 Mastin
Overland Park, KS 66212
cwolfe@national.edu

[E]   Newman University
3100 McCormick Avenue
Wichita, KS 67213-2087
conleej@newman.u.edu

[AE]   Washburn University
Legal Assistant Program
1700 College Ave.
Topeka, KS 66621
www.washburn.edu

KENTUCKY

[E]   Beckfield College
        Paralegal Studies
        16 Spiral Drive
        Florence, KY 41042
        www.beckfieldcollege.com

[AE]   Daymar College
        Paralegal Program
        3361 Buckland Sq.
        Owensboro, KY 42304
        www.daymarcollege.com

[AE]   Eastern Kentucky University
        Paralegal Program
        McCreary 113
        521 Lancaster Avenue
        Richmond, KY 40475-3102
        www.paralegal.eku.edu

[AE]   Morehead State University
        Paralegal Program
        350 Rader Hall, University
          Boulevard
        Morehead, KY 40351
        www.morehead-st.edu

[AE]   Sullivan College-Lexington
          Campus
        2355 Harrodsburg Rd.
        Lexington, KY 40504
        www.sullivan.edu/lexington

[AE]   Sullivan College-Louisville
        Legal Studies
        3101 Bardstown Rd.
        Louisville, KY 40205
        www.sullivan.edu

[AE]   University of Louisville
        Paralegal Studies
        104 Ford Hall
        Louisville, KY 40292
        www.louisville.edu/a-s/polsci/paralegal

[AE]   Western Kentucky University-
        Bowling Green Community
          College
        Paralegal Studies Program
        2355 Nashville Rd. Room 139K

Bowling Green, KY 42101
www.wku.edu

LOUISIANA

[AE]   Herzing College
        Legal Assisting/Paralegal Studies
          Program
        2400 Veterans Blvd., Ste. 410
        Kenner, LA 70062
        www.herzing.edu

[AE]   Louisiana State University
        Paralegal Studies Program
        1115 Pleasant Hall
        Baton Rouge, LA 70803-1530
        www.outreach.lsu.edu

[AE]   University of New Orleans
        226 Carondelet St. #310L
        New Orleans, LA 70130
        www.uno.edu

MAINE

[E]   Andover College
        901 Washington Ave.
        Portland, ME 04103
        www.andovercollege.edu

[E]   Husson College
        One College Circle
        Bangor, ME 04401-2929
        hansenm@husson.edu

[E]   University of Maine
        85 Texas Ave.
        Bangor, ME 04401
        www.uma.maine.edu

MARYLAND

[AE]   Anne Arundel Community College
        Paralegal Studies Program
        101 College Pkwy. (Flrs 202A)
        Arnold, MD 21012
        www.aacc.cc.md.us/criminist

[E] Chesapeake College
PO Box 8
Wye Mills, MD 21679
www.chesapeake.edu

[E] College Of Southern Maryland
Business Department
PO Box 910
8730 MitchellRd
La Plata, MD 20646
www.csm.cc.md.us

[AE] Community College of Baltimore
County—Dundalk Campus
Paralegal Program
7200 Sollers Point Rd.
Baltimore, MD 21222
www.ccbc.cc.md.us

[E] Frederick Community College
7932 Opossumtown Pike
Frederick, MD 21793
www.frederick.edu

[AE] Harford Community College
Paralegal Studies Program
401 Thomas Run Rd.
Bel Air, MD 21015
www.harford.cc.md.us

[E] University of Maryland University
College
Paralegal Studies
3501 University Boulevard East
College Park, MD 20783
www.umuc.edu

[AE] Villa Julie College
Paralegal Program
1525 Green Spring Valley Rd.
Stevenson, MD 21153
www.vjc.edu

MASSACHUSETTS

[E] Anna Maria College
Paralegal Program
50 Sunset Lane
Paxton, MA 01612
www.annamaria.edu

[AE] Bay Path College
Legal Studies Program
588 Longmeadow St.
Longmeadow, MA 01106
www.baypath.edu

[AE] Elms College
Paralegal Institute
291 Springfield St.
Chicopee, MA 01013
www.elms.edu/academics/undergrad-uate/bl_paralegal

[E] Middlesex Community College
Legal Studies
33 Kearney Square
Lowell, MA 01852
www.middlesex.mass.edu

[AE] North Shore Community College
Paralegal Program
1 Ferncroft Rd.
Danvers, MA 01923
www.northshore.edu

[E] Northeastern University
360 Huntington Ave 269
Ryder Hall
Boston MA 02115
www.northeastern.edu

[AE] Northern Essex Community
College
Paralegal Studies Program
100 Elliot Street
Haverhill, MA 01830
www.necc.mass.edu

[AE] Suffolk University
Paralegal Studies, 41 Temple St.
Boston, MA 02114
www.suffolk.edu/cas/ehs/undergraduate

MICHIGAN

[E] Baker College of Auburn Hills
1500 University Drive
Auburn Hills, MI 48326
Melissa.manela@baker.edu

[E]   Baker College of Clinton
       Township
       Paralegal Program
       34950 Little Mack Ave.
       Clinton Township, ME 48035
       Kristi.wickerham@backer.edu

[E]   Backer College of Jackson
       2800 Springport Road
       Jackson, MI 48202
       Twilli13@backer.edu

[AE]   Davenport University
       Legal Assistant Program
       6191 Kraft.
       Grand Rapids, MI 49512
       www.davenport.edu

[E]   Davenport University
       Paralegal Program
       4123 W. Main St.
       Kalamazoo, MI 49006
       www.davenport.edu

[E]   Delta College
       Legal Assistant Studies
       1961 Delta Road, Office A-79
       University Center, MI 48710
       www.delta.edu

[AE]   Eastern Michigan University
       Legal Assistant/Paralegal
       Program
       14 Sill Hall
       Ypsilanti, MI 48197
       www.cot.emich.edu/legalassistant

[AE]   Ferris State University
       Legal Assistant Program
       College of Business
       119 South Street, Bus. 358
       Big Rapids, MI 49307
       *www.ferris.edu/htmls/colleges/
       business*

[E]   Grand Valley State University
       Legal Studies Department
       271-C Devos Center/401
       W. Fulton
       Grand Rapids, MI 49504
       www.gvsu.edu/ls

[AE]   Henry Ford Community College
       5101 Evergreen Rd.
       Dearborn, MI 48128
       kadams@hfcc.edu

[AE]   Kellogg Community College
       Legal Assistant Program
       450 North Ave.
       Battle Creek, MI 49016-3397
       www.kellogg.cc.mi.us

[AE]   Lake Superior University
       Legal Asst. Studies
       650 W. Easterday Ave.
       Sault Ste. Marie, MI 49783
       www.lssu.edu

[AE]   Lansing Community College
       Legal Assistant Program
       Po Box 40010-2100 Business
       Department
       Lansing, MI 48901-7201
       www.lcc.edu/legal

[AE]   Macomb Community College—
       South Campus
       Legal Assistant Program
       14500 Twelve Mile Rd.
       Warren, MI 48088
       www.macomb.cc.mi.us

[AE]   Madonna University
       Legal Assistant Program
       36600 Schoolcraft Rd.
       Livonia, MI 48150
       *www.madona.edu/pages/
       legalassistant.cfm*

[AE]   Northwestern Michigan College
       Legal Assistant Program
       1701 E. Front St.
       Traverse City, MI 49686
       www.nmc.edu/business

[AE]   Oakland Community College
       Legal Assistant Program
       27055 Orchard Lake Rd.
       Farmington Hills, MI 48334
       www.occ.cc.mi.us/lgl

[AE]   Oakland University
       Legal Assistant Program

238A Elliott Hall
Rochester, MI 48309-4963
*www.oakland,edu/contin-ed/
    legalassistant*

MINNESOTA

[E]   Alexandria Technical College
        1601 Jefferson street
        Alexandria, MN 56308
        mavisp@aix.tec.mn.us

[AE]   Hamline University
        Legal Studies Program
        1536 Hewitt Ave.
        St. Paul, MN 55104
        www.hamline.edu

[AE]   Inver Hills Community College
        Legal Assistant Program
        2500 80th St.
        Inver Grove Heights,
            MN 55076-3224
        www.ih.cc.mn.us/paralegal

[AE]   Minnesota Paralegal Institute
        13911 Ridgedale Drive, Suite 175
        Minnetonka, MN 55305
        www.mnparalegal.com

[E]   Minnesota School of
            Business/Globe College
        5910 Shingle Creek Pkwy.
        Brooklyn Center, MN 55305
        www.msbcollege.edu

[AE]   Minnesota State University
            Moorhead
        Legal Assistant Program
        1104 7th Ave. S.
        Moorhead, MN 56563
        www.mnstate.edu/paralegal

[AE]   North Hennepin Community
            College
        Legal Assistant Program
        7411 85th Ave. N.
        Brooklyn Park, MN 55445
        www.nh.cc.mn.us

[E]   St. Cloud Technical College
        1540 Northway Drive
        St. Cloud, MN 56301
        shensel@sctc.edu
        mmontreux@sctc.edu

[AE]   Winona State University
        Paralegal Program
        PO Box 5838
        Winona, MN 55987-5838
        www.winona.msus.edu

MISSISSIPPI

[AE]   Mississippi College
        Paralegal Studies Program
        PO Box 4030
        Clinton, MS 39058
        www.mc.edu/~clements

[E]   Mississippi Gulf Coast
            Community College
        2226 Switzer Road
        Gulfport, MS 39507-3894
        Kimberly.starks@mgccc.edu

[AE]   Mississippi University for Women
        Paralegal Program
        Cromwell Communications
            Building
        1100 College Street
        PO Box W-1634
        Columbus, MS 39701
        www.muw.edu/academics/paralegal

[E]   University of Mississippi
        Paralegal Studies Program
        PO Box 879
        University, MS 38675
        *www.olemiss.edu/depts/
            applied_sciences/ugprogramsis*

[AE]   University of Southern
            Mississippi
        Paralegal Studies Program
        118 College Drive #5108
        PO Box 5108
        Hattiesburg, MS 39406
        www.usm.edu

MISSOURI

[AE] Avila University
      Legal Assistant Program
      11901 Wornall Rd.
      Kansas City, MO 64145
      www.avila.edu

[E]   Hickey College
      940 W. Port Plaza
      St. Louis, MO 63146
      www.hickeycollege.edu

[AE] Maryville College
      Paralegal Studies
      13550 Conway Rd.
      St. Louis, MO 63141
      www.maryville.edu

[AE] Missouri Western State College
      Legal Studies
      4525 Downs Dr. Room PS204
      St. Joseph, MO 64507
      www.mwsc.edu

[E]   National American University—
      Independence
      Legal Studies
      3620 Arrowhead Avenue
      Independence, MO 64057
      cwolfe@national.edu

[E]   Patricia Stevens College
      330 N. 4th, #360
      St. Louis, MO 63102
      www.patriciastevenscollege.com

[E]   Penn Valley Community College
      Legal Technology Program
      3201 SW Traffic Way
      Kansas City, MO 64111
      www.kcmetro.edu

[E]   Rockhurst University
      1100 Rockhurst Rd.
      Kansas City, MO 64110
      www.rockhurst.edu

[E]   Sanford Brown College
      1203 Smizer Mill Road
      Fenton, MO 63026-3400
      kmurphy@sbc-fenton.com

[E]   St. Louis Community College
      Meramec
      Legal Assistant Program
      11333 Big Bend Blvd.
      St. Louis, MO 63122
      www.stlcc.edu

[E]   St. Louis Community College—
      Florissant Valley
      3400 Pershall Road
      St. Louis, MO 63135
      www.stlcc.cc.mo.us/fv

[AE] Webster University
      Legal Studies Program
      470 East Lockwood Ave.
      St. Louis, MO 63119
      www.webster.edu

[E]   William Woods College
      Paralegal Studies Program
      One University Avenue
      Fulton, MO 65251
      www.williamwoods.edu

MONTANA

[A]   University of Great Falls
      Paralegal Studies Program
      1301 20th Street South
      Great Falls, MT 59405
      www.ugf.edu

[AE] University of Montana
      College of Technology
      909 South Ave. W
      Missoula, MT 59801
      www.cte.umt.edu

NEBRASKA

[E]   Central Community College
      Paralegal Studies
      3134 West Highway 34
      Grand Island, NE 68802-4903
      www.ccneb.edu

[E]   Chadron State College
      Legal Studies

1000 Main Street
Chadron NE 69337
lleesch@csc.edu

[AE] College of St. Mary
Paralegal Studies Program
7000 Mercy Road
Omaha, NE 68106
www.csm.edu

[AE] Metropolitan Community College
Legal Asst. Program
PO Box 3777
Omaha, NE 68103
www.mccneb.edu

NEVADA

[E] Community College of Southern
Nevada
Legal Assistant Program
6375 W. Charleston Blvd., W2C
Las Vegas, NV 89146-1164
www.ccsn.edu

[E] Heritage College
Associate of Arts Degree Paralegal
Studies
3315 Spring Mountain Rd. #7
www.heritage.edu
Las Vegas, NV 89102

[AE] Truckee Meadows Community
College
1781 Three Mile Drive
Reno, NV 89509
kberning@tmcc.edu

NEW HAMPSHIRE

[E] Hesser College
3 Sundial Avenue
Manchester, NY 03103
www.hesser.edu

[E] McIntosh College
Legal Assistant Program
23 Cataract Ave.
Dover, NH 03820
www.mcintoshcollege.com

[E] New Hampshire Technical College
31 College Drive
Concord, NH 03301-7425
speters@nhctc.edu

[E] New Hampshire Community
Technical College at Nashua
Paralegal Studies Program
505 Amherst Street
Nashua, NH 03063
www.nashua.nhctc.edu

NEW JERSEY

[AE] Atlantic Cape Community
College
5100 Black Horse Pike
Mays Landing, NJ 08061
www.atlantic.edu

[AE] Bergen Community College
Paralegal Studies Program
400 Paramus Rd. Room A306
Paramus, NJ 07652
www.bergen.cc.nj.us

[AE] Berkeley College
Paralegal Studies Program
44 Rifle Camp Rd.
West Patterson, NJ 07424
www.berkeleycollege.edu

[AE] Brookdale Community College
Paralegal Technology Program
765 Newman Springs Rd.
Lincroft, NJ 07738-1597
*www.brookdale.cc.nj.us/fac/legal
studies*

[AE] Burlington County College
3331 State Route 38331 State
Route 38
Mt Laurel, NJ 08054
www.bcc.edu

[AE] Cumberland County College
Legal Assistant Program
College Drive-PO Box 1500
Vineland, NJ 08362-0517
www.cccnj.net

[AE] Essex County Community College
Paralegal Program
303 University Ave.
Newark, NJ 07102
www.essex.edu

[AE] Farleigh Dickinson University
Paralegal Studies Program
285 Madison Ave. M-DH2-02
Madison, NJ 07940
www.fdu.edu

[AE] Gloucester County College
Business Division
Paralegal Program
14000 Tanyard Rd.
Sewell, NJ 08619
www.gccnj.edu

[AE] Mercer County Community
College
Legal Assistant Program
PO Box B
Trenton, NJ 08690-1099
www.mccc.edu

[AE] Middlesex County College
Legal Studies Department
2600 Woodbridge Ave.
Edison, NJ 08818-3050
www.middlesexcc.edu

[E] Montclair State University
1037 Rte. 46 E.
Clifton, NJ 07013

[E] Montclair state University
Legal Studies Department
Montclair, NJ 07043
taylerm@mail.montclair.edu

[AE] Montclair State University
Legal Studies Department
Dickson Hall-DI-347
1 Normal Avenue
Upper Montclair, NJ 07043
www.chss.monclair.edu/leclair/msu2

[E] Ocean County College
Legal Assistant Technology
Program

PO Box 2001
Toms River, NJ 08754
*www.ocean.cc.nj.us/academics/
programs_of_study*

[AE] Raritan Valley Community College
Paralegal Studies Program
PO Box 3300
Somerville, NJ 08876
www.raritanval.edu

[E] Sussex County Community
College
One College Hill
Newton, NJ 07860
www.sussex.cc.nj.us

[E] Thomas Edison State College
101 West State Street
Trenton, NJ 08608-1101
jkrom@tesc.edu

[E] Union County College
1033 Springfield Ave.
Cranford, NJ 07016
www.ucc.edu

[E] Warren County Community
College
Legal Studies
475 Route 57 W
Washington, NJ 07882-4343
www.warren.cc.nj.us

NEW MEXICO

[E] Central New Mexico Community
College
525 Buena Vista SE
Business & Information
Technology Division
Albuquerque, NM 87106
www.cnm.edu

[E] Dona Ana Branch Community
College
Legal Assistant Program
Box 30001, Dept. 3DA
Las Cruces, NM 88003
http://dabcc-www.nmsu.edu

[E]   New Mexico State University,
        Alamogordo
        Paralegal Program
        2400 N. Scenic Dr.
        Alamogordo, NM 88310
        www.alamo.nmsu.edu

[E]   Sante Fe Community College
        Paralegal Studies
        Business & Technologies
          Department
        6401 Richards Avenue #322H
        Sante Fe, NM 87508
        dposen@sfccnm.edu

NEW YORK
·····································

[AE]   Berkeley College
        Paralegal Studies Program
        99 Church Street
        White Plains, NY 10601
        www.berkeleycollege.edu

[E]   Berkeley College of New York
          City
        Paralegal Studies
        3 East 43rd Street
        New York, NY 10017
        www.berkeleycollege.edu

[AE]   Bronx Community College
        Paralegal Studies Program
        University Ave. & West 181 St.
        Bronx, NY 10453
        www.bcc.cuny.edu

[E]   Corning Community College
        Paralegal Assistant Program
        1 Academic Dr.
        Corning, NY 14830-3297
        www.corning-cc.edu

[E]   Dutchess Community College
        53 Pendell Road
        Poughkeepsie, NY 12601-1595
        www.sunydutchess.edu

[E]   Erie Community College
        Paralegal Unit

121 Ellicott St.
Buffalo, NY 14209-2698
www.ecc.edu

[AE]   Finger Lakes Community College
        Paralegal Program
        4355 Lakeshore Dr.
        Canandaigua, NY 14424
        www.fingerlakes.edu

[E]   Fiorello H. LaGuardia
          Community College
        31-10 Thomson Avenue, Room
          E223F
        Long Island City, NY 11101
        www.lagcc.cuny.edu

[AE]   Genesee Community College
        Paralegal Program
        1 College Rd.
        Batavia, NY 14020
        www.sunygenesee.cc.ny.us

[AE]   Hilbert College
        Legal Assistant Program
        5200 South Park Ave.
        Hamburg, NY 14075
        www.hilbert.edu

[E]   Hofstra University
        Paralegal Certificate Legal Studies
          Program
        University of Continuing
          Education
        Hampstead, NY 11549
        www.hofstra.edu

[A]   Interboro Institute
        Paralegal Studies Program
        450 West 56th Street
        New York, NY 10019
        www.interboro.edu

[E]   Katherine Gibbs School
        232 West 40th Street
        New York, NY 10018
        cscaros@gibbsnewyork.com

[AE]   Lehman College/CUNY
        Paralegal Studies Program
        Office of Continuing Education

250 Bedford Park Blvd. West
Bronx, NY 10468-1589
www.lehman.cuny.edu

[AE] Long Island University
      Paralegal Studies Program
      1 University Plaza, LLC 302
      Brooklyn, NY 11201
      www.liu.edu

[AE] Long Island University—
         C.W. Post Campus
      Legal Studies Program
      720 Northern Blvd.
      Brookville, NY 11548
      www.liu.edu/legal

[AE] Marist College
      Paralegal Program
      400 Westage Business Center
      Fishkill, NY 12524
      www.marist.edu

[AE] Mercy College
      Paralegal Studies Program
      Dept. of Law, Criminal Justice
      555 Broadway
      Dobbs Ferry, NY 10522
      And
      E. 277 Maritine Ave.
      White Plains, NY 10601
      www.mercy.edu

[AE] Monroe Community College
      Law & Criminal Justice
      228 E. Main St.
      Rochester, NY 14604
      www.monroe.cc.edu

[AE] Nassau Community College
      Paralegal Program
      One Education Dr.
      Garden City, NY 11530
      www.sunynassau.edu

[AE] New York City Technical
         College
      Legal Assistant Studies
      300 Jay St., Room N 622
      Brooklyn, NY 11201
      www.nyctc.cuny.edu

[AE] New York University
      15 Barclay street, Room 220
      New York, NY 10007
      www.scps.nyu.edu/paralegal

[E]   Olean Business Institute
      301 North Union Street
      Olean, NY 14760
      www.obi.edu

[AE] Queens College/CEP
      Paralegal Program
      65-30 Kissena Blvd. Kiely
         Room 111
      Flushing, NY 11367
      www.qc.edu/cep

[AE] Rockland Community
         College/SUNY
      145 College Road
      Suffern, NY 10901
      www.sunyrockland.edu

[E]   Sage Colleges
      Legal Studies Program
      140 New Scotland Ave.
      Albany, NY 12208
      www.sage.edu

[AE] Schenectady County Community
         College
      Paralegal Program
      Department of Law and
         Business
      78 Washington Ave. Room 305
      Schenectady, NY 12305
      www.sunysccc.edu

[AE] St. John's University
      Legal Studies Program
      8000 Utopia Pkwy.
      Jamaica, NY 11439
      www.stjohns.edu

[AE] Suffolk County Community
         College
      Paralegal Program
      533 College Rd.
      Seldon, NY 11784
      www.sunysuffolk.edu

[AE]   SUNY/Westchester Community
College
Paralegal Studies
75 Grasslands Rd.
Valhalla, NY 10595-1698
www.sunywcc.edu

[AE]   Syracuse University
Legal Assistant Program
700 University Ave.
Syracuse, NY 13244-2530
www.suce.syr.edu/lap

[E]   Tompkins Cortland Community
College
Paralegal Program
170 N. St., Dryden, NY 13053
www.sunytccc.edu

NORTH CAROLINA

[AE]   Carteret Community College
Paralegal Program
3505 Arendell St.
Morehead City, NC 28557
www.cateret.edu

[AE]   Central Piedmont Community
College
Paralegal Program
PO Box 35009.
Charlotte, NC 28235
www.cpcc.edu/paralegal

[AE]   Fayetteville Tech. Community
College
Paralegal Technology Program
PO Box 35236
Fayetteville, NC 28303
www.faytechcc.edu

[E]   Guilford Technical Community
College
PO Box 309
Jamestown, NC 27282
richardsons@gtcc.edu

[E]   Kings College
Paralegal Program
322 Lamar Ave.

Charlotte, NC 28204
www.kingscollege.org

[AE]   Meredith College
Legal Assistant Program
3800 Hillsborough St.
Raleigh, NC 27607-5298
www.meredity.edu/legal

[AE]   Pitt Community College
Paralegal Technology Program
PO Drawer 7007
Greenville, NC 27835-7007
www.pittcc.edu

[E]   South College
Paralegal Studies
1567 Patton Avenue
Ashville, NC 28806
*www.lcpac.indiana.edu/education/
proprietary_schools*

[E]   South Piedmont Community
College
Paralegal Technology
4209 Old Charlotte Highway
Monroe, NC 28110
www.southpeidmont.org

[E]   Western Piedmont Community
College
Paralegal Technology
1001 Burkemont Ave.
Morganton, NC 28655-9978
www.wp.cc.nc.us/bustech/paralgl

NORTH DAKOTA

[E]   Lake Region State College
1801 N. College Dr.
Devils Lake, ND 58301
www.lrsc.nodak.edu

OHIO

[E]   713 *Training.com*
1601 W. 5th Avenue, Suite 123
Columbus, OH 43212-2310
www.713training.com

[AE]   Capital University Law Center
       Legal Assistant Program
       303 E. Broad St.
       Columbus, OH 43215
       www.law.capital.edu/programs/
            paralegal

[AE]   College of Mount St. Joseph
       Paralegal Studies Program
       5701 Delhi Rd.
       Cincinnati, OH 45233-1670
       www.msj.edu

[AE]   Columbus State Community
            College
       Legal Studies Department
       550 E. Spring St., Nestor Hall 425
       Columbus, OH 43215
       www.cscc.edu/docs/legalassist

[AE]   Cuyahoga Community College
       Paralegal Studies Program
       11000 Pleasant Valley Road
       Parma, OH 44130
       www.tri-c.cc.oh.us

[E]   East Michigan University
       7737 Lucretia Court
       Mentor, OH 44060
       www.emich.edu

[E]   Edison Community College
       Paralegal Studies
       1973 Edison Dr.
       Piqua, OH 45356
       www.edisonohio.edu

[E]   EHOVE Career Center
       Paralegal Program
       316 W. Mason Rd.
       Milan, OH 44846
       www.ehove-jvs.k12.oh.us

[A]   James A. Rhodes State College
       Paralegal/Legal Assisting Program
       4240 Campus Drive
       Lima, OH 45804
       www.rhodesstate.edu

[AE]   Kent State University
       Paralegal Studies Program

       113 Bowman Hall
       PO Box 5190
       Kent, OH 44242
       http://dept.kent.edu/cjst/
            paralegalstudies

[E]   Kent State University—
            East Liverpool
       Legal Assisting Technology
       400 East 4th St.
       East Liverpool, OH 43920
       www.kentliv.kent.edu

[AE]   Lake Erie College
       Legal Studies Program
       391 W. Washington St.
       Painesville, OH 440677
       www.lakeerie.edu

[AE]   Lakeland Community College
       Paralegal Studies Program
       7700 Clocktower Rd.
       Kirkland, OH 44094
       www.lakeland.cc.oh.us

[E]   Muskingum Area Technical College
       Paralegal Program
       1555 Newark Rd.
       Zanesville, OH 43701
       www.matc.tec.oh.us

[AE]   Myers University
       Paralegal Education Program
       112 Prospect Ave.
       Cleveland, OH 44115-1096
       www.dnmyers.edu

[E]   North Central State College
       2441 Kenwood Circle,
            P.O. Box 698
       Mansfield, OH 44901-4750
       www.ncstatecollege.edu

[E]   RETS Tech Center
       Paralegal Program
       555 East Alex Bell Rd.
       Centerville, OH 45459
       www.retstechcenter.com

[E]   Shawnee State University
       Legal Assisting Program

940 2nd St.
Portsmouth, OH 45662
www.shawnee.edu

[AE] Sinclair Community College
Legal Assisting Program
444 West Third St.
Dayton, OH 45402
www.sinclair.edu

[E] University of Akron
Legal Assisting Technology
The Polsky Bldg. 161
Akron, OH 44325-4304
*www.commtech.uakron.edu/2k/
    publicservice/legalassisting*

[AE] University of Cincinnati—
        Clermont
Paralegal Technology Program
UC Clermont 4200 College Drive
Batavia, OH 45103
www.ucclermont.com

[AE] University of Cincinnati
Legal Assisting Program,
    University College
105 Farmridge Road
Springboro, OH 45066
www.uc.edu

[E] University of Cincinnati,
        University College
PO Box 207
Cincinnati, OH 45221-0207
www.uccollege.uc.edu

[AE] University of Toledo
College of Health & Human
    Services
Legal Specialities
2801 W. Bancroft St.
Scott Park Campus MS #400
Toledo, OH 43606
www.utoledo.hhs/legal

[AE] Ursuline College
Legal Studies
2550 Lander Rd.
Pepper Pike, OH 44124
www.ursuline.edu

OKLAHOMABB

[AE] East Central University
Legal Studies Program
200 Stadium Dr., Box N6
Ada, OK 74820
www.ecok.edu/dept/polisci/leglstud

[E] Metropolitan College
Legal Assistant Program
10820 East 45th Street, Suite B-101
Tulsa, OK 74146
www.metropolitancollege.edu

[E] Metropolitan College
1900 NW Expressway, Suite R-302
Oklahoma City, OK 73118
www.metropolitancollege.edu

[AE] Rose State College
6420 Southeast 15th St.
Midwest City, OK 73110
www.rose.cc.ok.us/busdiv/la

[AE] Tulsa Community College
Legal Assistant Program, Business
    Service Division
909 South Boston Ave., MC #425
Tulsa, OK 74119
www.tulsa.cc.ok.us

[AE] University of Oklahoma Law Center
Legal Assisting Education
300 Timberdell Rd., #314
Norman, OK 73019
www.law.ou.edu

[AE] University of Tulsa
Paralegal Studies
Division of Continuing Education
Tulsa, OK 74104-3189
www.walkabout@utulsa.edu

OREGON

[E] Pioneer Pacific College
Paralegal Program
27501 SW Parkway Ave.
Wilsonville, OR 97070-9296
www.pioneerpacific.edu

PENNSYLVANIA

[E] Academy of Medical Arts &
Business
Paralegal Programs
2301 Academy Dr.
Harrisburg, PA 17112
www.acadcampus.com

[E] Berks Technical Institute
2205 Ridgewood Rd.
Reading, PA 19610
www.berkstechnical.com

[AE] Bucks County Community College
Paralegal Studies Program
275 Swamp Rd.
Newtown, PA 18940
www.bucks.edu

[E] California University of
Pennsylvania
Regional Enterprise Tower
425 6th Avenue, Suite 430
Pittsburgh, PA 15219
nemeth@cop.edu

[E] Cedar Crest College
Paralegal Studies Program
100 College Dr.
Allentown, PA 18104-6196
www.cedarcrest.edu

[AE] Central Pennsylvania College
Legal Assistant Program
College Hill Rd.
Summerdale, PA 17093
www.centralpenn.edu

[AE] Clarion University
of Pennsylvania
Legal Business Studies Program
1801 W. 1st St.
Oil City, PA 16301
www.clarion.edu

[AE] Community College
of Philadelphia
Paralegal Studies Program
1700 Spring Garden St.
Philadelphia, PA 19130-3991
www.ccp.cc.pa.us

[E] Consolidated School of Business
2124 Ambassador Circle
Lancaster, PA 17603
www.csb.edu

[AE] Delaware County Community
College
Paralegal Studies Program
901 S. Media Lane Rd.
Media, PA 19063-1094
www.dccc.edu

[AE] Duquesne University
Paralegal Institute
600 Forbes Avenue, Rockwell Hall
Pittsburgh, PA 15282-0102
www.leadership.duq.edu/paralegal

[AE] Gannon University
Lawyer's Assistant Program
Box 3221, University Square
Erie, PA 16541
www.gannon.edu

[AE] Harrisburg Area Community
College
Legal Assistant Program
108 Martel Circle
Dillsburg, PA 17019
www.hacc.edu

[AE] Lehigh Carbon Community
College
Paralegal Studies Program
4525 Education Park Dr.
Schnecksville, PA 18078
www.lccc.edu

[AE] Manor College
Legal Studies Program
700 Fox Chase Rd.
Jenkintown, PA 19046
www.manor.edu

[AE] Marywood College
Legal Assistant Program
2300 Adams Ave.
Scranton, PA 18509
www.marywood.edu

[E] McCann School of Business
Paralegal Program

2650 Woodglen Rd.
Pottsville, PA 17901
www.mccannschool.com

[AE] Northampton Community
     College
     Paralegal Studies
     3835 Green Pond Rd.
     Bethlehem, PA 18020
     www.northampton.edu

[AE] Peirce College
     Paralegal Studies
     1420 Pine St.
     Philadelphia, PA 19102
     www.peirce.edu

[AE] Pennsylvania College
     of Technology
     Legal Assistant Program
     One College Ave.
     Williamsport, PA 17701
     www.pct.edu

[E]   The PJA School
     7900 W. Chester Pike
     Upper Darby, PA 19082
     www.pjaschool.com

[AE] Villanova University
     Paralegal Education Program
     Stanford Hall, Ground Floor
     800 Lancaster Avenue
     Villanova, PA 19085
     www.vilanova.edu

RHODE ISLAND

[E]   Johnson & Wales University
     Center for Legal Studies
     8 Abbott Park Pl.
     Providence, RI 02903
     www.jwu.edu

[AE] Roger Williams University
     Paralegal Studies
     150 Washington Street
     Providence, RI 02803
     www.rwu.edu

SOUTH CAROLINA

[E]   Aiken Technical College
     Paralegal Studies
     PO Drawer 696
     Aiken, SC 29802
     www.alk.tec.sc.us

[AE] Central Carolina Technical College
     Legal Assistant Program
     506 N. Guignard Dr.
     Sumter, SC 29150
     www.sum.tech.sc.us

[AE] Florence Darlington Technical
     College
     Legal Assistant/Paralegal Program
     PO Box 100548, Highway 42
     Florence, SC 29501-0548
     www.fdtc.edu

[AE] Greenville Technical College
     Paralegal Department
     506 South Pleasantburg Drive,
     CJ 122
     Greenville, SC 29607
     www.greenvilletech.com

[AE] Horry-Georgetown Technical
     College
     Paralegal Program
     339 Pampas Drive.
     Myrtle Beach, SC 29577
     www.hor.tec.sc.us

[AE] Midlands Technical College
     Legal Assistant/Paralegal Program
     PO Box 2408
     Columbia, SC 29202
     www.midlandstech.com

[AE] Orangeburg-Calhoun Technical
     College
     Public Service
     3250 St. Matthews Rd. N.E.
     Orangeburg, SC 29118-8299
     www.octech.org

[AE] South University—Columbia
     Paralegal Studies
     3810 N. Main St.
     Columbia, SC 29203
     www.southuniversity.edu

[AE] Technical College of the Low
Country
Legal Assistant Program
921 Ribaut Rd.
PO Box 1288
Beaufort, SC 29901
www.tclonline.org

[AE] Trident Technical College
Paralegal/Legal Assistant Program
PO Box 11867
66 Columbus Street
Charleston, SC 29423-8067
www.tridenttech.edu

SOUTH DAKOTA

[AE] National American University
Paralegal Studies Program
321 Kansas City St., Box 1780
Rapid City, SD 57709
www.national.edu

[AE] Western Dakota Technical Institute
Paralegal Program
800 Mickelson Dr.
Rapid City, SD 57703
www.wdti.tec.ed.us

TENNESSEE

[A] Chattanooga State Technical
Community College
Legal Assistant Technology
Program
7158 Lee Hwy.
Chattanooga, TN 37421
www.cstcc.cc.tn.us

[E] Cleveland State Community
College
Legal Assistant Program
3535 Adkisson Dr., PO Box 3570
Cleveland, TN 37320-3570
www.clscc.cc.tn.us

[E] Draughons Junior college
340 Plus Park Blvd.

Nashville, TN 37217
www.draughons.org

[E] Draughons Junior College
1860 Wilma Rudolph Boulevard
Clarksville, TN 37040
www.draughons.org

[E] Miller Motte Business College
Paralegal Program
1820 Business Park Dr.
Clarksville, TN 37040
www.miller-motte.com

[AE] Pellissippi State Technical
Community College
Legal Assistant Technology
Program
10915 Hardin Valley Rd.
PO Box 22990
Knoxville, TN 37933-0990
www.pstcc.edu

[E] Roane State Community College
Paralegal Studies
276 Patton Lane
Harriman, TN 37748
www.roanestate.edu

[AE] South College
Paralegal Studies Program
720 N. 5th Ave.
Knoxville, TN 37917
www.southcollegetn.edu

[AE] Southeastern Career College
Paralegal Studies Program
719 Thompson Lane, Ste. 600
Nashville, TN 37204
www.southeasterncareercollege.edu

[AE] Southwest Tennessee Community
College
Legal Assistant Program
5983 Macon Cove
Memphis, TN 38134-7693
www.southwest.tn.edu

[AE] University of Memphis
Paralegal Studies
1 Johnson Hall

Memphis, TN 38152
www.people.memphis.edu/
paralegalstudies

[AE]   University of Tennessee—
Chattanooga
Legal Assistant Studies
615 McCallie Ave., Dept. 3203
Chattanooga, TN 37403-2598
www.utc.edu/legalast

[AE]   Volunteer State Community
College
Paralegal Studies Program
1480 Nashville Pike
Gallatin, TN 37066-3188
www.volstate.edu

[AE]   Walters State Community College
Legal Assisting Program
500 S. Davy Crockett Pkwy.
Morristown, TN 37813-5899
www.wscc.tn.us

TEXAS

[AE]   Amarillo College
Paralegal Studies
PO Box 447
Amarillo, TX 79178-0001
www.actx.edu

[E]   Blinn College
Legal Assistant Program
PO Box 6500
Bryan, TX 77805-6030
www.blinncol.edu

[AE]   Center for Advanced Legal
Studies
Paralegal Program
3910 Kirby Dr., Ste. 200
Houston, TX 77098
www.paralegalpeople.com

[AE]   Central Texas College
Paralegal Studies Program
PO Box 1800
Killeen, TX 76540
www.ctcd/lap

[E]   Del Mar College
Legal Assistant Program
101 Baldwin Blvd.
Corpus Christi, TX 78404-3897
www.viking.delmar.edu

[AE]   El Centro College
Legal Assistant Program
801 Main Street, 5th Floor.
Dallas, TX 75202-3604
www.ecc.dccd.ed/health-l/
paralegal/aralegal

[E]   Lamar Institute of Technology
PO Box 10043
Beaumont, TX 77710
spencert@lit.edu

[AE]   Lamar University-Port Arthur
Legal Assisting Program
PO Box 310
Port Arthur, TX 77641-0310
www.pa.lamar.edu

[AE]   Lee College
Legal Assistant Program
PO Box 818
Baytown, TX 77520-0818
www.lee.edu

[E]   McLennan Community College
Legal Assistant Program
1400 College Dr.
Waco, TX 76708
www.mcc.cc.tx.us

[E]   Midland College
Legal Assistant Program
3600 N. Garfield St.
Midland, TX 79705
www.midland.cc.tx.us

[AE]   North Harris College
Legal Assistant Program
2700 W. Thorne, A-133
Houston, TX 77073
http://paralegal.northharriscollege.com

[E]   San Antonio College
Legal Assistant Program
1300 San Pedro Ave.

San Antonio, TX 78212
www.accd.edu/sac

[AE] San Jacinto College
North Campus
Legal Assistant Program
5800 Uvalde
Houston, TX 77062
www.sjcd.edu/paralegal

[E] South Plains College
828 Gilbert Drive
Lubbock, TX 79416
jkline@spc.cc.tx.us

[E] South Texas Community
College
3201 W. Pecan
McAllen, TX 78501
www.stcc.cc.tx.us

[AE] Southeastern Career Institute
5440 Harvest Hill Rd., Ste. 200
Dallas, TX 75230
www.southeasterncareerinstitute.com

[AE] Southwestern Professional
Institute
3033 Chimney Rock, Ste. 200
Houston, TX 77056
www.spi-careers.com

[E] Stephen F. Austin St. University
Legal Assistant Program
Box 13064
Nacogdoches, TX 75962-3064
www.sfasu.edu/crimilj

[E] Tarrant County College
828 W. Harwood Rd.
Hurst, TX 76054
www.tccd.net

[AE] Texas A & M University at
Commerce
Paralegal Studies Program
Dept. of Political Science
PO Box 3100
Commerce, TX 75429
*http://orgs.tamu-commerce.edu/
paralegal*

[AE] Texas State University-San Marcos
Legal Studies
601 University Dr.
San Marcos, TX 78666-4616
www.swt.edu

[E] Texas Woman's University
Legal Studies Program
Box 425889
Denton, TX 76204-5889
*www.twu.edu/as/histgov/undplan.
htm#basparalegal*

[E] University of Texas at
Brownsville/Southmost College
Legal Assistant Department
80 Fort Brown
Brownsville, TX 78520
ljones@south.edu

[E] Virginia College at Austin
Paralegal Studies
6301 E. Highway 290, Ste. 200
Austin, TX 78723
www.vc.edu

[E] Wharton County Junior College
5333 FM 1640, Room 140F
Richmond, TX 77469
candacew@wcjc.edu

UTAH

[E] Mountain West College
Paralegal Studies Program
3280 W. 3500 S.
West Valley City, UT 84119
www.mwcollege.com

[E] Utah Career College
1902 West 7800 South
West Jordan, UT 84088
www.tuahcollege.edu

[AE] Utah Valley State College
Legal Assistant Program
800 West University Parkway,
MS 205
Orem, UT 84058
www.unvnet.uvsc.edu/legl/

VERMONT

[E]   Woodbury College
        Paralegal Program
        660 Elm St.
        Montpelier, VT 05602
        www.woodbury-college.edu

VIRGINIA

[E]   Bryant & Stratton College
        Paralegal Studies
        8141 Hull Street Rd.
        Richmond, VA 23235
        www.bryantstratton.edu

[AE]   J. Sergeant Reynolds Community
        College
        Legal Assistant Program
        Parham Rd. Campus
        PO Box 85622
        Richmond, VA 23285-5622
        www.jsr.vccs.edu

[AE]   Marymount University
        Paralegal Studies Program
        2807 North Glebe Rd.
        Arlington, VA 22207-4299
        www.marymount.edu

[E]   Mountain Empire Community
        College
        3441 Mountain Empire road
        Big Stone Gap, VA 24219-4634
        bsnodgrass@me.vccs.edu

[E]   National College of Business &
        Technology
        Paralegal Studies
        1813 E. Main St.
        Salem, VA 24153
        www.ncbt.edu.

[A]   Northern Virginia Community
        College
        Paralegal Studies / Legal Assisting
        Program
        3001 North Beauregard
        Alexandria, VA 22311

*www.nvcc.edu/alexandria/visual/
legal/index2.htm*

WASHINGTON

[E]   Columbia Basin College
        2600 North 20th Avenue
        Pasco, WA 99301
        www.cbc2.org/insturct/bus/para

[AE]   Edmonds Community College
        Legal Assistant Program
        20000 68th Ave. West
        Lynnwood, WA 98036
        www.edcc.edu

[AE]   Highline Community College
        Paralegal Program
        2400 S. 240th St. MS18-1
        Des Moines, WA 98198-9800
        *www.flightline.highline.ctc.edu/
        paralegal*

[E]   Pierce College
        Paralegal Studies Program
        9401 Farwest Dr. SW
        Tacoma, WA 98498-1999
        www.pierce.ctc.edu

[AE]   Skagit Valley College
        Paralegal Program
        2405 E. College Way N-207
        Mt. Vernon, WA 98273-5899
        www.skagit.edu

[E]   South Puget Sound College
        Paralegal Program
        2011 Mottman Rd. SW
        Olympia, WA 98512-6292
        www.spscc.ctc.edu

[AE]   Spokane Community College
        Paralegal Program
        1810 North Greene St., MS 2011
        Spokane, WA 99207-5399
        www.scc.spokane.edu

[AE]   Tacoma Community College
        6501 S. 19th, Bldg. 19
        Tacoma, WA 98466
        www.tacomacc.edu

WEST VIRGINIA

[AE] Marshall University &
      Community Technical College
      Legal Assistant Program
      One John Marshall Drive
      Huntington, WV 25755-2700
      www.marshall.edu

[E]   Mountain State University
      Paralegal Studies
      PO Box AG
      Beckley, WV 25802
      www.mountainstate.edu

WISCONSIN

[AE] Chippewa Valley Technical
      College
      Legal Assistant Program
      620 W. Clairemont Ave.
      Eau Claire, WI 54701
      www.cvtc.edu

[AE] Lakeshore Technical College
      Paralegal Program
      1290 North Ave.
      Cleveland, WI 53015
      www.gotoltc.edu

[E]   Madison Area Technical College
      3550 Anderson St.
      Madison, WI 53704
      www.madison.tec.wi.us

[AE] Milwaukee Area Technical
      College
      Legal Assistant Program
      700 W. State St.
      Milwaukee, WI 53233
      www.westweb.matc.edu/para

[AE] Northeast Wisconsin Technical
      College
      Paralegal Studies
      2740 W. Mason St.
      Green Bay, WI 54307-9042
      www.nwtc.tec.wi.us

[AE] Western Wisconsin Technical
      College
      Paralegal Program
      304 6th St. N.
      La Crosse, WI 54602
      www.western.tec.wi.us

WYOMING

[AE] Casper College
      Legal Assistant Program
      125 College Dr.
      Casper, WY 82601
      www.caspercollege.edu

[AE] Laramie County Community
      College
      Legal Assistant Program
      1400 E. College Dr.
      Cheyenne, WY 82007
      www.lccc.cc.wy.us

appendix C

Legal Assistant and Paralegal Associations List

The following list includes members of NFPA, NALS, and NALA. There are several organizations that are not members of either that you can find by networking in your city.

NFPA members are indicated by **, NALA members by *, and NALS by +. If no Web site or e-mail address is listed, please contact NALA, NALS, or NFPA for current information. Several of the NALS chapters do not have their own Web sites. Information about them can be found on the main state Web site. I have indented those organizations that are under the auspices of the state Web site.

NATIONAL ORGANIZATIONS

The American Alliance of Paralegals, Inc.
www.aapipara.org

American Association of Law Libraries
www.aallnet.org

American Association for Paralegal Education
www.aafpe.org

American Bar Association
www.abanet.org/

Association of Legal Administrators
www.alanet.org

International Paralegal Managers Association
www.ipma..org

National Association of Legal Assistants (NALA)
www.nala.org

National Federation of Paralegal Associations
www.paralegals.org

National Paralegal Association
www.nationalparalegal.org

National Association of Legal Professionals (NALS)
www.nals.org

ALABAMA
···

*Alabama Association of Paralegals
www.aala.net

+Alabama Association of Legal Professionals
www.alabama-aals.org

   Baldwin County Association of Legals Professionals

   Birmingham Association of Legal Professionals

   Dallas County Legal Secretaries Association

   Mobile Legal Secretaries Association

   NALS of Shelby County

   Tuscaloosa County Legal Professionals Association

*Legal Assistant Society of Virginia College-Virginia College

*Northeast Alabama Litigation Support Association

*Samford Paralegal Association
www.samford.edu

ALASKA
···

**Alaska Association of Paralegals
www.alaskaparalegals.org

*Fairbanks Association of Legal Assistants

+NALS of Anchorage
www.nalsofanchorage.org

ARIZONA
···

*Arizona Paralegal Association
www.azparalegal.org

*Legal Assistants of Metropolitan Phoenix
www.geocities.com/azlamp

+NALS of Arizona
www.nalsofarizona.org

+NALS of Yavapai County

+NALS of Phoenix
www.nalsofphoenix.org

+NALS of Tuscon and South AZ
www.tusconlegalsupport.org

*Tucson Association of Legal Assistants
www.azstarnet.com/nonprofit/tala

ARKANSAS

+AALS-The Association for Arkansas Legal Support Professionals
www.arkansasals.org

  Jefferson County Association of Legal Support Professionals

  Saline County Legal Support Professionals

  White County Association of Legal Support Professionals

*Arkansas Association of Legal Assistants
www.aala-legal.org

**Arkansas Paralegal Association
www.arparalegal.org

+Garland County Legal Support Professionals
www.gclsp.org

+Greater Little Rock Legal Support Professionals
www.geocities.com/glrlsp

+Northeast Arkansas Legal Support Professionals
www.nealsp.org

CALIFORNIA

California Alliance of Paralegal Associations
www.caparalegal.org

California Association of Independent Paralegals
CAIndependent@paralegals.org

+CAMAL Association of Legal Professionals

Central Coast Paralegal Association
www.caparalegal.org

*Fresno Paralegal Association
www.fresnoparalegal.org

Inland Counties Paralegal Association
www.icaparalegal.org

Kern County Paralegal Association
www.kcpaonline.org

*Los Angeles Paralegal Association
www.lapa.org

+NALS of Orange County
www.nalsoc.com

+NALS of San Diego

*Orange County Paralegal Association
www.ocparalegal.org

*Paralegal Association of Santa Clara County
www.sccparalegal.org

+Pomona Valley-Citrus LSA

+Port Stockton LSA

Redwood Empire Association of Paralegals
www.redwoodempirelegalassistants.com

**Sacramento Valley Paralegal Association
www.svpa.org

San Diego Paralegal Association
www.sdparalegals.org

**San Francisco Paralegal Association
www.sfpa.com

*Santa Barbara Paralegal Association
www.sbparalegals.org

Sequoia Paralegal Association
www.caparalegal.org/spa.html

*Ventura County Association of Legal Assistants
www.vcparalegal.org

COLORADO

*Colorado Association of Professional Paralegals and Legal Assistants
www.capplaweb.org

*Legal Assistants of the Western Slope

+NALS of Colorado
www.nalsofcolorado.org

*Pikes Peak Paralegal
www.pikespeakparalegals.org

**Rocky Mountain Paralegal Association
www.rockymtnparalegal.org

CONNECTICUT

**Central Connecticut Paralegal Association
www.CentralConnecticut@paralegals.org

**Connecticut Association of Paralegals, Inc.
www.paralegals.org/Connecticut/

**New Haven County Association of Paralegals
www.NewHaven@paralegals.org

DELAWARE

Delaware Paralegal Association
www.delaware@paralegals.org

DISTRICT OF COLUMBIA

+D.C. Legal Secretaries Association

**National Capital Area Paralegal Association
www.nationalcapital@paralegals.org

FLORIDA

*Central Florida Paralegal Association
www.fpainc.com/pages/718816/index.htm

Gainesville Association of Legal Assistants
www.afn.org/~gala

+NALS of Central Florida

*Northeast Florida Paralegal Association
www.nefpa.org

*Northwest Florida Paralegal Association
www.nwfpa.com

*Paralegal Association of Florida
www.pafinc.org

*South Florida Paralegal Association
www.sfpa.info/

*Southwest Florida Paralegal Association
www.swfloridaparalegals.com

**Tampa Bay Paralegal Association
www.tbpa.org

*Volusia Association of Paralegals
www.volusiaparalegals.com

GEORGIA
....

+Cobb County Legal Secretaries Association
www.cobblsa.org

**Georgia Association of Paralegals, Inc.
www.gaparalegal.org

+NALS of Atlanta
www.nalsofatlanta.org

+NALS of Georgia

*Southeastern Association of Legal Assistants
www.seala.org

HAWAII
....

+Hawaii Legal Support Professional
www.hawaiilasp.org

**Hawaii Paralegal Association
www.hawaiiparalegal.org

ILLINOIS
....

*Central Illinois Paralegal Association
www.hometown.aol.com/cipainfo/myhomepage/club.html

**Illinois Paralegal Association
www.ipaonline.org

+NALS of Illinois
www.nalsofillinois.org

IDAHO
....

+Idaho Legal Secretaries Association
www.idals.net

+Boise Legal Secretaries Association
www.blsa.net

+Lewiston Legal Secretaries Association

+North Idaho Legal Secretaries Association

INDIANA

**Indiana Paralegal Association
www.indianaparalegals.org

**Michiana Paralegal Association
www.michiana@paralegals.org

**Northeast Indiana Paralegal Association
www.neindianaparalegal.org

IOWA

*Iowa Association of Legal Assistants
www.ialanet.org

KANSAS

*Heartland Association of Legal Assistants
www.accesskansas.org/hala

*Kansas Association of Legal Assistants
www.accesskansas.org/kala

**Kansas Paralegal Association
www.accesskansas.org/ksparalegals

KENTUCKY

Greater Appalacian Paralegal Association
www.kypa.org/gapaapp

**Greater Lexington Paralegal Association, Inc.
www.lexingtonparalegals.com

Kentucky Paralegal Association
www.kypa.org

Louisville Association of Paralegals
www.loupara.com

Northern Kentucky Association of Paralegals
www.kypa.org/nkap

*Western Kentucky Paralegals
www.kypa.org/wkp

LOUISIANA

Baton Rouge Paralegal Association
www.brparalegals.org

Lafayette Paralegal Association
www.lpa-la.org

*Louisiana State Paralegal Association
www.la-paralegals.org

**New Orleans Paralegal Association
www.neworleans@paralegals.org

*Northwest Louisiana Paralegal Association
www.PE.ast.@la-paralegals.org

MAINE

+NALS of Maine
www.nalsofmaine.org

NALS of Southern Maine

NALS of Midcoast Maine

NALS of Central Maine

NALS of Northeast Maine

MARYLAND

*Baltimore City Paralegal Association

**Maryland Association of Paralegals
www.maryland@paralegals.org

MASSACHUSETTS

**Central Massachusetts Paralegal Association
www.centralmassachusetts@paralegals.org

**Massachusetts Paralegal Association
www.massparalegal.org

**Western Massachusetts Paralegal Association
www.westernmassachusetts@paralegals.org

MICHIGAN

+NALS of Michigan
www.nalsofmichigan.org

Berrien Case LSP
www.nalsofmichigan.org/berrien-case

NALS of Calhoun County
www.nalsofmichigan.org/chapterspage1

NALS of Detroit
www.nalsofdetroit.org

Genessee Association of Legal Support Professionals
www.gcbalaw.org/assoc_galsp

Grand Traverse County LP
www.nalsofmichigan.org/chapterspage2

NALS of Greater Kalamazoo
www.nalsofgreaterkalamazoo.org/

Jackson County Legal Support Professionals
www.geocities.com/pamfeb55_511

NALS of Lansing
www.nalsoflansing.org

Livingston County Legal Secretaries Association
www.nalsofmichigan.org/chapterspage3

Mid Michigan Association of LSP
www.nalsofmichigan/mid-michigan

NALS of Northern Michigan
www.nalsofmichigan.org/chapterspage4

NALS of West Michigan
www.nalsofwmi.org

NALS of Washtenaw County
www.absims.com/wcalsp

NALS of Oakland County
www.nalsofmichigan/oakland

MINNESOTA

**Minnesota Paralegal Association
www.mnparalegals.org

+NALS of Greater Minnesota

+NALS Twin Cities

MISSISSIPPI

*Mississippi Association of Legal Assistants
www.msmala.org

+Mississippi Division of NALS
www.msnals.org

Greenwood Legal Professionals Association
www.msnals.org/page4

Gulf Coast ALP
www.msnals.org/page5

Jackson Legal Professionals Association
www.msnals.org/page6

Metro Legal Professionals Associaton
www.msnals.org/page7

Pinebelt Legal Professionals
www.msnals.org/page8

Tri-County LSPA
www.msnals.org/page9

MISSOURI

Student Chapter of the Mid-Missouri Paralegal Association
www.wmwoods.edu/Info.asp?2934

Missouri Paralegal Association
www.missouriparalegalassoc.org

*St. Louis Association of Legal Assistants
www.slala.org

**Springfield Paralegal Association

Southwest Missouri Paralegal Association
www.communityconnection.org/resource_pages/34107

+NALS of Missouri

Central Ozarks Legal Secretaries Association

Franklin County ALSP

Heart of America Legal Professionals Association

Kansas City Legal Secretaries Association
www.kclsa.net

Lakes Area Legal Support Association

NALS of Greater St. Louis

St. Louis County Association of Legal Professionals

Springfield Area Legal Support Professionals

MONTANA

*Montana Association of Legal Assistants
www.malanet.org

+NALS of Montana
www.nalsofmontana.org

NEBRASKA

*Nebraska Association of Legal Assistants
www.neala.org

NEVADA

+NALS of Nevada

+Douglas-Carson Legal Professionals

+NALS of Las Vegas, a professional legal association
www.Nalsoflasvegas.org

+NALS of Washoe County
www.nalsofwashoecounty.com

*Nevada Paralegal Association
www.nevadaparalegal.org

**Paralegal Association of Southern Nevada
www.southernnevada@paralegals.org

*Sierra Nevada Association of Paralegals
www.snapreno.com

NEW HAMPSHIRE

**Paralegal Association of New Hampshire
www.panh.org

NEW JERSEY

*Legal Assistants Association of New Jersey
www.laanj.org/pages/1/index.htm

+NJALS...the association for legal professionals
www.njals.org

   Union Essex Legal Professional Association

   Hunterdon County Legal Secretaries Association

   Monmouth Legal Secretaries Association

   Morris County Legal Secretaries Association

   Somerset County Legal Secretaries Association

**South Jersey Paralegal Association
www.southjersey@paralegals.org

NEW MEXICO

+Albuquerque Association of Legal Professionals

State Bar of New Mexico, Paralegal Division
www.nmbar.org

NEW YORK

Adirondack Paralegal Association
mprovost@jwlawoffice.com

**Capital District Paralegal Association
www.cdpa.info

Empire State Alliance of Paralegal Associations
www.geocities.com/empirestateparalegals

**Long Island Paralegal Association
www.longisland@paralegals.org

+NALS of New York
www.nalsofnewyorkinc.org

+NALS of Nassau County
www.nalsofnewyorkinc.org/nassau

+NALS of New York City
www.nalsofnewyorkinc.org/newyorkcity

+CNY Chapter of NALS
www.nalsofnewyorkinc.org/onondaga

+NALS of Suffolk County
www.nalsofnewyorkinc.org/suffolk

+Westchester County Legal Secretaries Association
www.nalsofnewyorkinc.org/lowerhudsonvalley

Onondgaga County Bar Association Legal Assistants' Committee
http://www.onbar2.org/sect-comms/paralegals/index.htm

Oswego County Paralegal Association
cwade@hancocklaw.com

**Paralegal Association of Rochester
www.par.itgo.com

**Western New York Paralegal Association
www.wnyparalegals.org

NORTH CAROLINA

*Metrolina Paralegal Association
www.charlotteareaparalegals.com

*North Carolina Paralegal Association
www.ncparalegal.org

NORTH DAKOTA

+NALS of Fargo-Moorhead

+Minot Legal Secretaries Association

*Red River Valley Paralegal Association
www.rrvpa.org

*Western Dakota Association of Legal Assistants
www.wdala.org

OHIO

Cincinnati Paralegal Association
www.cincinnatiparalegals.org

**Cleveland Association of Paralegals
www.capohio.org

**Greater Dayton Paralegal Association
www.dayton@paralegals.org

+NALS of Ohio
www.nalsofohio.org

NALS of Central Ohio

Medina County Association for Legal Professionals
www.medinalegalprofessionals.org

Stark County Association for Legal Professionals

*Paralegal Association of Northwest Ohio
www.panonet.org

**Paralegal Association of Central Ohio
www.pac.paralegals.org

OKLAHOMA
••

*City College Legal Association

+NALS of Oklahoma
www.nalsorok.org

*Oklahoma Paralegal Association
www.okparalegal.org

*TCC Student Association of Legal Assistants
www.tulsacc.edu

*Tulsa Association of Legal Assistants
www.tulsatala.org

OREGON
••

+NALS of Oregon
www.nalsor.org

Central Oregon Legal Professionals
www.nalsor.org/colp

NALS of Lane County
www.nalsor.org/lane

Legal Professionals of Douglas County
www.nalsor.org/douglas

NALS of Mid-Willamette Valley
www.nalsor.org/mwvalley

Mt. Hood Legal Professionals
www.nalsorrg/mt_hood

NALS of Portland
www.nalsor.org/portland

NALS of Southern Oregon Coast
www.nalsor.org/soc

**Oregon Paralegal Association
www.oregonparalegals.org

*Pacific Northwest Legal Assistants Association PO Box 1835 Eugene, OR 97440

PENNSYLVANIA

**Central Pennsylvania Paralegal Association
www.centralpennsylvania@paralegals.org

Chester County Paralegal Association
www.chescoparalegal.org

Lancaster Area Paralegal Association
www.lapaparalegals.org

**Lycoming County Paralegal Association

**Montgomery County Paralegal Association
www.montgomery@paralegals.org

+NALS of Pennsylvania
www.palegal.org

Capital Area Association of Legal Professionals
kimschracknals@verizon.net

Lehigh-Northhampton Counties Legal Secretaries Association

Philadelphia Legal Secretaries Association
www.philalsa.org

Pittsburgh Legal Secretaries Association
kimwork@comcast.net

Schuylkill County LSA
phyllis@lmbtlaw.com

**Philadelphia Association of Paralegals
www.philaparalegals.com

**Pittsburgh Paralegal Association
www.pghparalegals.org

RHODE ISLAND

**Rhode Island Paralegal Association
www.rhodeisland@paralegals.org

SOUTH CAROLINA

* *

*Charleston Association of Legal Assistants

Legal Staff Professionals of South Carolina
www.lspsc.org

Legal Staff Professionals of the Low Country
echaney@hsblawfirm.com

Legal Staff Professionals of the Midlands
sharon.wotherspoon@nelsonmullins.com

Legal Staff Professionals of Greenville
www.lspg.org

Hilton Head Legal Staff Professionals
susanolmstead@adelphia.net

Legal Staff Professionals of Orangeburg
sonia@hbrllp.com

Spartanburg County Legal Staff Professionals
lallison@jshwlaw.com

**Palmetto Paralegal Association
www.palmetto@paralegals.org

*South Carolina Upstate Paralegal Association
www.scupa.org

SOUTH DAKOTA

* *

+Black Hills Legal Professional Association

*South Dakota Paralegal Association
www.sdparalegals.com

TENNESSEE

* *

East Tennessee Chapter
www.tnparalegal.org/east

*Greater Memphis Legal Alliance
www.memphisparalegals.org

**Memphis Paralegal Association
www.paralegal.org/memphis

**Middle Tennessee Paralegal Association
www.mtpaonline.com

*Smokey Mountain Paralegal Association
www.smparalegal.org

Southeast Tennessee Chapter
www.tnparalega.org/southeast

+TALS...Legal Professionals of Tennessee
www.talstn.org

Chattanooga Legal Professionals

Memphis Legal Secretaries Association
www.memphislsa.org

NALS of Nashville
www.talsn.org/nashvillenews

Rutherford/Cannon County ALS

*Tennessee Paralegal Association
www.tnparalegal.org

West Tennessee Chapter
www.tnparalegal.org/west

TEXAS

*Capitol Area Paralegal Association
www.capatx.org

**Dallas Area Paralegal Association
www.dallasparalegals.org

*El Paso Association of Legal Assistants
www.epala.org

*Houston Corporate Paralegal Association

Houston Legal Assistants Association
www.hlaa.net

*Houston Paralegal Association
www.houstonparalegalassociation.org

+Texas Association of Legal Professionals
www.texasalp.org

NALS of Amarillo

Arlington Legal Secretaries Association

Austin Legal Secretaries Association
www.austinlsa.org

Rio Grand Valley Legal Support Professionals

Dallam-Hartley-Moore Counties Legal Secretaries Association

Dallas Association of Legal Secretaries

El Paso County Legal Support Professionals
www.epclsa.org

Fort Worth Legal Secretaries Association

Greater Dallas Association of Legal Professionals
www.gdalp.org

Houston Association of Legal Professionals
www.houstonalp.org

Lubbock Legal Secretaries Association

Corpus Christi Association of Legal Professionals
www.ccalp.com

San Antonio Legal Secretaries Association
www.sanantoniolsa.org

Waco Legal Professionals Association
www.wacolpa.org

Wichita County Legal Secretaries Association

East Texas Area Legal Professionals Association

Beaumont Legal Secretaries Association

Midland Legal Secretaries Association

NALS of TSTC Harlingen Student Chapter

*North Texas Paralegal Association

*Northeast Texas Association of Legal Assistants
www.ntala.net

*Paralegal Association/Permian Basin
www.paralgalspb.org

*South Texas Organization of Paralegals
www.southtexasparalegals.org

*Southeast Texas Association of Paralgals
www.setala.org

*Texas Panhandle Association of Legal Assistants
www.members.cox.net/tppa

*Tyler Area Association of Legal Assistants

*West Texas Association of Legal Assistants, Laredo, TX

UTAH

*Legal Assistants Association of Utah
www.laau.info

+Utah Legal Professionals Association

VERMONT

**Vermont Paralegal Organization
www.vermont@paralegals.org

VIRGINIA

+VALS— the Association for Legal Professionals
www.v-a-l-s.org

Charlottesville-Albemarle Legal Secretaries Association
www.monticello.avenue.org/calsa

Fredericksburg Area Legal Secretaries Association

New River Valley Legal Secretaries Association

Norfolk-Portsmouth Area Legal Secretaries Association

Northern Virginia Legal Secretaries Association
www.nvlsa.org

Peninsula Legal Secretaries Association

Prince William County Association for Legal Professionals

Richmond Legal Secretaries Association

Roanoke Valley Legal Secretaries Association

Virginia Beach Legal Staff Association
www.vblsa.org

Virginia Highlands LSA

*Richmond Association of Legal Assistants
www.ralanet.org

*Roanoke Valley Paralegal Association
www.rvpa.org

*Tidewater Paralegal Association

*Virginia Peninsula Paralegal Association
www.vappa.org

WASHINGTON

+NALS of Washington
www.nalsofwashington.org

 NALS of Greater Wenatchee

 East King County Legal Support Professionals

 NALS of Greater Seattle

 NALS of Kitsap County
 www.nalsofkitsap.org

 NALS of Snohomish County

 NALS of Pierce County

 NALS of Thurston County

 NALS of Spokane

 NALS of Yakima County

**Washington State Paralegal Association
www.wspaonline.com

WEST VIRGINIA

*Association of West Virginia Paralegals
www.lawv.org

*Legal Assistants/Paralegals of Southern West Virginia
www.lapswv.org

*Ohio Valley Paralegal Organization

WISCONSIN

*Madison Area Legal Assistant Association
www.madisonparalegal.org

+Wisconsin Association for Legal Professionals
www.wisconsinalp.org

 Brown County Association for Legal Professionals

 Fox Valley Association for Legal Professionals

 Greater Milwaukee Association of Legal Professionals

 Lakeshore Area Association for Legal Professionals

 Legal Professionals Association—East Central

Racine-Kenosha Legal Professionals

St. Croix Valley Legal Professionals

Legal Personnel of South Central Wisconsin
www.lpscw.org

Northcentral Association of Legal Professionals

WYOMING

*Legal Assistants of Wyoming
www.lawyo.com

*NALA member

**NFPA member

+NALS member

appendix D

Suggested Reading

Bolles, Richard N. *What Color is Your Parachute?* California: Ten Speed Press, updated yearly.

The Directory of Executive Recruiters. Fitzwilliam, NH: Consultants News, updated yearly.

Bixler, Susan and Nancy Nix-Rice. *The New Professional Image: Your Best for Every Business Situation,* 2nd Edition. Massachusetts: Adams Media, 2005.

Enslow, Wendy S. and Arnold G. Boldt. *No-Nonsense Cover Letters: The Essential Guide to Creating Attention-Grabbing Cover Letters that Get Interviews and Job Offers (no Nonsense).* New York: Career Press, Inc., 2007.

Epstein, Lorne. *You're Hired! Interview Skills to Get the Job.* Virginia: E3 Publishing, 2005.

Harrington, Betty. *Games Mother Never Taught You.* New York: Warner Books, 1977.

Jackson, Tom. *Guerrilla Tactics in the New Job Market,* 2nd Edition. New York: Bantam Books, 1991.

Levinson, Jay Conrad and David E. Perry. *Guerilla Marketing for Job Hunters.* New Jersey: John Wiley & Sons, 2005.

Morem, Susan. *How to Gain the Professional Edge, Achieve the Personal and Professional Image You Want.* Minnesota: Better Books, 1997.

Parker, Yana. *Damned Good Resume Guide: A Crash Course in Resume Writing,* 4th Edition. California: 10 Speed Press, 2002.

Smith, Rebecca. *Electronic Resumes and Online Networking: How to Use the Internet to Do a Better Job Search, Including a Complete Up-to-Date Resource Guide,* 2nd Edition. Franklin Lakes, NJ: Career Press, 2000.

Van Devender, John and Gloria Van Devender-Graves. *Savvy Interviews: How to Ace the Interviews and Get the Job.* Virginia: Capitol Books, Inc., 2007.

Yates, Martin John. *Knock 'em Dead* series. Avon, MA: Adams Media, 2003.

About the Author

Andrea Wagner's extensive background in the paralegal field as a teacher and placement specialist has given her a unique understanding of the legal profession.

She has a bachelor's and master's degree in theater and an ABA-approved paralegal certificate. She is on the advisory board of several LA-area paralegal schools and was a charter member of the Commission for the California Advanced Paralegal Specialization. She has also taught at several paralegal schools. Currently she is the Human Resources Manager for a major human rights organization. She resides with her family in Los Angeles.

Please contact her at awresume@hotmail.com about your comments, corrections and criticisms of the book.

Index